STUDIES IN IRISH LITERATURE, CINEMA AND CULTURE

Series editor: Dr. Pilar Villar-Argáiz, Senior Lecturer in British and Irish Literature, the Department of English Philology, University of Granada

1. Kathryn Laing and Sinéad Mooney (editors), *Irish Women Writers At the Turn of the 20th Century: Alternative Histories, New Narratives.*
2. Constanza del Río and José Carregal (editors), *Revolutionary Ireland, 1916–2016. Historical Facts & Social Transformations Re-Assessed.*
3. Adela Flamarike, *Women, Art And Nationalism in the Irish Revival. Presence And Absence.*
4. James Gallacher, *Bohemian Belfast and Dublin. Two Artistic and Literary Worlds in the Work of Gerard Keenan.*
5. A. J. Francisco Elices *Irish Dystopian Fiction*
6. Carlos M. Otero, *Ireland and the Irish in 20th Century British Cinema.*
7. Marjan Shokouhi, *Irishness in the Context of Current Environmental Discourse.*

We invite further submission for titles to be published in the series.

STUDIES IN IRISH LITERATURE, CINEMA AND CULTURE
No. 1
Series editor: Dr. Pilar Villar-Argáiz,

Irish Women Writers at the Turn of the 20th Century

Alternative Histories, New Narratives

Irish Women Writers at the Turn of the 20th Century

Alternative Histories, New Narratives

Edited by Kathryn Laing and Sinéad Mooney

EER

EDWARD EVERETT ROOT PUBLISHERS, BRIGHTON 2020

In association with the Irish Women's Writing Network

EER

Edward Everett Root, Publishers, Co. Ltd.,
30 New Road, Brighton, Sussex, BN1 1BN, England.

Details of our overseas agents and how to buy our books are given on our website.

www.eerpublishing.com

edwardeverettroot@yahoo.co.uk

*Irish Women Writers at the Turn of the Twentieth Century:
Alternative Histories, New Narratives*

Edited by Kathryn Laing and Sinéad Mooney

Studies in Irish Literature, Cinema and Culture series, volume 1.

ISBN 9781911454182 Paperback
ISBN 9781911454212 Hardback
ISBN 9781911454243 eBook

First published in England 2020.

This edition © Edward Everett Root Publishers, 2020.

Cover design by Pageset Limited, High Wycombe, Buckinghamshire.

Book production by Amanda Helm, St Leonards-on-Sea, East Sussex.

Printed and bound in Great Britain by TJ International Ltd, Padstow, Cornwall

Contents

Recoveries

Acknowledgements

This volume would not have been possible without the enthusiastic cooperation and scholarship of our contributors, the knowledgeability and helpfulness of our peer reviewers and the advice and assistance of the Series Editor, Pilar Villar-Argáiz. We are grateful to James H. Murphy and Whitney Standlee for their generous and insightful readings of the introduction. Our thanks are also due to John Spiers and all involved in the publication of the volume at Edward Everett Root. We also acknowledge with gratitude the University of Limerick/NUI Galway Gender Arc and the Institute for Irish Studies, Mary Immaculate College, who contributed to the funding of the 2016 symposium, *Occluded Narratives: Irish Women's Writing 1880–1910,* held at Mary Immaculate College, which generated several of the essays in the collection. That event also inaugurated the Irish Women's Writing Network (1880–1920) – https://irishwomenswritingnetwork.com – which continues to bring together the work of a transnational group of scholars in the field, and which would not be possible without the work of the Network website administrator Deirdre Flynn and the team as a whole – Anna Pilz, Whitney Standlee, Julie Anne Stevens, Caoilfhionn Ní Beacháin, Kathleen Williams, Elizabeth Tilley and postgraduate assistant researchers Geraldine Brassil and Sophie von Os.

Introduction:
"A Palpable Energy"

Kathryn Laing and Sinéad Mooney

Silenced female voices, the gendered gaps and absences in archives and literary histories, and silence as theme and technique, all feature in many of the essays included in this collection. Addressing these occlusions and retrieving these voices is the chief thread that connects this project to numerous predecessors, not least the groundbreaking publication in 2002 of volumes IV and V of the *Field Day Anthology of Irish Writing*, dedicated to women's writing and traditions in response to their underrepresentation in the original three volumes. However, *Irish Women Writers at the Turn of the Twentieth Century: Alternative Histories, New Narratives*, while still addressing itself to issues of representation, retrieval and reconsideration of the silenced, ironically finds itself participating in a rich and multi-voiced critical conversation.

Assessing the future impact of Irish feminism in the wake of the Field Day volumes IV and V, Linda Connolly warned in 2004 that internal "discontents and divisions," and debate about canons and feminist anthologising projects required continued navigating, and that "[w]hat is now *done* with this anthology is crucial to the future of feminism in mainstream studies" (2004, 154). What has been *done* and achieved since is considerable. Citing a range of publications and the success of recent anthologies of Irish women's writing, Margaret Kelleher in 2016 asserted that "we are in a better place as critics and teachers," identifying a "palpable energy" in Irish writing, publishing and indeed criticism.[1] It is not an exaggeration to say that this energy is not only palpable but clearly now a powerful feminist force in Irish studies. This energy

---

1   "Literary Cabinets and 'Who's in, Who's Out': Katharine Tynan (1902) and her Successors." This plenary lecture is available as a podcast on the Irish Women's Writing Network website. The network was launched at the "Occluded Narratives: Irish women's writing 1880–1910" Symposium, 25–26 November 2016, Mary Immaculate College, Limerick.

charge, evident in contemporary feminist literary and cultural recovery projects, continues to initiate new of ways reading, teaching and conceptualising the work of Irish women writers, poets, dramatists, historians and other neglected figures from diverse disciplines.

Patricia Coughlan's assertion that "the harvests of canon expansion must be continually reaped by active work specifically within criticism, if the writers and texts which research recovers are to be integrated into the literary–historical narrative" remains pertinent ("Introduction" 2008, 2). Significant occlusions and exclusions still exist. However, it is now possible to describe and celebrate, without complacency, the extraordinary flourishing of scholarship on Irish women writers broadly and more specifically on turn-of-the-twentieth century women writers—and to identify coordinates on a map of pioneering scholarship in a necessarily fluid and flexible field of intellectual and critical enquiry. Key coordinates are, significantly, too numerous to list in their entirety here, but must include anthologies, dictionaries, databases and the multiple interventions and publications by critics including J. W. Foster, James H. Murphy, Heidi Hansson, Gerardine Meaney and Margaret Kelleher, to name but a few.[2] Scholars continue to build on these legacies, from Heather Ingman's *Irish Women's Fiction: From Edgeworth to Enright* (2015) to Tina O'Toole's recoveries of the Irish contexts of numerous "New Woman" writers in *The Irish New Woman* (2013) and Whitney Standlee's attention to underrated writers including Katharine Tynan, L. T. Meade, and Katherine Cecil Thurston in *Power to Observe: Irish Women Novelists in Britain, 1890–1916* (2015).

This critical landscape also comprises a considerable body of scholarship dedicated to individual writers of the turn of the twentieth-century period, recently recovered or examined anew, including Eva Gore Booth, Emily Lawless, Constance Markievicz and Hannah Lynch, for example. Anthologies such as Lucy Collins's *Poetry by Women in Ireland: A Critical Anthology, 1870–1970* (2012) or Sinéad Gleeson's *The Long Gaze Back* (2015) continue the work of recuperating neglected poets and poetry, short story writers and their work respectively. Activist movements including the "#Waking the Feminists Campaign" and "Fired! Irish Women Poets and the Canon," launched to challenge gender equality issues as well as the academic and cultural status quo, conferences, newly developed databases, and a flourishing of edited collections of scholarship have all contributed to the continued activity of "opening the field."[3] These collections have often focused on a particular theme, genre or

2   For example, the *Field Day* volumes IV and V (Cork 2002), the *Dictionary of Munster Women Writers, 1800–2000* (Tina O'Toole, ed. 2005); *A Database of Irish Women's Writing, 1800–2005* (Maria Luddy and Gerardine Meaney 2007).

3   *Opening the Field: Irish Women, Texts and Contexts* (Haberstroh, ed., 2007) is one of the many works of scholarship to follow on from the publication of the *Field Day Anthologies* volumes IV and V. Foundational edited collections include *Irish Literature:*

talismanic moment, *Fictions of the Irish Land War* (Hansson and Murphy, eds., 2014), for example, while the essays gathered in *Irish Writing 1878–1922: Advancing the Cause of Liberty* (Pilz and Standlee, eds., 2016) are framed by specific attention to "the political engagement, both direct and oblique, of texts written by Irish women during the pivotal historical period between 1878–1922" (2). In the contexts of the "Decade of Centenaries, a series of commemorations remembering key historic events in the 1912–22 period," *Women Writing War* uncovers "the work of a range of women who were active cultural producers and agents, deeply invested in the political and military struggles of their day" (O'Toole, McIntosh and O'Cinnéide, eds., 2016, 1). *A History of Modern Irish Women's Literature*, the most recent co-ordinate on the rapidly expanding and shifting map of pioneering scholarship, marks a pivotal moment: "We are now at a point in time where a fruitful dialogue between feminist literary scholarship and new practices in literary history and literary criticism in Ireland can combine to generate a history of modern Irish women's literature" (Ingman and Ó Gallchoir 2018, 4).

Featuring acts of recuperation and innovative readings of recovered writing, *Irish Women Writers at the Turn of the Twentieth Century* contributes to the creation of new narratives and insights into the history of Irish women's writing during this specific period. In this volume, our aims are dual: firstly to give readers a flavour of the "palpable energy" that is currently driving scholarship in this field and the diverse body of writing dedicated to both recovery work and, secondly, to shaping original critical perspectives on writers who have been made visible and around whom a critical field is continuing to develop. Published in association with the Irish Women's Writing Network, 1880–1920 (https://irishwomenswritingnetwork.com), the objective of this particular volume is also to illustrate and to build on the ethos of the Network: developing further international and interdisciplinary conversations and connections between scholars who are already established in their field, early career scholars, postgraduates and researchers whose area of expertise crosses disciplines. The research of contributors working in differing disciplines and based across the world, examining diverse writers, dramatists, poets, novelists, journalists, travel writers, children's writers, visual artists and historians, is collected here, establishing unexpected crossings and intersections, and dialogues between essays and critical approaches. The shifting nature of this critical ground, and the fact that the contributions include both initial recovery work which lays the foundations for subsequent scholars and also more "established" names which can now be considered in multiple contexts, we offer as evidence of a vibrant and rapidly evolving field. This collection thus offers a snapshot of new

---

Feminist Perspectives (Coughlan and O'Toole, eds., 2008); *New Contexts: Re-Framing Nineteenth-Century Irish Women's Prose,* (Hansson ed., 2008); and *Irish Women Writers: New Critical Perspectives* (D'hoker, Ingelbien, and Schwall,. eds., 2011).

directions and voices in current research on Irish women's writing at the turn of the twentieth century.

In this collection, like Ingman and Ó Gallchoir, we employ a policy of "generous inclusion" in relation to the term "Irish writer" (2018, 5). Lindsay Janssen's essay considers the journalism of a member of the Irish diaspora, Margaret Dixon McDougall (1828–1899), who was commissioned by the *Montreal Witness* to travel to Ireland as a special correspondent and report on the famine and Land War of 1879–82, while Barry Montgomery presents his research on the Lithuanian-born Hannah Berman, one of the earliest Irish Jewish writers, who immigrated to Dublin as a child around the year 1892, and who, as well as being a short story writer, novelist, and a prolific translator from Yiddish, was active in Dublin literary networks which aimed to establish common ground between the Irish and Yiddish revivals, and the cultural concerns of indigenous and newly-arrived communities. Still other writers considered here have been sidelined because of their marginality to the Irish Revival's imperative of establishing a distinct national identity, because of what was perceived to be their too-close concern with the commercial demands of the British marketplace, or simply because of a lack of sufficient "Irish credentials," whether those were judged by a sufficient quotient of recognisably Irish subject matter or residence.

Some essays concern comparatively well-known Irish women writers considered from fresh perspectives: Seán Hewitt reads Emily Lawless as a natural historian; Julie Anne Stevens' essay on Edith Somerville uses her 1928 *roman d'atelier French Leave*, 1880s diaries and sketchbooks as a way of exploring female visual artists' international networks; Sinéad Mooney considers the Cork New Woman novelist Katherine Cecil Thurston's diseased and deranged male characters in terms of the *fin-de-siècle* discourse of degeneration; Matthew Reznicek returns to Thurston's "transgressive *Künstlerroman*," *Max*, from a different angle, paying particular attention to the ways in which "the novel's representation of the transnational European railroad as fluid destabilises heteronormative identities" (87). Other essays concern authors or bodies of work seldom or never critically considered before now, grounded in archival research and the patient combing of periodicals and identification of the writers behind pseudonyms. Mary Pierse is eloquent on the difficulty of determining the most basic biographical facts about her subject, the Co. Down suffragist, feminist critic and journalist L. A. M. Priestley, in county archives and libraries, while Patrick Maume traces similar difficulties in retrieving the life and work of the Donegal Presbyterian "kailyard" writer Erminda Rentoul Esler (*c.*1860–1924), identifying her as a subject for further research. Essays on other unfamiliar writers, such as Lisa Weihman's discussion of Theodosia Hickey, a children's writer whose comedic 1933 *roman á clef* of the 1916 Rising, *Easter Week*, speak eloquently both to recent research on Irish women's writing about war and the Irish revolutionary movement (O'Toole, McIntosh and O'Cinnéide 2016) and to two other essays in this collection: Lia Mills' account of Eva Gore-Booth's radical poetic engagement with the Rising and WWI and Maureen O'Connor's eco-critical contextualisation of Gore-Booth's pacifism with her other progressive causes alongside the work of fellow Irish first-wave feminists such as Alice Stopford Green, Margaret Cousins, and Charlotte Despard.

The "Decade of Commemorations" is in fact a constant presence behind much of the research presented here: issues concerning bearing witness and acts of memory are at the core of Lindsay Janssen's investigation of how Dixon McDougall's writing on the Land War variously navigates the "reality boundary" and the historicity of the events she witnessed as a journalist, and Christopher Cusack's argument that the persistent belief that the memory of the Famine has been repressed in Irish literature "is at least partially inflected by the gender dynamics of canon formation" and his counter-examples of its portrayal in forgotten writing such novels and short stories by Jane Barlow, Louise Field, L. T. Meade and Mildred Darby (39). Lia Mills' tracing of the pacifist Eva Gore-Booth's ambivalent idealisation of the 1916 Rising crystallises around Esther Roper's witnessing of the dramatic meeting at Mountjoy jail between Gore-Booth and her rebel sister Constance Markievicz, whose execution had just been commuted to life imprisonment, and Gore-Booth's subsequent attempts to prevent the execution of Roger Casement.

Heidi Hansson's rich essay builds on and charts new fields of enquiry on *The Nineteenth Century*, further exploring how Irish woman contributors over the periodical's first quarter-century negotiate the traditional female "modesty topos" by framing their claims to authority in terms of eye-witness accounts of travel and late Victorian imperial philanthropy as strategies for the gradual negotiation of a female public voice. Many contributors' essays further foreground literary endeavours as a form of activism strongly engaged with the issues of the day, be they nationalist, anti-imperial, suffragist or other. L. A. M. Priestley's writings on votes for women appeared in journals as widely different as the *Irish Citizen* and the *Vote*, *The Irish Presbyterian* and in the theosophist journal *The Herald of the Star*, as documented in Mary Pierse's essay. For Maureen O'Connor, Eva Gore-Booth's anti-conscription activities align closely with her vegetarianism and her mystical poetry and verse drama, while the feminist historian Alice Stopford Green was "a member of Cumann na mBan, and contributed frequently to advanced Nationalist newspapers in the period leading up to the Rising, was a close friend of Roger Casement, and was one of two women who provided the funds for the Howth gun-running trip" (20–1). If nationalism, while it inhibited or sidelined some women writers, provided others of the period with a position from which to write, it is clearly far from the whole story.

Other contributions draw out a more oblique but no less compelling politics from their subjects, setting up some intriguing dialogues between essays. An eco-critical approach connects Maureen O'Connor with Seán Hewitt's reading of Emily Lawless's fictional portrayal of the natural world in terms of her work as a natural historian whose interests "ranged across entomology, botany, marine zoology and geology" (29); the Irish landscape also features in Matthew Reznicek's account of Max (1910), which he reads in terms of a feminist "geographics" of nomadism between variously oppressive Irish and Russian topographies. George Egerton and Emily Lawless considered as Irish "New Woman" writers form the subject of Aintzane Legarreta Mentxaka's essay on early modernist deployments of silence, which can never be apolitical in a period of Irish nationalist literary production which privileged woman as sorrowing mother or imperilled maiden, both static and silent icons of national identity. Anne Jamison's consideration of Edith Somerville's subversive adult fairytale "Little Red Riding-Hood in Kerry" (1934) explores the construction of a "modern, Irish equestrian 'New Girl'" in the context of female empowerment through foxhunting, the economic exploitation of young women under the renewed agitation for land centred on Ireland's 1933 Land Act and the highly coded narratives of Irish folklore.

Even contributions dealing with bodies of work less obviously grounded in the major national or international debates or events of the turn of the twentieth century in Ireland, such as Elke D'hoker's discussion of the work of the Co. Cork short story writer, biographer, translator and novelist Ethel Colburn Mayne (1865–1941), nonetheless testify to a declining Anglo-Irish social order and the stultifying conditions in which impoverished daughters lived. Pre-empting not only the desperate daughters, devouring mothers and decaying Big Houses of Elizabeth Bowen, Molly Keane and Jennifer Johnston, her maternal portraits also resonate strikingly with the "weak, miserable creatures who obsess over their sons and resent their daughters" in Theodosia Hickey's *Easter Week* (209). Colburn Mayne has hitherto been chiefly remembered for her association with *The Yellow Book* in the 1890s, but a consideration of her work necessarily involves, as Heather Laird argues, the stipulation of "[a]n historical framework that decentres familiar notions of power and the political and, consequently, expands the category of the historically relevant," hence automatically producing "a body of scholarship more attuned to that which is at the margins" (2018, 18). Such a decentring is key to the concerns of this collection.

If there is, finally, as our collection's title suggests, no one single story of Irish women's writing any more than there is a monolithic "Irish writing," *Irish Women Writers at the Turn of the Twentieth Century: Alternative Histories, New Narratives* represents one initiative among many in an increasingly rich and complex scholarly and publishing landscape. The Irish Women's Writing Network (1880–1920), whose inaugural symposium in 2016 provided the initial impetus for the collection, continues to gather momentum as an interdisciplinary association for the sharing of research among members across the world, with bibliography and archive pages under development and regular postings of blogs contributed by established, early career scholars and postgraduates on their current research. Now available on its website is a new series of blogs, interviews with some of the pioneering scholars in the field of Irish women's writing.[4]

Other projects involve the inauguration of two new Irish women's writing series with Edward Everett Root Press. "Key Irish Women Writers" offers comprehensive accounts of significant individual careers focusing on the long nineteenth century and the first half of the twentieth; the first volumes to appear will be *Maria Edgeworth* by Clíona Ó Gallchoir, *Elizabeth Bowen* by Heather Ingman, *Jane Wilde* by Eibhear Walshe and *Kate O'Brien* by Aintzane Legarreta Mentxaka. A second series, "Irish Women Writers: Texts and Contexts," aims to make forgotten, out of print, or uncollected texts by Irish women writers available for the purposes of teaching and research; the first volumes include *Ethel Colburn Mayne: Selected Stories*, edited by Elke D'hoker, *Hannah Lynch's Irish Girl Rebels: "A Girl Revolutionist" and "Marjory Maurice,"* edited by Kathryn Laing, and *Rosa Mulholland (1842–1921), Feminist, Victorian, Catholic and Patriot*, edited by James H. Murphy. Together with other ongoing recovery initiatives by Tramp Press and others, and a new Museum of Irish Literature (MoLI, https://moli.ie) which opened with an exhibition on Kate O'Brien, there is, if not yet sufficient reason for outright celebration, at least the basis for fruitful ongoing collaborations and conversations. To this evidence of the "palpable energy" identified by Margaret Kelleher, *Irish Women Writers at the Turn of the Twentieth Century: Alternative Histories, New Narratives*, contributes a diverse range of material in order to further such dialogues.

References

Bourke, Angela et al., eds. 2002. *The Field Day Anthology of Irish Writing Volumes IV and V: Irish Women's Writing and Traditions*. Cork: Cork University Press.

Collins, Lucy, ed. 2014. *Poetry by Women in Ireland: A Critical Anthology, 1870–1970*. Liverpool: Liverpool University Press.

Connolly, Linda. 2004. "The Limits of 'Irish Studies': Historicism, Culturalism, Paternalism," *Irish Studies Review* 12, No. 2: 139–62, DOI: 10.1080/0967088042000228914.

Coughlan, Patricia. 2008. "Introduction." *Irish Literature: Feminist Perspectives*,

---

4   Mapping pioneering scholarship in this field is a new Network project launched by Anna Pilz and Whitney Standlee in 2019. See "Research Pioneers", https://irishwomenswritingnetwork.com/category/research-pioneers/

edited by Patricia Coughlan and Tina O'Toole, 1–16. Dublin: Carysfort.

D'hoker, Elke, Raphaël Ingelbien and Hedwig Schwall, eds. 2011. *Irish Women Writers: New Critical Perspectives*. Switzerland: Bern.

Foster, John Wilson. 2008. *Irish Novels 1890–1940: New Bearings in Culture and Fiction*. Oxford: Oxford University Press.

Gleeson, Sinéad, ed. 2015. *The Long Gaze Back: An Anthology of Irish Women Writers*. Rearsby: W F Howes.

Haberstroh, Patricia Boyle, ed. 2007. *Opening the Field: Irish Women, Texts and Contexts*. Cork: Cork University Press.

Hansson, Heidi, ed. 2008. *New Contexts: Re-Framing Nineteenth-Century Irish Women's Prose*. Cork: Cork University Press.

——, and James H. Murphy, eds. 2014. *Fictions of the Irish Land War*. Bern: Peter Lang.

Ingman, Heather. 2015. *Irish Women's Fiction: From Edgeworth to Enright*. Dublin: Irish Academic Press.

——, and Clíona Ó Gallchoir, eds. 2018. *A History of Modern Irish Women's Literature*. Cambridge: Cambridge University Press.

Kelleher, Margaret. 2001. "Writing Irish Women's Literary History." *Irish Studies Review* Volume 9, Number 1: 5–14.

——. 2016. "Literary Cabinets and 'Who's in, Who's Out': Katharine Tynan (1902) and her Successors." Irish Women's Writing Network (1880–1920). Podcast audio, https://irishwomenswritingnetwork.com/podcasts/

Laird, Heather. 2018. *Commemoration*. Cork: Cork University Press.

Luddy, Maria and Gerardine Meaney. 2007. *A Database of Irish Women's Writing, 1800–2005*. https://warwick.ac.uk/fac/arts/history/irishwomenwriters/

Murphy, James H. 2011. *Irish Novelists and the Victorian Age*. Oxford: Oxford University Press.

O'Toole, Tina, ed. 2005. *Dictionary of Munster Women Writers, 1800–2000*. Cork: Cork University Press.

——. 2013. *The Irish New Woman*. New York: Palgrave Macmillan.

O'Toole, Tina, Gillian McIntosh and Muireann O'Cinnéide, eds., 2016, *Women Writing War: Ireland 1880–1922*. Dublin: University College Dublin Press.

Pilz, Anna and Standlee, Whitney, eds. 2016. *Irish Women's Writing, 1878–1922*. Manchester: Manchester University Press.

Standlee, Whitney. 2015. *Power to Observe: Irish Women Novelists in Britain, 1890*. Oxford: Peter Lang.

New Perspectives

1

"The Wind is Our Confederate": Nation and Nature in the Work of First-Wave Irish Feminists

Maureen O'Connor

In environmental philosophy and ecological humanities there has been what is referred to as a "material" turn in the twenty-first century, with especially urgent interventions being made by feminists, led by the groundbreaking work of theorists like Karen Barad, Stacy Alaimo, Iris van der Tuin, Serenella Iovino and Serpil Opperman. The last two writers often collaborate, and have characterised this turn as a "search for new conceptual models to theorise the connections between matter and agency on the one side, and the intertwining of bodies, natures, and meanings on the other side" (2012, 450). Alaimo describes "feminist new materialism" as scrambling the "conventional notions of subjectivity that separate the rational human from the external environment" (2014, 15). Barad's foundational theory of agential realism argues that there are no independent entities but, rather, phenomena in an ongoing process of "becoming" through relationships and interactions with other phenomena, or "beings in our differential becoming" (2003, 818). Her account of performativity "calls into question the givenness of the differential categories of 'human' and 'nonhuman'" (2003, 808). So, in brief, the material turn is one that theorises a co-extensivity of the human subject with the non-human. Van der Tuin has warned of the dangers of this kind of materialist approach if conducted outside of a feminist frame, when it would deny subjectivity to those whose accession to both human and subject status in Western discourse is recent and insecure. She names specifically (if far from exhaustively), "women, lesbians, gays, blacks, and post-colonial people" (2014, 233), this last category of significance in an Irish context. Rather than erase the subject, feminist new materialism would posit it as multiplicitous and dynamic. A century ago, Eva Gore-Booth, Margaret Cousins, Charlotte Despard, and Alice Stopford Green anticipated much of this contemporary debate in the ways they imagined the subject in relation to its environment and the liberatory possibilities inherent in such a revised understanding of that relationship. While space does not allow for a full discussion of each woman's work in this regard, it is worth drawing connections between their positions and identifying something specific in Irish feminist rhetoric when it is informed by anti-imperialist convictions as well as what we would today call "green" sensibilities. Unlike their Anglo-American contemporaries, first-wave feminists who were also animal advocates and vegetarians, these Irish women's relationship to power was complicated by Ireland's colonial history, a history marked by periods of starvation and shortages that made the choice of a vegetarian diet uniquely confrontational.

Since the onset of the modern-day ecology movement in the 1960s and '70s, usually identified with hippies and other counter-culturalists, the popular picture of vegetarians is of tree-hugging, whey-faced weaklings. In the previous century, there was a (perhaps surprisingly) robust vegetarian movement beginning in the 1850s lasting through the early twentieth century. If one were to go by some of the contemporary cartoons on the subject—featuring diners being carried into vegetarian restaurants on stretchers, or people turning into vegetables on display, for example—the impression might be of a similarly dismissive popular response to the phenomenon. Far from a passing fad, however, vegetarianism was a widespread movement reaching all parts of the United Kingdom. It is remarkable to see how many articles and letters to the editor in newspapers across Britain are on the topic of vegetarianism, including coverage of the many local and national meetings and the foundation of organisations like the Irish Vegetarian Union, which began in Belfast in 1890. (According to Charles W. Forward, editor of *The Vegetarian Review*, the first Vegetarian Society met in Kent, on 30 September 1847.) As early as 1848, *Punch* reported on "The Vegetarian Movement," noting the existence of "a vegetarian press, a vegetarian society, a vegetarian boarding-house, a vegetarian school, two or three vegetarian hotels" (1848, 182). The names and locations of vegetarian cafés and restaurants in towns and villages across the British Isles can be found in reviewing newspaper coverage of suffrage activity in the late-nineteenth and early twentieth centuries. Suffrage meetings and talks were regularly held in vegetarian establishments, including the famous café in Dublin, which appears in James Joyce's *Ulysses*, and where many historically significant conversations took place, including those involved in planning the Easter Rising. Advertisements for this café appear in the back pages of nearly every issue of the *Irish Citizen,* the nationalist suffrage newspaper, founded by the Irish Women's Franchise League, which ran from 1912 until 1920.

No late Victorian observer would be surprised at an association between rebellion and a meatless diet. By the late nineteenth century there was growing alarm about vegetarianism, at this point an internationally coordinated movement, vocal as well as visible. In Britain it was sometimes seen as a threat to empire and to the increasingly fragile construct of Western masculinity, placed under serious pressure by the Boer War, and its revelations regarding the poor physical state of a majority of adult English males. In *Degeneration*, Max Nordau identified vegetarianism as one of the "hysterical" decadent tendencies of the modern age (1898, 210). Over the *fin-de-siècle* period, vegetarianism came to be associated with anarchism, amongst its famous advocates being Leo Tolstoy and Edward Carpenter, whose zoophilia, according to Leela Gandhi, was closely linked to his socialist class critique and to his anticolonialism (2006, 36). James Gregory observes that "above all[,] food reform was identified as a threatening component of counter culture, especially socialist movements, across Europe" (2014, 13). The welcome address to the first international vegetarian conference held in Cologne in 1889, delivered by its president, Ernest Hering, gives an indication of the socialist element of the vegetarian "mission":

> Our work concerns the whole people, humanity at large; it is of an international character, entirely devoid of selfish interests. No title, no cross of any order, no social position of high account is to be gained here and anyone seeking for such will be disappointed. The welfare of the whole people, of the entire population in all its classes, nay, all of mankind, is to be the only and single object of our work here; and therefore we call upon all, to whatever class or nation they may belong, to grant us their assistance and co-operation.[1]

This is more of a call to arms than might be expected from a vegetarian meeting, but, in the words of Forward, writing about the virtues of the "Edenic diet" in 1898, "One of the most noticeable features of the Vegetarian movement is the fact that so large a proportion of those who have been associated with it were advocates—and in many cases, very active advocates—of other moral and social reforms" (1898, 62).

Understanding this context affects our reading of a letter that Oscar Wilde wrote to the writer Violet Fane in 1887, in which he notes vegetarianism's "curious" connection:

> with modern socialism, atheism, nihilism, anarchy and other political creeds. It is strange that the most violent republicans I know are all vegetarians: Brussels sprouts seem to make people bloodthirsty, and those who live on lentils and artichokes are always calling for the gore of the aristocracy and for the severed heads of kings. ... [I]n the political sphere a diet of green beans seems dangerous. (2000, 334)

As an article in the *Yorkshire Gazette* from 1885 observes, all vegetarians are

---

1   Originally published in *Vegetarian*, 28 September 1889; quoted in Gregory (2014, 1).

radicals or dissenters (1885, 4), so Wilde is not being as outrageous or ironic as the modern-day reader might assume, though he is parodying the sometimes overwrought response to vegetarianism, alternately dismissed as "humbug" and taken seriously, especially in the context of empire and fear of fomenting revolution. Some pro-vegetarian propaganda of the mid-nineteenth century defended the diet by looking to the Irish labourer, on average larger and stronger than his Scottish or English coeval, a physical superiority achieved through an unintentionally vegetarian diet, as John Smith suggests when citing "English farmers" who testify that Irish labourers "are capable of performing a much greater amount of agricultural work on their simple meal of potatoes and buttermilk than the English labourer, though feeding on an abundance of flesh-meat" (1854, 184–5). This same hearty Irishman, however, can serve as an example in an anti-vegetarian argument. While reference to the Famine is not explicit in either use of the figure of the Irish vegetarian, Andrew Combe's reference in his 1849 book on digestion is obliquely informed by agrarian unrest of some kind:

> The Hindoos are frequently quoted as a remarkable instance of the effects of a vegetarian diet in producing a mild and inoffensive disposition; but mention is forgotten to be made of the Irish peasantry, whose diet is perhaps as exclusively vegetable, and who are notorious for committing deeds of savage barbarity. (1849, 147)

"Hindoo" here is a homogenizing reference to the empire's Indian subjects, who could function as exemplars of the wholesomeness of the diet or be portrayed as "vegetarians who are at once cruel without valour, seditious without cause, and fanatical without sincerity," as they were in *Dundee, Perth and Cupar Advertiser* in 1857, the year of the Indian rebellion, or Sepoy Mutiny (1857, 3). An argument against vegetarianism mounted in *The Globe* from 1905, suggests that "a vegetarian nation suffers morally unless it makes up its quantum of nastiness in some other way" (1905, 1), echoing Wilde's characterization of vegetarians as bloodthirsty, and offering a telling instance of recourse to man's animal nature as needing an outlet, positioning him firmly in the realm of "nature, red in tooth and claw," in Tennyson's phrase.[2]

I turn now to some radical Irish women who were feminists, workers' advocates, Irish nationalists, and vegetarians. In Anglo-American iterations of first-wave feminism, to espouse and practise vegetarianism was a radical act of subversion, of cultural and economic revolt. Holloway Prison, for example, began catering for vegetarians once suffragettes were being gaoled in significant numbers. In Ireland, the history of politically charged periods of disastrous hunger and the colonial practice of alleging the inferiority of subject peoples

---

2   On rather flimsy evidence, Forward suggests that Tennyson was at least interested in vegetarianism, if not a practitioner, as such (1898, 129–30).

like the Irish as eaters of grass, rice, and potatoes, versus the virile intellectual meat-eaters of England, makes the dietary choice a particularly defiant one. In the Irish context, the adaptation of a vegetarian diet by privileged women of the Ascendancy suggests, *inter alia*, a sense of solidarity across sectarian and class divisions, one of the ways in which Irish first-wave feminism is distinguished from its English counterpart. Leah Leneman's 1997 article, "The Awakened Instinct: Vegetarianism and the Women's Suffrage Movement in Britain," includes three of the women I am discussing in its valuable documentation and rediscovery of the virtually constitutive link between early feminism and animal activism/vegetarianism. The feminist journal *Shafts*, for example, took anti-vivisection and vegetarianism as a central part of its feminist remit (though the idea that preparing meals without meat would require less housewifely labour might come as a surprise to the vegetarian cook). Leneman is one of the first scholars to note Eva Gore-Booth's vegetarianism. Not only was Gore-Booth less public about her diet than Cousins or Despard, it was not the kind of detail that seemed important in the early days of reclaiming these forgotten figures.

Eva Gore-Booth (1870–1926), poet and playwright, was born in Sligo, which she left in 1897 to join her partner, Esther Roper, in Manchester and to work defending the rights of working-class women to equal pay and access to education, in addition to her suffrage activities. She is perhaps best-known for her posthumous appearance in a Yeats poem and for being the sister of Constance Markievicz, though, as her biographer Sonja Tiernan has demonstrated, Eva was the more radical of the two women, and inspired the activism of her older sister. My title is taken from a poem by Gore-Booth to Markievicz while the latter was imprisoned and facing a death sentence after the Easter Rising:

Comrades

To Con

The peaceful night that round me flows,
    Breaks through your iron prison doors,
Free through the world your spirit goes,
    Forbidden hands are clasping yours.

The wind is our confederate,
    The night has left her doors ajar,
We meet beyond earth's barrèd gate,
    Where all the world's wild Rebels are. (1929, 511)

In this account of the sisters' telepathic connection, bodies are not, to quote Barad, "objects with inherent boundaries and properties" (2003, 815). The radical openness to alternative modes of being, not restricted by conventional notions of embodiment, is shared by all of the women I am discussing, influenced to some extent, in the case of Gore-Booth, Cousins, and Despard, by

Theosophy, the mystical order founded in 1875 by Helena Petrovna Blavatsky which drew on Eastern religions and was popular amongst Irish intellectuals and artists in the *fin-de-siècle* period. Theosophy's theories regarding the syncretism of creation, the subatomic connection between all material (and immaterial) forms and the ever-changing differentiation between forms bears many similarities to feminist new materialism. It certainly offered to these women a way out of what Barad and others have described as a representational bind. It potentially allows for the independence of reality outside of the language of masculinist structures and introduces friction and drag into the smooth juridical production of the western subject. Catherine Candy, writing about Cousins, describes Theosophy as "magic, science and philosophy syncretised in a broadly anti-colonial challenge to European reason" (2009, 29).

Gore-Booth's own anti-colonial struggle emerged most publicly in her anti-conscription activities and support for the 1916 Easter Rising. Like many participants in the Rising, she was opposed to the Great War, figured by Irish nationalists as the slaughtering of millions in the name of colonialist aggression. Gore-Booth was especially concerned that conscription not be established in Ireland. Declaring a republic, even if the effort failed, could delay and possibly foreclose such a development. Her volume of poetry *Broken Glory* (1917), written in response to the Rising, is dedicated to Roger Casement, and links various forms of rebellion. Amongst the paeans to the rebel dead, including the homosexual Casement, are more perverse poems that possibly queer the Rising, including the poem "To C. A.," which describes a non-binary figure, who is sometimes a woman with richly coiling hair, other times an "Umbrian monk": "Gorgeous in silky robes of blue and green, / Hair in soft shining coils, white throat bepearled. / It is not true, you are what you have been" (1929, 516–7). Also in 1916, Gore-Booth co-founded a journal named *Urania*, a title drawn from contemporary sexological discourse. According to Havelock Ellis, in the 1896 edition of *Sexual Inversion,* "inverts" of both sexes exhibit "decided preference for green" (1915, 299). That green, the colour of the "natural" world, can also function as the colour of the outsider to masculine heteronormativity reveals the contradictions and ambiguities that circulate around the colour and by extension, the natural. Kate Soper defines "nature," in "its commonest and most fundamental sense," as "opposed to culture, history, convention, … in short, to everything which is defining of the order of humanity" (1995, 15). It is through the idea of "nature" that "we conceptualise what is 'other' to ourselves"; yet, as Soper goes on to note, this same idea of "nature" "has been used to condemn the 'perversity' of human behavior" (1995, 28), an enlistment of "nature's" authority to enforce conformity, even while it is other to the human. Green as the colour of the outsider in an Irish context is at least as complex as Anglo-Irish identity, already poised between insider and outsider. It was the choice of colour, for example, for Wilde's carnation to signal queerness, clearly drawing on sexological theories about the colour's attractions for the marginalised.

In distinct ways, the women I am discussing were unconventional in their navigation of the heterosexual imperative, including Margaret Cousins (née Gillespie; 1878–1954). Cousins, like Gore-Booth, was an eminent first-wave Irish feminist activist and writer, though not of fiction or poetry; she was a journalist and wrote historic/sociological treatises on women. Like Gore-Booth, Cousins was from an isolated, rural part of the country, from the mid-sized market town of Boyle in County Roscommon, only twenty-five miles distant from Lissadell. Though a member of the bourgeoisie rather than the gentry, like Gore-Booth, and like Despard, Cousins abandoned and renounced a life of privilege, built on empire, in order to live among and serve the powerless and the poor. Cousins left rural Ireland to pursue a music degree in Dublin where she met the poet James Cousins, whom she married in 1903. Cousins was the first secretary of the Irish Vegetarian Society, which introduced her to the struggle for women's rights when she was a delegate to a vegetarian conference in Manchester in 1906. A conference of the National Council of Women was being held in the city at the same time, and she recalled this moment as a "turning-point" in her life when the links between the many liberatory causes she would pursue first became apparent. Cousins was a founder, with Hanna Sheehy Skeffington, of the Irish Women's Franchise League in 1908, acting as its first treasurer. Like the Sheehy Skeffingtons, Cousins distinguished between the Irish and English struggles for women's suffrage. In *We Two Together,* the duo-autobiography she wrote with her husband, Cousins recalls that "Hannah asked me and some other friends to join in working out a scheme for a militant suffrage society suitable to the different political situation of Ireland, as between a subject country seeking freedom from England and England, a free country … we had no desire to work under English women leaders; we could lead ourselves" (1950, 164). The couple left Ireland permanently in 1913, first to work for Annie Besant in Liverpool and then to settle in India in 1915, where they lived the rest of their lives. In India Margaret became the first woman magistrate in the country, was gaoled for her work with Gandhi, and was prominently active in international women's (and girls') issues, including helping to found the All Asia Women's conference.

Cousins was a dedicated anti-imperialist in every one of her advocacies, including her vegetarianism. Self-determination could not be gained piecemeal: "The cause of Freedom is single and indivisible. No one facet of it can be sacrificed to expediency in favour of another without radical danger to the whole cause and to those who place expediency before principle" (1950, 186). Ariel Salleh has argued in a similarly syncretic way that "[a]n ecofeminist theory of value will use a libidinally informed economics joining together socialist, feminist, indigenous, and ecological concerns" (1999, 209). As an ecofeminist

17

critic, Salleh operates within a postcolonial framework, as does Helen Tiffin who links "the question of animals, racism and colonialism" (2001, 31). Cousins gave up meat-eating on her wedding day when she married James, a long-time vegetarian. According to Cousins, at their wedding breakfast the bride and bridegroom, "were happy to look the animal kingdom innocently in the face" (1950, 91), while in another sense Margaret was to remain "innocent" throughout her "white" (that is, sexless) marriage, an avoidance of one particular "degrad[ing] ... demand of nature" (1950, 108). Cousins's syncretic vision united the suffering and oppression of women and animals, and she saw as inseparable nationalism and women's suffrage, causes for which she was gaoled in England, in Ireland, and in India. Candy has observed that, especially after the move to India, Cousins "came more and more to see systemic colonial cruelty against women and animals as her explicit target" (2007, 166). For Gore-Booth and Cousins the political was bodily, even through the body's evolutionary history. As Salleh observes, "ecofeminists ... see how political practices are fundamentally cathected by bodily energy and drives" (1997, 118). Cousins and Gore-Booth shared a belief, not uncommon in early feminist circles, in the evolution of humanity away from sexual difference, both psychic and physical. To this end Cousins coined the term "femaculine," thereby setting a fundamental challenge to the purity of western subjectivity, predicated on masculinity and the maintenance of its integrity. Vegetarianism is a part of this challenge, because, as Cathryn Bailey has demonstrated, "the reproduction of the privileged body comes about partly through the regulation of human eating practices" (2007, 44).

Both Cousins and Gore-Booth were friends and admirers of Charlotte Despard (1844–1939). Cousins is especially adoring in her descriptions of the older woman. She quotes the *Liverpool Express*'s November 1913 report of Despard's address to Liverpool Vegetarian Society, which was throwing a lunch in honour of her twenty years of work in food reform: "Vegetarianism was really at the base of a great many things: food seemed only a humble thing but if they realised what did and might go through them through the body, then perhaps they would think the question of food was one of the greatest importance" (1950, 227). Despard was not born in Ireland but in Kent; however, her father was a French of Frenchpark, in County Roscommon, and she identified with the country passionately, visiting it often, until moving there to stay in the last thirty years of her life, in answer to "the call of my blood" (quoted in Linklater 1979, 220). She lived for a time with Maud Gonne, whom she met in 1917. Despard was also a writer, occasionally of fiction and poetry, but most frequently on the "Woman Question," especially in numerous pamphlets, but also in her fiction. She was a feminist and vegetarian, anti-vivisectionist, a workers' advocate, and Irish Nationalist who supported Sinn Féin and the IRA during the War of Independence, and was identified as a "dangerous subversive" by the Free State government under the 1927 Public Safety Act. Decades older than Cousins and Gore-Booth, she was nonetheless even more dismissive of convention than they were, aggressively inserting herself into public spaces in support of controversial and unpopular causes much to the chagrin of her Ascendancy relations, who held high positions in the colonial administration of Ireland, both military and political, including her brother, Field Marshall Lord French, who became Viceroy of Ireland in 1918. She was both heedless and exploitative of her elite connections, using them, for example, to get Gore-Booth and Roper into Ireland soon after the Rising, when no civilians were allowed entry into the country, so that Eva could visit her sister in gaol. Her unorthodox appearance was frequently remarked upon. She wore open sandals whenever possible and never wore a hat. One of her biographers, Andro Linklater, describes her as famously "unhusbanded," widowed, a woman who, once she had nominally fulfilled her heterosexual obligations, discovered "the thread of love" among other women dedicated to their own cause (1979, 244). In this new era, she was struck by the fact that "women understand women, love women, admire women, as they never did before" (quoted in Linklater 1979, 235).

Like the other women under discussion, Despard saw oppression as structural and as affecting all marginalised groups:

> The Women's Movement is related also with the other great movements of the world. ... The awakened instinct which feels the call of the sub-human which says:— "I am the voice of the voiceless. Through me the dumb shall speak," is a modern phenomenon that cannot be denied. It works itself out as food reform on the one hand, and on the other, in strong protest against the cruel methods of experimental research. Both these are in close unison with the demands being made by women. (1913, 44)

The word "instinct" is one often also used by Cousins, pointing to these women's grounding of intellection and ethics in the thoroughly animalised body. One of Gore-Booth's late poems, "Animals," uses similar imagery:

> You really think they cannot feel like you or I?
> Ah me, I know not; yet one said, so legends tell,
> "Alas for him who cannot hear the dumb things cry,
> How shall he see the Light Invisible?" (1929, 29)

Both writers provide examples of what Carrie Rohman has identified as "antiepistemology," that is, "a means of knowing that operates outside of the constraints of language" (2008, 132). Rohman tracks the effect of Darwin's work, which radically linked humans to other animals, making it increasingly difficult to "deny the fundamental interology of human and animal" (2008, 22). Of course, this same theory could be wielded to link only certain kinds of humans—that is, non-white and other inferior races, such as the Irish—

with the animal in a scientifically sanctioned way. Animality was displaced onto marginalised groups with special intensity in the wake of Darwin's theories in order to protect the western subject and "maintain the imperialist power dynamic" (2008, 29). Rohman argues that the figure of the animal is particularly threatening in this imperial context, as it evokes an irreducible multiplicity and plurality threatening to the sanctity of the individual subject. She sees some writers of the period, however, defying this in their use of the animal, embracing the radical mystery the animal both represents and embodies.

We can see the revolutionary import of a particular post-Darwinian deployment of the animal in a passage from Alice Stopford Green's 1897 text, "A Woman's Place in the World of Letters," originally published as a lengthy article in *Nineteenth Century*, reissued as a slim hard-bound pamphlet in 1913:

> Even in her literary ventures woman remains essentially mysterious. ... Fearing to venture out into the open unprotected and bare to attack ..., she seeks safety in what is known in Nature as protective mimicry—one recalls the touching forms of beautiful creatures that, dwelling in the arid desert, have shrouded themselves in the dull hue of the soil, or in arctic cold have taken on a snowy whiteness; of live breathing things that have made themselves after the likeness of a dead twig, and harmless beings who in their alarm have donned the gay air of predatory insects and poisonous reptiles. (1913, 7–8)

Once again, there is an evocation of animalistic instincts, of specific significance to Stopford Green, "profound instincts whose roots go down into the deep of unconscious Being" (1913, 19), more accessible to Woman than to hyper-civilised Man, who has alienated himself from "that elemental power which inspires the whole of unconscious Being [that] reaches in her its highest expression, welling up from hidden springs of Nature," springs connected to "the ultimate depths of woman's nature" (1913, 11–2). While fully aware of the dangers of the essentializing binaries that place women and nature on one side, men and culture on the other, Stopford Green, like the other women discussed so far, embraced and transvalued the longstanding association between women and the natural. As Helen Kingstone notes, Stopford Green both "draws on and rails against ... this binary in her analysis of the challenge facing women writers" (2014, 445).

Alice Stopford Green (1847–1929), was a prolific historian, a native of Kells, County Meath, and of Anglo-Irish background, like the other women discussed here. Her family was particularly distinguished for its service to the Church of Ireland, including producing a bishop. She became a member of Cumann na mBan, and contributed frequently to advanced Nationalist newspapers in the period leading up to the Rising, was a close friend of Roger Casement, and was one of two women who provided the funds for the Howth gun-running trip, that is, the purchase and transportation of arms from Germany to Ireland in 1914. She was branded a "red hot revolutionist" by British intelligence in April 1916, according to Angus Mitchell (2006, 20), one of the foremost experts on Stopford Green and the source of recent research revealing her vegetarianism.[3] Stopford Green's revolutionary activity began after the death of her husband, historian John Richard Green, in 1883, which is also when her own historiographical interests shifted from English material. According to Sandra Holton, at the same time as she began to redirect her focus to Ireland, Stopford Green also began to "articulate far more definitely than ever before the significance of gender in the field of letters" (2002, 123).

Kingstone argues that Stopford Green anticipated *écriture féminine* (2014, 442), an understanding of women's writing as, to use Stopford Green's own phrase, "beyond Law" (1913, 23), a word she capitalises throughout, prefiguring a Kristevan/Lacanian understanding of the "Law" as the father's language which excludes women. Reality, or "the visible established order," in "Woman's Place," has been so structured as to cast woman as a "strayed wanderer from some different sphere—a witness, a herald it might be, of another system lying on the marge and confines of Space and Time. Man is no stranger in this sense" (1913, 19). He is not a stranger, but is limited in his interactions with other phenomena. Woman's experience on the other hand, cannot be expressed through "mere language" (1913, 12), which is inadequate to express those experiences and modes of experience understood by women and ignored by man, "[h]ence her strange inarticulateness" (1913, 12). Woman is a being from the future where "she imagines ceaselessly another Life which shall utterly efface old codes and systems," making common cause with all Others, "who, like herself, were seeking something different from what they know" (1913, 23). Stopford Green places pressure on what counts as "knowing" for women and other outsiders, including "the poor, the slaves, … and sinners" (1913, 23). Despite being an accomplished, widely published, articulate, and well-regarded historian for whom, according to Holton, "the quality of the writing mattered as much to her as its accuracy" (2002, 124), nevertheless, "[s]he does not speak the tongue of this world, nor does she in her heart think its thoughts" (1913, 20).

The essay's consistent characterisation of woman as an alien, as other to the world of reason and civilisation, to the ordered representations possible through language, recalls Barad's challenge to language's primacy. Barad's question—"What compels the belief that we have direct access to cultural representations

---

3   In the National Library of Ireland, Mitchell has discovered a conversation between Stopford Green and her husband recorded in an 1874 diary, in which Stopford Green defends her vegetarianism: "Talking of cruelty to animals I said one did not like to take their lives, because one's love for life gave one a bond to all living things. We were joined to them in life, & tragic force was added from the feeling that we were joined to them in death too" (National Library of Ireland, Ms 43,327).

and their content that we lack toward the things represented?" (2003, 801)—echoes through Stopford Green's essay, which argues that Woman is, in fact, more vitally engaged in the world's "becoming" than Man, despite her official exclusion. Stopford Green concludes, "Man's vision has stopped short" (1913, 32). Woman, on the other hand "reveals herself as intensely modern" and necessarily future-oriented (1913, 18). The women discussed here defy mere chronology, continue to be our contemporaries and our educators, providing the re-discovered "insights" of present-day feminist new materialists, who, with Stopford Green, would argue that woman "is herself perhaps Nature's chief witness to the truth that humanity is not the centre of the universe" (1913, 29).

References

Alaimo, Stacy. 2014. "Thinking as the Stuff of the World." *O-Zone: A Journal of Object-Oriented Studies* 1: 13–21.

Bailey, Cathryn. 2007. "We Are What We Eat: Feminist Vegetarianism and the Reproduction of Racial Identity." *Hypatia* 22, no 2: 35–59.

Barad, Karen. 2003. "Posthumanist Performativity: Toward an Understanding of How Matter Comes to Matter." *Signs: Journal of Women in Culture and Society* 2, no. 3: 801–831.

Candy, Catherine. 2007. "'Untouchability': Vegetarianism and the Suffragist Ideology of Margaret Cousins." In *Irish Women and the Vote: Becoming Citizens*, edited by Louise Ryan and Margaret Ward. 136–70. Dublin: Irish Academic Press.

Candy, Catherine. 2009. "Mystical Internationalism in Margaret Cousins's Feminist World." *Women's Studies International Forum* 32, no 1: 29–34.

Combe, Andrew. 1849. *The Physiology of Digestion, Considered with Relation to the Principles of Dietetics*. Edinburgh: Royal College of Physicians.

Cousins, Margaret and James. 1950. *We Two Together: A Duography*. Madras: Ganesh.

Despard, Charlotte. 1913. *Theosophy and the Woman's Movement*. London: Theosophical Publishing Society.

Ellis, Havelock. 1915. *Studies in the Psychology of Sex, Volume II: Sexual Inversion,* Third Edition, Revised and Enlarged. Philadelphia: F. A. Davis Company.

Forward, Charles W. 1898. *Fifty Years of Food Reform: A History of the Vegetarian Movement in England*. London: Ideal Pub. Union.

Ghandi, Leela. 2006. *Affective Communities: Anti-Colonial Thought and the Politics of Friendship*. Durham: Duke University Press.

Gore-Booth, Eva. 1929. *Poems of Eva Gore-Booth: Complete Edition*, edited by Esther Roper. London: Longmans, Green and Co.

Gregory, James. 2004/rev 2014. "Vegetarianism as an International Movement,

c.1840–1915." Academia.edu.116.https://www.academia.edu/4120418/
Vegetarianism_as_an_international_movement_c.1840_1915

Holton, Sandra. 2002. "Gender Difference, National Identity and Professing History: The Case of Alice Stopford Green." *History Workshop Journal* 53: 118–27.

Iovino, Serenella and Serpil Opperman. 2012. "Theorizing Material Ecocriticism: A Diptych." *ISLE: Interdisciplinary Studies in Literature and Environment* 19, no. 3: 448–75.

Kingstone, Helen. 2014. "Feminism, Nationalism, Separatism? The Case of Alice Stopford Green." *Journal of Victorian Culture* 19, no. 4: 442–56.

Leneman, Leah. 1997. "The Awakened Instinct: Vegetarianism and the Women's Suffrage Movement in Britain." *Women's History Review* 6, no. 2: 271–87.

Linklater, Andro. 1979. *An Unhusbanded Life: Charlotte Despard: Suffragette, Socialist, and Sinn Feiner.* London: Hutchinson.

Mitchell, Angus. 2006. "Alice Stopford Green and the Origins of the African Society." *History Ireland* 14: 19–24.

Nordau, Max. 1898. *Degeneration.* London: William Heinemann.

"Our Indian Empire and the Lessons It Teaches." 1857. *Dundee, Perth and Cupar Advertiser,* 21 August 1857.

Rohman, Carrie. 2008. *Stalking the Subject: Modernism and the Animal.* New York: Columbia University Press.

Smith, John. 1854. *Fruits and Farinacea, the Proper Food of Man; Being an Attempt to Prove, from History, Anatomy, Physiology, and Chemistry, that the Original and Best Diet of Man Is Derived from the Vegetable Kingdom.* New York: Fowler and Wells.

"Some Curious Headings Are Appearing in the Newspapers Just Now." 1885. *Yorkshire Gazette,* 19 January 1885.

Salleh, Ariel. 1997. *Ecofeminism as Politics: Nature, Marx, and the Postmodern.* London and New York: Zed Books.

Salleh, Ariel. 1999. "In Conversation with Meira Hanson: On Production and Reproduction: Identity and Nonidentity in Ecofeminist Theory." *Organization and Environment* 12, no. 2: 207–18.

Soper, Kate. 1995. *What is Nature: Culture, Politics, and the Non-Human.* Oxford: Blackwell.

Stopford Green, Alice. 1913. *Woman's Place in the World of Letters.* London: MacMillan and Co.

Tiernan, Sonja. 2012. *Eva Gore-Booth: An Image of Such Politics.* Manchester: Manchester University Press.

Tiffin, Helen, 2001. "Unjust Relations: Post-Colonialism and the Species Boundary." In *Compr(om)ising Postcolonialism(s): Challenging Narratives and Practices,* edited by Greg Ratcliffe and Gerry Turcotte, 30–41.

Sydney: Dungaroo.

"The Vegetarian Movement." 1848. *Punch,* XIV.

Van der Tuin, Iris. 2014. "Diffraction as a Methodology for Feminist Onto-Epistemology: On Encountering Chantal Chawaf and Posthuman Interpellation." *Parallax* 20, no. 3: 231–44.

"Vicious Vegetarianism." 1905. *Globe,* 29 May 1905.

Wilde, Oscar. 2000. *The Complete Letters,* edited by Merlin Holland and Rupert Hart-Davis. New York: Henry Holt and Co.

2

Emily Lawless: The Child as Natural Historian

Seán Hewitt

Writing in *A Garden Diary*, a set of notes and thoughts on nature, science, and literature composed during 1899 and 1900, Emily Lawless (1845–1913) gives a striking account of one May morning in particular. Beginning with the post-Darwinian caveat that nature is undoubtedly "cruel," in this passage Lawless turns our attention to a peculiarly spiritualised scene:

> This morning at a very early hour there was a tenderness, a kind of hovering serenity over everything, that appealed to one like a benediction. The air itself seemed changed; sanctified. The familiar little paths one walked along were like the approaches to some as yet invisible Temple. (Lawless 1901, 196)

Lawless continues by way of a reflection on the paintings of Jean François Millet: "in certain pictures … this quality of sanctity is the first thing that strikes one, the more so that the obviously religious element is conspicuously absent from them" (Lawless 1901, 196). Throughout Lawless's prose writings, this is a recurring reflection. That the natural world might be in some way "sanctified," and a site of spiritual awe which does not make recourse to orthodox religion, is rooted in Lawless's study and practice of natural history, and pervades her literary oeuvre. In her adult writings, Lawless repeatedly returns to the figure of the child (whether her own earlier self, or through fictional characters) in order to process and frame this sense of the numinous in nature, establishing the pursuit of natural history as a way of recovering a sort of pre-modern ecological connectedness and enchantment. By positing the close study of nature as a way of recovering a lost sense of the religious, Lawless inverts the materialism of positivist science by positing that materialism as a form of access to the spiritual.

Recent developments in ecocritical theory bring into new focus Lawless's innovations as a writer engaged with the materiality of the natural world. As Heidi Hansson has noted of Lawless's approach to the natural world in her poetry (though this is equally, if not more applicable to her prose writings), in dealing with nature as "real," she is writing against a *fin-de-siècle* tradition which viewed nature primarily in symbolic terms. Furthermore, through her natural historical study, she "differs from pre-Modernist and Modernist writers who primarily use aspects of nature as a metaphor for the inner life of the mind" (Hansson 2014, 6). Here, Hansson is following a line of criticism established by Edith Sichel, one of Lawless's early champions. Writing in the preface to the poems posthumously collected in *The Inalienable Heritage* (1914), Sichel summarised Lawless's verse as exhibiting a "twofold relation to nature," namely a focus on the external aspect, developed through years of scientific study, and an "inward relation," based on personal, national and intellectual history. Sichel characterised Lawless's attractions as a writer as being to "the visible pagan nature of the senses, and the search into Nature which means science, and the search concerning Nature which means thought" (Sichel 1914 , v–vi). This insightful analysis, which emphasises the sensuousness of Lawless's ecologies while also foregrounding their scientific basis, is an early expression of her innovative approach to nature writing which new critical and theoretical work brings into renewed light.

Throughout her works, as this chapter shows, Lawless foregrounds the figure of the child as a method of reinstating wonder at the heart of scientific study, using natural historical study in her work as a mode of countering post-Enlightenment disenchantment. The recent spiritual turn in ecocriticism foregrounds an unpicking of Enlightenment notions of a desacralised natural world. As Jane Bennett summarises:

> The eighteenth-century Enlightenment sought to demystify the world according to faith, where nature was God's text, filled with divine signs, intrinsic meaning, and intelligible order. In the face of belief in an enchanted cosmos, the Enlightenment sought to push God to a more distant social location; in the face of unreflective allegiance to tradition, it sought self-determination and self-conscious reason; in the face of a view of knowledge as mysterious divine hints, it sought a transparent, certain science; in the face of a sacralised nature, it sought a fund of useful natural resources. (Bennett 1987, 7)

Philosophers and critics such as Mary Midgley, Richard Kearney, George Levine, W.J.T. Mitchell, and Val Plumwood have all emphasised the necessity for re-thinking human/non-human relations, with many advocating a return to spiritually-inclined ways of viewing the world as autonomous, sacred, animated or otherwise "enchanted." In this way, a counter-Enlightenment turn is seen as necessary for the development of a new, ecologically-minded future. Richard Kearney, who argues that "the shortest route from wonder to wonder is loss," coins the term "anatheism" as "an invitation to revisit what might be termed a primary scene of religion: the encounter with a radical Stranger who we choose, or don't choose, to call God" (Kearney 2011, 7, 13). Jane Bennett follows a similar objective by developing a social theory which foregrounds "enchantment," by which she understands "a state of wonder, and one of the distinctions of this state is the temporary suspension of chronological time and bodily movement. To be enchanted, then, is to participate in a momentarily immobilizing encounter; it is to be transfixed, spellbound" (Bennett 2001, 5). Philip Fisher, similarly, describes a "moment of pure presence within wonder [which] lies in the object's difference and uniqueness" (Fisher 1998, 131). Thus, enchantment in the natural world also comes with a sense of the uncanny, of one's default temporal and sensory state being suspended (Bennett 2001, 5). Reading Lawless's work, wonder, and particularly childhood wonder in nature, is fundamental, and the way in which her texts negotiate the materiality of nature along with a sense of the numinous illumines them as particularly innovative in their navigating of natural science and spiritual awe.

In "An Entomological Adventure," a long personal essay included in *Traits and Confidences* (1898), Lawless begins by framing her childhood joy, her "most transcendent depths of rapture," as being linked to a peculiar uncanniness in the bog landscape. The bog, for her, was "a region full of bewitching suggestions, of haunting mystery, of dim, untravelled possibilities. A region from which no amount of after-familiarity ever entirely succeeded in stripping away the glamour" (Lawless 1898, 4). Throughout the essay, which recounts an incident in which the young Lawless finds herself trapped in a hayrick whilst out moth-hunting after dark, this sense of a gothic uncanny is used to foreground the alterity of the natural world. As Derek Gladwin has shown, this use of the bog to signal an uncanny and productive *difference* between observer and observed is prominent in the Irish Gothic (see Gladwin 2016). Thus, Lawless's recreation of "enchantment" finds its correlative in her use of the gothic mode. At nine years old, the child is, for Lawless, both far from the "first premonitory chill of disillusion," and from a sense of their own "unaccountably imposed limitations" (Lawless 1898, 6–7). She has a spiritual sensibility not limited by rationality or doubt, and is able to pursue natural historical activities in ways that might be curtailed by gender norms imposed more fully at a later age. Even the stars, in childhood, "twinkle encouraging remarks, addressed to you, and to you alone" (Lawless 1898, 7). "An Entomological Adventure" links, in this way, Lawless's spiritual and scientific pursuits as a child, where the universe retains a simple but majestic wonder in the particularity and physicality encouraged by natural historical study.

In recounting her childhood love for nature, and her trajectory towards entomological study, Lawless foregrounds the restrictions applied to her as a young woman as being instrumental in her focus on insects, rather than mammals or birds:

> If less pressing upon her than upon others, there still were certain respects in which the long-recognised limitations of her sex continued to assert themselves. The most formidable, perhaps, of these was the early recognition of the fact that under no circumstances, by no possible stretch of indulgence, would this Cuvier or Buffon in short frocks ever be entrusted with a gun! This plainly tyrannical, and heartless regulation had the natural effect of curtailing at one fell swoop the entire realm over which her future activities were to range, and in which she was to record her triumphs. Although, despite this humiliating restriction, woods, flower-beds, kitchen-garden walks, the back of the stables, the croquet ground, the rabbit yard, and other probable places were still daily scanned in full expectation that some bird or quadruped "new to science" would shortly present itself for her to discover, still by degrees she began to see that the wider fields being interdicted, it would be necessary to confine herself within narrower ones. From this cause it came to pass that winged insects, especially butterflies, and, close behind butterflies, moths, grew to occupy the foremost place in her affections, and from that day, for many a year to come, their education—as caterpillars—their capture, the exploration and contemplation of their haunts, habits, manners, customs, history, and civilization generally, became fixed in her mind, not only as the highest, but I may even go so far as to say the only really important object of human study. (Lawless 1898, 8–9)

The consequential logic of this passage, which begins with this naturalist "in short frocks" having her scope curtailed, and links this both to an obsession with moths and butterflies and, later, a rejection of "puerile frivolities" such as painting, music and literature, is actually an inversion. A social pressure which is put in place to prevent the young Lawless from becoming too "boyish" in fact leads her to reject the polite "accomplishments" of her class and sex. In other essays, particularly "On the Pursuit of Marine Zoology as an Incentive to Gossip" (included in *Traits and Confidences*, 1898), Lawless's natural historical study (this time, as an adult) is rebellious, with the co-option of kitchen crockery as containers for captured marine life being both a symbolic and literal disruption of the domestic space. Lawless's depiction of her childhood self as a natural historian is thus a method of tracing her apparent peculiarity in the object of her studies to a pervasive gender bias, but it is also one which allows her to retain a "child-like" wonder in the minutiae of nature (and a sense of gothic adventure in its pursuit) into adulthood. Her "enchantment" with the natural world—a key facet of all her texts—is both gendered and disruptive: she is restricted from gun-sports and hunting because of her sex, and turns instead towards the minutiae of "winged insects." In later works, discussed below, Lawless's retention of a Romantic awe in nature is figured as a protest against the abstractions of taxonomy (the language of science being unsuited to describe the intangible qualities of a thing) and against the positivist, patriarchal scientific gaze. If the Romantic will is to seek the transcendent experience in nature, Lawless retains this; however, she also supplements it with an attention to (and respect for) a materiality in nature which does not reflect the self, but is decidedly uncanny, strange, or different.

As the younger Lawless receives a bull's-eye lantern, pill-boxes and a net, and goes out on a nocturnal adventure replete with Gothic undertones (complete with an "ivy-mantled ruin" at dusk), so the older Lawless retains, and even outdoes, the sense of enchantment in entomological adventuring:

> The same bull's-eye lantern, carried along the naked top of a sea cliff, from over whose edge winged objects keep whizzing; while a hoarse roar from the Atlantic booms in thunderous accents out of the void, and the ground yawns and quivers in unexpected places underfoot, is a yet more entrancing performance, but that particular form of rapture had not at this time grown to be part of our heroine's daily experiences. (Lawless 1898, 11)

Again, for Lawless here the world is "entrancing," animated (it "yawns and quivers"), and moth-hunting is a form of adventure, suitably undertaken by a "heroine." It is dangerous and dramatic, and retains for the adult the same sense of excitement and wonder that held the child. In highlighting this continuity, both in her autobiographical essays and in her verse and fiction, Lawless uses the figure of the child as natural historian as a way of subverting strictly positivist, masculinist ways of knowing. In retaining a Romantic awe in nature, but supplementing this with a concerted focus on materiality, she deploys a gendered critique of both contemporary science and contemporary literature.

As a natural historian, Lawless's interests ranged across entomology, botany, marine zoology, and geology. Alongside publications in *Entomologist's Weekly*, contributions to Alexander Goodman More's *Cybele Hibernica* and numerous references in the *Illustrated History of British Butterflies and Moths* (1874), her frequent contributions to *Nineteenth Century*, as Brendan Prunty notes, show a familiarity and dialogue with other eminent contributors to that magazine during the 1890s, including Thomas Henry Huxley's interventions in the ongoing debate between evolutionists with regards to the place of religion in scientific study (Prunty 2009, 175). Although botany, and popular botanical writing, had been encoded from the late eighteenth century onwards as a suitably feminine pursuit, remaining outside the norms of scientific writing particularly through the inclusion of poetic glosses, the gradual professionalisation of science, and its institutionalisation over the course of the nineteenth century, led to its masculinisation, particularly in the realm of system-building and modification

(George 2007, 11). As Heidi Hansson has shown, Lawless's contributions to scientific journals usually adhere to scientific conventions; however, Lawless's fiction often posits a proto-feminist critique of scientific knowledge, subverting the totalising aims of Linnaean taxonomy and even playfully referring to certain flowers by male rather than female pronouns. The scarlet anemone, in one anonymous contribution to *Notes and Queries*, is both "he" and, more colloquially, a "fellow" (Hansson 2011, 60, 64).

Lawless's "unwillingness to subscribe to any kind of taxonomical system" is at the heart of her innovative approach to environmental writing (Hansson 2007, 8). In her autobiographical essays, and in her final single-authored novel *The Book of Gilly: Four Months out of a Life* (1906)—*The Race of Castlebar* (1913) was a collaboration with Shan Bullock—, it is the figure of the child who, being exposed to different forms of scientific knowledge-making, is at the centre of Lawless's critique of a de-spiritualised, masculinist approach to both language and natural history. Mary Midgley has suggested that gender bias has been integral to the rejection of spiritually-inclined approaches to the environment in scientific circles, and Val Plumwood has detailed the ways in which the "officially gender-neutral concept of reason" is inflected with a "masculine presence" (Midgley 2001, 171; Plumwood 1993, 5). Elsewhere, the development of ecofeminist critiques in literary studies have sought to uncover the ways in which writers have rendered the natural world as a "speaking subject," valuing its alterity, its autonomy, rather than its subjugated position in a patriarchal worldview (Murphy 1995, 12). In Lawless's work, the spirituality of nature is emphasised in opposition to a more systematic, positivist approach, and the childlike state of wonder, awe, and fantasy is privileged in opposition to the supposedly cold rationality of the adult or gatekeeper.

In *The Book of Gilly*, Lawless reasserts in fictional form many of the ideas about the natural world which she presents in her non-fictional essays, thus building up a corpus of spiritually-inclined notions regarding the natural world which posits a continuity between the Romantic awe (or enchantment) of the child and the sensitive practice of the adult natural historian. In the novel, Lawless narrates the four months which Gilly, an English schoolboy, spends on his family property on Inishbeg. During his sojourn in the West of Ireland, Gilly is assigned a tutor, Mr. Griggs, who is a professional natural historian researching an article on "The Respiratory Action of the Dytiscidæ." He also meets Tim, a young companion, and a disabled Oxford graduate, Phil Acton, who acts as a foil to Griggs's stark rationalism. The two adults, in fact, are said to "stand at exactly opposite poles of the intellectual sphere" (Lawless 1906, 180). For the young Gilly, who is excited by an imperially-minded sense of adventure and romance in his new landscape, Mr. Griggs becomes an incongruous figure when set against this mysterious, spiritually-imminent island. The Atlantic, a dominant presence in the book, becomes emblematic of the essence of mystery and concealment: it is full of life that cannot be seen from the surface, and the processes of dredging and fishing are correlates of the spiritual faith or mythical belief. In the second chapter of the novel, which "Introduces His Island," the "earliest of the island people to awaken" are actually the "smaller members of the zoophyte family—hydroids and their allies—whose home there is in the three deep rock-pools which fill the long trough lying between the outer and the inner reef" (Lawless 1906, 13). This initial ecological expansion of "people" to include all things which "people" the landscape allows Lawless, in later chapters, to blur national and natural history, to include within a "Celtic" sensitivity to myth and Romance a scientific attention to the details of the material world. Such ideas of the ecological consciousness pushing against national identities and borders prefigures ecocritical notions of the Anthropocene as a crisis which requires new frames and scales, though for Lawless this is also a political sleight of hand which helps to accommodate a Unionist, Anglo-Irish identity within the Irish landscape (Chakravarty 2009, 207).

In her essay "A Note on the Ethics of Literary Forgery," published in *The Nineteenth Century* in January 1897, Lawless describes the process of reading antiquarian literature as being akin to dredging in the Atlantic. The creatures therein are "extremely uncanny to look at," and defy easy categorisation: "Are they of the nature of bells? or of the nature of flowers? or of balloons? or what? And this odd, convulsive, heaving movement—this systole and diastole, as of a heart acting on its own account, without any body to sustain it?" (Lawless 1897, 88–9). Such is the process by which writers attempt to recreate an historical context by seeking to name the unknowables of a vanished existence. The world is full of "unseen presences," and the Atlantic is a conjuror:

> The Atlantic is perhaps of all still extant and surviving magicians the most potent in this art of conjuring up and rejuvenating a world which has never entirely ceased to rustle and whisper along his shores. Place yourself also there, and listen with sufficient docility to his rather inarticulate teachings, and there is no knowing what important secrets he may not some day murmur suddenly into your ears. Emanations with the very thinnest of white misty finger-tips may be seen to flit silently out of the seaweeds, as you crunch your way homeward towards evening over the rocks. Incorporeal presences—which can be perfectly well seen so long as you do not look directly at them—peer suddenly at you from behind some glittering rock, or glide away into deeper water as you run your boat inshore. (Lawless 1897, 91–2)

Rather than the natural world being a tool for the exploration of the psyche of the speaker, or being merely emblematic or metaphorical, it is framed as autonomous, imminent with knowledge, and able to act independently of the human observer. Staring into the ocean, the onlooker is met with a striking alterity. Not only are the creatures therein difficult or impossible to classify in natural historical terms, but they are also given an otherworldly quality, suggesting the spirituality of nature alongside its materiality. It is this dual presence (noted in Edith Sichel's phrase as a "twofold relation to nature" (Sichel 1914, v–vi)) that Lawless emphasises, and which her child protagonists, unhindered by the adult expectation of rationality, most fully embody.

The same basic ideas from "On the Ethics of Literary Forgery" are repeated in *The Book of Gilly* as Gilly looks out of his bedroom window at night over the island's creek and enters onto a rumination which becomes the source of a night terror. Looking at the creek, Gilly imagines that he sees the seaweed "shining with dots and sparkles of phosphorescence," and begins to think about a conversation he has had with his Irish friend, Tim, who has informed him about the presence of certain "*things*," known as "Thim Ould Wans," who live in the caves around the island (Lawless 1906, 121). Tim's reference to the sídh is misconstrued by Gilly, who begins to imagine nightmarish animals such as sea anemones with eyes like those of a peacock butterfly. In this passage, through a set of terrors which is produced from the natural workings of the environment and the folk beliefs of its inhabitants, Gilly becomes aware of the spiritual or psychical immensity of the natural world, and Lawless prepares a stark contrast to the arrival of the rational Mr. Griggs, who appears for the first time in the following chapter.

Gilly's potential for imaginative excitement is fundamental to what is perhaps the key scene in the novel, related in a chapter "In which the Hero studies Zoology beside a Lake and the Cosmos Upon a Rocking Stone." Here, Lawless puts forward an image of acute enchantment in the natural world, what Philip Fisher would call a "moment of pure presence," or what Richard Kearney might deem an anatheistic encounter with the "radical stranger" (Fisher 1998, 131; Kearney 2011, 7). What is most notable is that this is contrasted both to any religious encounter and to the sterile methods of scientific enquiry being taught by Mr. Griggs. Standing on a stone by a lake, Gilly feels it rock, and all of a sudden becomes aware of the earth moving beneath him, and "a sense of something remote from himself, something planetary, something crushingly vast and incomprehensible" (Lawless 1906, 176). Importantly, Lawless qualifies the ensuing revery as based wholly in the material world: "it was a natural, not a religious awe" (Lawless 1906, 176). When Gilly finally is reawakened into the "real" world, it is by Mr. Griggs, who is "sitting cross-legged upon a dry tussock, writing away at feverish speed, and with a very stumpy pencil, his notes upon the Respiratory action of the Dytiscidæ" (Lawless 1906, 177). The language used here, even down to the "dry tussock," is suggestive of the joyless scientific practice of Griggs set in opposition to Gilly's revelatory and transcendent experience of the cosmos.

To the romantic figure of Phil Acton, the young idealistic Oxford graduate, Mr. Griggs's view of the world is "a crass crudity, a hardened philistinism," and to Mr. Griggs "reverence" is nothing but "an exploded superstition; idealism another way of spelling idiocy" (Lawless 1906, 180). In another formulation, Lawless delineates a common assumption that humanity exists on a binary between the Sancho Panzas of the world (who have "a sound grip on reality but no ideals") and the Don Quixotes (who have "the instinct of ideals, but without any decent hold on reality") (Lawless 1906, 181). It is clear which side of the binary Lawless errs on: her fiction, and her childhood figures, persistently emphasise "reverence" in nature as fundamental to any proper scientific or literary investigation. For Lawless, the pursuit of natural history, properly conducted, should be a mediator between the two, employing the childlike awe and spiritual reverence in nature with the scientist's grasp on "reality." In contrast, Mr. Griggs is a figure for whom "his honest scorn was at the service of all who were capable of even uttering words like 'mystery' or 'riddle'" (Lawless 1906, 180).

As in "An Entomological Adventure," in *The Book of Gilly* it is the mind of the child which is positioned as most instructive in combatting a sterile scientific positivism. For "that small personage," Gilly, the scientific pursuit of trying to define the indefinable is futile. What Lawless recognises as the boundary-bending nature of the sea creatures (and the literary and historical past) in "On the Ethics of Literary Forgery" is fundamental to Gilly's development in her bildungsroman:

> Let us dissect, if we can, the last thrill of a thrush's song; write down, if we flatter ourselves we can do so, in the language of science the precise meaning of the colours and scents of flowers, but let us in heaven's name leave alone that intangible product of moods and fancies, a child's or young boy's mind! (Lawless 1906, 181)

In this neat inversion, Lawless comes close to turning her gaze against the bildungsroman form itself. The project of defining Gilly's mind and its growth, as with classifying and dissecting the natural world, must be given over in part to an acknowledgment of intangibility, of mysteries and riddles. Thus, Lawless's critique of the masculinist desire for positive knowledge is also a literary critique, and a call for the acceptance of language's ability to describe or relay the world, whether "real" or imagined or both. If the binary of Phil Acton and Mr. Griggs or Sancho Panza and Don Quixote (with Gilly sitting somewhere in the middle) is unsatisfactory, it is because neither effectively blends the idealistic vision with the realistic vision: "If for Phil Acton the veil of things was too often a wearisomely inscrutable mystery, for Mr. Griggs there was no veil at all, merely a set of serviceable partitions, a sign-boarded over with useful knowledge, planking out the universe" (Lawless 1906, 188).

During a period when writers such as W. B. Yeats and A. E. were promoting forms of "Celtic" mysticism appropriated from a variety of international traditions, Lawless's language of a veiled world beyond material reality is surely pointed. Like Yeats, she rejects a scientific positivism which sees "no veil at all"; however, she also promotes a focused, spiritual attention on materiality. Where she wrote in her *Garden Diary* of "the wonder, the mystery, of those ordinary processes of nature," Lawless also sought to draw a link between the awe in nature of her childhood self and her child protagonist Gilly in order to counter "adult" rationality. In that diary, Lawless persistently advocates for an ecological spirituality:

> Assuredly man is by nature a devotional creature, however little of the dogmatic may mingle with his devotions. He may avert his ear from the church-going bell, he may refuse to label himself with the label of any particular denomination, but it is only to be overtaken with awe in the heart of a forest, and to fall on his knees, as it were, in some green secluded spot of the wilderness. (Lawless 1901, 197)

In her presentation of children practicing natural historical study in ways contrary to the positivism of scientific orthodoxy, Lawless argues in her prose works for the retention of wonder, reverence, and spirituality. Such an "enchanted" worldview is brought into new focus by the recent spiritual turn in eco-theory, and Lawless's innovations as a writer-naturalist are made clearer. Though, as Heidi Hansson notes, "Lawless's political conservatism means that it is easy to regard her literary output as equally unadventurous," the ecologies of her works show her modernity (Hansson 2016, 50). Returning to the figure of the child, Lawless finds an instructive example for both literature and science, seeking out a time before those "unaccountably imposed limitations" distinguished natural historical practice from spiritual consciousness and positing the mindset of the child as a counter to the post-Enlightenment rationalism of contemporary professionalised science (Lawless 1898, 6–7).

References

Bennett, Jane. 1987. *Unthinking Faith and Enlightenment: Nature and the State in a Post-Hegelian Era*. New York and London: New York University Press.

——. 2001. *The Enchantment of Modern Life: Attachments, Crossings, and Ethics*. Princeton and Oxford: Princeton University Press.

Chakravarty, Dipesh. 2009. "The Climate of History: Four Theses." *Critical Inquiry* 35: 197–222.

Fisher, Philip. 1998. *Wonder, the Rainbow, and the Aesthetics of Rare Experiences.*

Harvard University Press.

George, Sam. 2007. *Botany, Sexuality, and Women's Writing 1760–1830: From Modest Shoot to Forward Plant.* Manchester and New York: Manchester University Press.

Gladwin, Derek. 2016. *Contentious Terrains: Boglands, Ireland, Postcolonial Gothic.* Cork: Cork University Press.

Hansson, Heidi. 2007. *Emily Lawless, 1845–1913: Writing the Interspace.* Cork: Cork University Press.

———. 2011. "Emily Lawless and Botany as Foreign Science." *Journal of Literature and Science* 4, no. 1: 59–73.

———. 2014. "Kinship: People and Nature in Emily Lawless's Poetry." *Nordic Journal of English Studies* 13, no. 2: 6–22.

———. 2016. "Nature, Education, and Liberty in *The Book of Gilly* by Emily Lawless." In *Irish Women's Writing, 1878–1922: Advancing the Cause of Liberty*, edited by Anna Pilz and Whitney Standlee, 49–64. Manchester: Manchester University Press.

Kearney, Richard. 2011. *Anatheism: Returning to God after God.* New York: Columbia University Press.

Lawless, Emily. 1898. *Traits and Confidences.* London: Methuen.

———. 1897. "A Note on the Ethics of Literary Forgery." *The Nineteenth Century: a Monthly Review* 41, no. 239 (January): 84–95.

———. 1901. *A Garden Diary, September 1899–September 1900.* London: Methuen & Co.

———. 1906. *The Book of Gilly: Four Months out of a Life.* London: Smith, Elder, & Co.

———. 1914. *The Inalienable Heritage, and Other Poems.* Privately Printed.

Midgley, Mary. 2001. *Science and Poetry.* London: Routledge.

Murphy, Patrick D. 1995. *Literature, Nature, and Other: Ecofeminist Critiques.* Albany and New York: State University of New York Press.

Plumwood, Val. 1993. *Feminism and the Mastery of Nature.* London and New York: Routledge.

Prunty, Brendan. 2009. "The Irish Fiction of Emily Lawless: A Narrative Analysis." PhD Diss., National University of Ireland, Maynooth.

Sichel, Edith. 1914. "Preface" in Emily Lawless, *The Inalienable Heritage, and Other Poems.* Privately Printed.

3

Sunk in the Mainstream: Irish Women Writers, Canonicity, and Famine Memory, 1892–1917

Christopher Cusack

Where is the Famine in the literature of the Revival?
—Terry Eagleton (1995, 13)

A girl did not dare to be original in 1846.
—L. T. Meade (1909, 2)

It feels curiously anachronistic, thirty years after Chris Morash's *The Hungry Voice* (1989), to begin an essay about the literature of the Great Irish Famine by adverting to Terry Eagleton's oft-cited reflections on the representation of the crisis in Irish writing. However, his observations perfectly frame the argument this essay will develop regarding the relation between canon, gender, and memory. In *Heathcliff and the Great Hunger*, his influential contribution to the 1990s post-revisionist movement in Irish Studies, Eagleton argues that "repression or evasion would seem to be at work in Irish literary culture, which is hardly rife with allusions to the event" (1995, 12). He is asking an important question, but while he partly qualifies his argument by focusing on the canon, the notion that the Famine is absent from the oeuvres of the great white males whose faces adorn the famous Irish Writers souvenir poster is itself doubtful (see Cusack and Goss 2006). More importantly, though, Eagleton's argument is problematic in general. As this essay will argue by considering examples of Famine fiction published by Irish women between 1892 and 1917, processes of canonisation, and particularly its gendered dynamics, have significantly influenced the cultural memory of the Famine.

Eagleton was certainly aware of the existence of a body of Famine literature, as demonstrated by his references to Chris Morash's studies on the subject, but he argues that the memory of the Famine is mainly hidden in the margins of canonical texts such as Emily Brontë's *Wuthering Heights* (1847). However, this suggestion has been strongly qualified by scholars such as Morash (1989 and 1995), Margaret Kelleher (1997), Melissa Fegan (2002), and most recently Marguérite Corporaal (2017), as well as doctoral research by Lindsay Janssen (2016) and myself (2018). Such work shows that there are at least 130 examples of literary fiction from pre-Independence Ireland and the Irish diaspora that engage very explicitly with the Famine past. Such texts, many of which were once widely read and in that sense not simply "minor," demonstrate that it is incorrect to argue that silence has been the primary modality of the memory of the event. This is indeed confirmed by the many hundreds of references to the crisis in newspapers and magazines down the decades, and by the prevalence of Famine narratives in the National Folklore Collection.

Yet the myth of silence continues to have mainstream traction, as Mary McAleese's preface to the monumental *Atlas of the Great Irish Famine* shows. The former President states that:

> Writing about and representing the Great Irish Famine, the most tragic event in Irish history[,] has not been straightforward. For many years the event was cloaked in silence, its memory for the most part buried or neglected. (McAleese 2012, ix)

McAleese's gambit, with its emphatic sense of pathos, prioritises its rhetorical purpose over accuracy. After all, in the same volume, Chris Morash, summarising two decades of scholarship, observes that "the old cliché that the Famine was a silence in Irish writing is not really sustainable" (2012, 644).

The trope of silence itself, rather than any actual lack of textual mediations of Famine memory, is a major reason why this view persists. A common critical strategy is to emphasise what is, purportedly, the Famine's traumatic unrepresentability, and then to describe the event in detail. The proliferation of this rhetorical posture in turn has given shape to the dominant narrative of the Famine on a meta-discursive level, particularly in the context of the preoccupations of the Revival, even if it inevitably disproves itself by its own example, as I will show (see also Cusack 2018, 20–21, 45–52).

This strategy is, however, not the only causative factor in the aetiology of silence, as Eagleton's focus on the canon unwittingly establishes. As Margaret Kelleher states, a major cause of the belief that the Famine has not really been represented is that "[t]he extent to which Irish literature contains references to the famine depends, very simply, on where one looks" (1997, 4). While there are few texts now considered canonical from the late nineteenth and early twentieth century that have a central focus on the Famine, there is a large trove of pre-independence Famine writing, especially fiction, that was banished to the cultural hinterlands in the wake of the Irish Revival. Even though they were once highly popular, authors such as Patrick Sheehan, Justin McCarthy, and

Joseph Guinan, in whose works the Famine features at length, have not become canonical, unlike contemporaries such as Stoker, Wilde, Yeats, and Synge (see also Murphy 1997).

An exploration of canon formation also brings into focus another dimension. As I argue in this essay, one of the reasons why the myth of Famine silence became so forceful is the silencing of women's voices in the Irish canon. Some of the most popular Irish writers from the latter decades of the nineteenth century and first two decades of the twentieth, such as L. T. Meade (1844–1914), Jane Barlow (1857–1917), Katharine Tynan (1859–1931), and Emily Lawless (1845–1913), engaged deeply with the memory of the Famine, as did less famous authors such as Mildred Darby (1867–1932), Louise Field (1856–1940), Máire Ní Chillín (1874–1956), and the pseudonymous "Slieve Foy," in addition to diasporic authors such as the Irish-American Mary Synon (dates unknown) (Cusack 2018). None of these authors remain widely read today.

In her contribution to *A History of Modern Irish Women's Literature*, Paige Reynolds shows how Irish Revivalism contributed in no small degree to reducing the visibility of women in Irish society and culture beyond predominantly symbolical iterations of femininity as "the vulnerable virgin and self-abnegating mother" (2018, 131). Such tropes were part of binaries that encouraged images of Irishness rooted in masculinity and virility, which were meant to prove Ireland's fitness for self-government (see Beatty 2016). Despite the numerous Irish women writers who critiqued such patriarchal dualism, Irish womanhood became both religiously and culturally increasingly formalised as a highly idealised—and thus inherently reductive—iteration of domestic femininity at the service of an emergent sense of masculine nationhood.

As James H. Murphy points out, literary production during this era showed near "parity" in terms of authors' genders (2011, 17). Indeed, Stephen Gwynn, an important advocate of Irish Revivalism during the *fin de siècle*, remarked in 1897 that "[t]he roll of Irish novelists is more than half made up of women's names," highlighting Emily Lawless and Jane Barlow, both writing about the Famine at the time, as the two exemplars "who stand out prominently among contemporary writers of Irish fiction" (1897, 16, 21). But as literature was considered the pre-eminent vehicle for new ideals of Irishness, the Irish canon grew ever more androcentric, particularly as some of the major writers of the Revival in turn became the bedrock of post-Independence forms of national self-imagination. For the apotheosis of every Synge or Yeats, it seems, a Lawless or Barlow had to be consigned to oblivion, and their versions of the Irish past, including their examinations of Famine memory, erased.

The process of canon formation is obviously not a zero-sum game, but in the context of the Famine it is notable that several women writers from this era who wrote about it, such as L. T. Meade and Katharine Tynan, had greater fame than most of the men doing so, and were indeed among the bestselling Irish writers of their day. Moreover, many, including Tynan and Jane Barlow, were part of the same côteries as male contemporaries who are now more famous. Despite this, they are no longer known outside the specialist repertoire. By and large, the authors from this period who still garner attention beyond academic contexts are male.

Given the number of Irish women who wrote fiction about the Famine around the *fin de siècle* and indeed the fame some of them enjoyed, it would appear that the consolidation of the persistent Famine narrative about traumatic repression is at least partially inflected by the gender dynamics of canon formation. Gendered processes of sociocultural consecration and marginalisation have in this sense deeply influenced the creation and proliferation of narratives of Irish cultural forgetting, all in the service of new and proudly resistant narratives of nationhood. By this token, Famine memory is not typified primarily by silence, but rather by a lack of visibility that is culturally engineered.

However, Terry Eagleton's argument about the apparent absence of the Famine in Irish literary culture is premised on the notion that the Revival was, as Kevin Whelan suggests, "the creation of a series of radical responses to the Famine legacy" (2005, 137). Scholars such as Whelan, Eagleton, and Seamus Deane conceptualise the Famine as a cultural trauma that was repressed to enhance the viability of the Irish nation-building project (Whelan 2005; Deane 1997, 51).

Numerous texts from the late nineteenth and early twentieth century indeed seem to suggest that the memory of the Famine was the subject of cultural forgetting. In his 1908 tract *The Famine Years*, Canon Joseph Guinan states that "the bitter memories" of the crisis "are now well nigh forgotten" (1908, 32). In the preface to *The Hunger* (1910), Mildred Darby claims that "[f]ew people of the present generation know more of the appalling catastrophe than its broad outlines, gathered from some attenuated volume of Irish History; and those very outlines have probably grown vague" (Merry 1910, 1). In her biography of temperance reformer Father Theobald Mathew, Katharine Tynan describes the crisis as "a holocaust of a million dead of starvation" during which things happened "too horrible to be told" (1908, 144, 150).

Further examples abound, but what is interesting here is that Guinan, Darby, and Tynan, and indeed numerous others who advocate such theories about the attrition of Famine memory, contradict their own assertions. Guinan states that "there is no use now in indulging in bitter reflections" (1908, 4), but then spends another thirty pages doing exactly that. Darby remarks that the Famine is "unforgettable" and "burnt by personal suffering upon the memory" (Merry 1910, 3). And Tynan's chapter on things "too horrible to be told" covers a full fourteen pages. These works, like so many other examples of Famine literature, are typical examples of apophasis. This discursive emphasis on silence is actually a highly conventional manifestation of Famine memory and a marker of its propagation rather than elision or sublimation. It provides an idiom and range of imagery for the description of the Famine that validates its epistemological conceptualisation as the ground zero of Irish culture.

Post-Famine silence is frequently, though not exclusively, coded as feminine, by male and female authors alike. Famine narratives often feature upper (-middle) class female characters who use the crisis to chip away at the strictures of their social position, as in L. T. Meade's *The Stormy Petrel* (1909), but it can also mute female protagonists. Such stories allegorise the death of Irish culture through the familiar representation of Ireland as a young woman. For instance, the protagonist of Emily Lawless' short story "After the Famine" (1898), Eleanor D'Arcy, is an impoverished gentry daughter who is severely traumatised by the death of her father and sisters as a result of their charitable efforts. She is objectified as a largely voiceless victim whose only utterances are either faltering descriptions of the way her loved ones died, or exclamations directed at the dead. Eileen Fitzmaurice, the protagonist of Jane Barlow's story "The Keys of the Chest" (1897), is very similar in terms of age and class, but she is literally silenced by the Famine, as she accidentally dies in an explosion ordered by an officer of the Public Works to destroy a large rock that is the focus of Eileen's childhood fancies. In these texts, as in many other works, the death of culture and the traumatic silence it engenders are imagined as feminine.

In *Forgetful Remembrance*, Guy Beiner demonstrates how cultural amnesia is usually fraught with contradiction. His study of the memory of 1798 in Ulster highlights how "disremembering," an ostensibly negative manifestation of memory usually rooted in social tensions, in many ways actually cements the legacy of the history it is trying to repress (Beiner 2018). The memory of the Famine is a major example of this: the emphasis on silence and trauma is in fact a performative strategy which results in the consolidation and distribution of a particular type of narrative about Ireland's past. While the idea that the Famine was so traumatic that it muted an entire culture may have been a validatory strategy for the Revivalist project, as a cultural index it is recursive and misleading.

It is mostly their shared theme and the vagaries of canon formation that bring together works like Jane Barlow's *Kerrigan's Quality* (1894) and "The Keys of the Chest" (1897), Louise Field's *Denis* (1896), L. T. Meade's *The Stormy Petrel* (1909), Mildred Darby's *The Hunger* (1910), and assorted short stories by Katharine Tynan, Emily Lawless, and others (for a full overview, see Cusack 2018). These texts do not constitute a subset within the larger domain of Famine fiction other than by virtue of their authors' gender. Nor are they, with the exception of Meade's novel (Cusack 2019), more explicitly gendered in the way they engage with the memory of the crisis than some Famine fiction by male writers, such as Anthony Trollope's *Castle Richmond* (1860) or Justin McCarthy's *Mononia* (1901). And while most of these women writers came from broadly similar class backgrounds in the upper-middle or upper classes, their political and religious backgrounds and views are by no means identical.

These works resemble other Famine fiction in the repertoire of images and representational strategies they employ. Like the vast majority of Famine fiction from the 1850s onwards, many instrumentalise the memory of the crisis to make points about other social, political, or cultural issues, using the Famine as a "blank canvas on which to explore their own anxieties" (Fegan 2002, 209). Louise Field's novel *Denis*, for example, is set during the crisis but harnesses its associations to address "that vast and ever-recurring problem, the Irish Question" still defining Irish society at the end of the nineteenth century (Field 1896, v), particularly in terms of class (Cusack 2019). Jane Barlow's *Kerrigan's Quality* (1894) also appropriates the memory of the crisis to discuss the position of the upper classes in *fin-de-siècle* Ireland. And Máire Ní Chillín's obscure tale "On the Bog Road" (1917), published in the M. H. Gill collection *On Tiptoe: A Collection of Stories and Sketches by Irish Women*, reduces the Famine to a moral lesson for children about faith and fortitude during the First World War. All of these authors use the Famine as a cipher, a vessel for a myriad concerns not directly related to the event itself.

In the context of this essay, L. T. Meade's *The Stormy Petrel* (1909) is thematically perhaps the most interesting text. Meade was a hugely prolific and popular author who published scores of self-consciously modern tales about female agency. As suggested by the second epigraph to this chapter, "[a] girl did not dare to be original in 1846" (Meade 1909, 2). However, in *The Stormy Petrel*, Meade uses the Famine past to introduce a powerful female protagonist who embraces philanthropy as a means of increasing her autonomy, though the novel soon becomes mired in a convoluted romantic plot. Meade's feminist interest in the Famine demonstrates that she was familiar with the most regular type of protagonist of Irish Famine fiction, namely the charitable young lady of upper-middle or upper class background who uses philanthropy for self-assertion, found throughout the entire corpus of pre-Independence Famine fiction (see Kelleher 1997 and Cusack 2019). Though Meade is surely, given her explicitly feminist rhetoric, a modern writer, her ostensibly radical protagonist is actually not that "original" within the context of Famine literature.

As a bestselling author, Meade had a good sense of her market, so her choice to devote an entire novel to the Famine is significant. Like numerous other Famine novels, *The Stormy Petrel*, published a few years before Meade's death in 1914, was reviewed in leading literary periodicals, including *The Academy*, which concluded slightly cattily that Meade's fans "will find that she has given good measure, and that the quality of interest which she invariably manages to impart to her books remains, despite many verbal infelicities, at its usual high level" (*The Academy*, 30 January 1909). Yet in her essential study *The Irish New Woman*, Tina O'Toole claims that "we find no traces of it [the Famine] in her later writing, which perhaps suggests an unwillingness to engage with the fractured history of her homeland" (2013, 46). The fact that O'Toole, the most prominent critic of Irish New Woman writing today, overlooked this novel, and thus a very prominent manifestation of Famine memory, betrays the extent to which the literary memory of the Famine is defined by the myth of absence.

Meade and others wrote a type of Irish realist fiction that was rejected by (self-proclaimed) arbiters of Revivalist taste such as W. B. Yeats and Stephen Gwynn, and Maurice Egan in the US. While acknowledging its influence, they considered it too focused on marketing particular versions of Irish life, often to non-Irish audiences, to the detriment of literary and cultural value. "Literature … in Ireland," Gwynn remarked in 1897, "is almost inextricably connected with considerations foreign to art" (1897, 8). In his view, the vast majority of nineteenth-century Irish fiction straddles narrative fiction and journalism, which affects its aesthetic value, yet it rarely manages to represent what he considers to be the quintessence of Irishness, since such novels often reduce Irishness to particular generalities.

Other critics from this era also asserted that the programmatic literary reappraisal promoted by the Revival would fix "the factors that had restricted the quality of Irish writing—its overly sociological, poorly literary and market-driven character" (Kelleher 2005, 195). In order to achieve a higher degree of authenticity, and thus realism, Gwynn believed authors should focus on the specificities of different iterations—social, geographical, cultural—of Irish identity and resist the temptation to present the Irish as a completely homogeneous and pathologically joyous people. Importantly, as examples of this approach, he discusses Jane Barlow, whose tales produce finely-grained representations of Irishness through careful explorations of discrete regional identities, and Lawless, who largely rejects the type of blatant stereotyping that sold particularly well outside Ireland in order to develop more nuanced depictions of Irishness (Gwynn 1897, 21–3).

Yet, though Gwynn considered these two authors especially praiseworthy, their reputations did not endure. Indeed, around the same time Yeats dismissed Barlow precisely for the qualities for which Gwynn commends her: "despite her genius for recording the externals of Irish peasant life, I do not feel that she has got deep into the heart of things" (Yeats 1895). Given that Revival-era women writers in particular were often dismissed for these putative transgressions and that most works of Famine fiction discussed in this essay match these criteria, it is highly probable that these ostensibly aesthetic considerations also masked restrictive gender norms, which thus helped shape the canon that propped up new constructions of Irish history and identity.

These processes also affected the reputations of earlier writers of Famine fiction. An important case in point is Annie Keary, whose Famine novel *Castle Daly* (1875) is promoted by Rosa Mulholland as "[t]he best Irish story written in later years" in her influential essay "Wanted an Irish Novelist" ('R. M.' 1891, 371). Neither Keary nor Mulholland, who also wrote about famine, remain well-known today, and accordingly their tales of Irish history too no longer find any audience outside academic contexts.

All of these examples are instructive: not only does their success demonstrate that these Irish women writers were much more popular than their current reputations suggest, but the fact that so many bestselling writers wrote successful fiction about the Famine emphatically gives the lie to the idea that the memory of the crisis was marked by a wholesale cultural silence. On the contrary, the Great Famine was a theme that sold, yet as their writers were lost from view, so did some of the concerns they addressed in their works.

But what is ultimately at stake here? Do we lose anything at all if these texts are no longer read today? Though it would be possible to make a case for the literary quality of some of the texts referenced in this essay, this certainly does not apply to all of these works. The longueurs of L. T. Meade's boilerplate romance or the filiopietistic orthodoxies of Máire Ní Chillín's Famine tale ensure that these texts were unlikely candidates for canonisation anyway, even if in terms of sales the literary marketplace is seldom defined primarily by such concerns. But this is not intended as a belated sally in the canon wars that were infamously fought over the *Field Day Anthology* in the 1990s and is not, per se, a form of "retrieval work" (Kelleher 2003, 87), even if that white whale or holy grail of Irish Victorianists, an Irish *Middlemarch*, might yet be hiding among a bevy of its lesser brethren.

From the 1990s onwards, historians have been labouring to reconsider the position of women in the Irish revolutionary movement and cultural revival (Pašeta 2013, 1–16; O'Toole, McIntosh, and O'Cinnéide 2016, 1–9). Such work stresses the importance of querying traditional narratives, as these often foreground exclusionary perspectives. As Heather Laird argues, "[a]n historical framework that decentres familiar notions of power and the political and, consequently, expands the category of the historically relevant would automatically produce a body of scholarship more attuned to that which is at the margins of conventional history writing" (2018, 18). Renewed attention to neglected sources or engagements with familiar material that highlight themes such as gender, sexuality, and class will enable us to demythologise narratives about the Irish past premised on zero-sum conceptions of victimhood and cultural trauma. Instead, we will be able to promote more diverse and balanced interpretations of the history of Ireland and its diaspora.

Literary history has a major role to play in such processes. In *Scholars and Rebels*, Terry Eagleton argues that Irish fiction from the nineteenth century should be considered "an *ersatz* form of sociology" (Eagleton 1999, 32). This, in fact, dovetails with some of the criticisms directed at Irish authors by Gwynn, Yeats, and others, but is actually a major argument for returning to them today. Often, canonical fiction, which only rarely started life as popular fiction, is not necessarily the best place to look for the record of a society's ideologies, mentalities, and mnemonic preoccupations (see Foster 2008, 1–24). Instead of seeking to revise the canon in order to reclaim lost literary luminaries, I suggest we reframe the way we think about the uses of literature and the process of canon formation, and consider the implications this may have for our conceptualisation of Irish history. What is the upshot if the notion of canonicity, with all that entails, is used as a normative heuristic category for the study of the Irish past?

In a sense, the case of Mildred Darby can figure as a metaphor for the way the cultural reinvention of Ireland resulted in the deletion of many women writers from the Irish literary canon and, consequently, the neglect of the issues they wrote about. In Darby's case, this silencing was literal, and was in fact a direct result of the cruelties of patriarchy. While she used the male pseudonym Andrew Merry, reviews of *The Hunger* (1910) show that many people were privy to the author's background – indeed, the *Irish Book Lover* of May 1910 named her outright (133). Following the publication of *The Hunger*, her husband Jonathon forbade her from publishing any further works. He felt that the novel, a *roman à clef* about the history of the Darby family, their estate, and their ancestral home, Leap Castle in Coolderry, Co. Offaly, had damaged his reputation (see Reilly 2018).

Though no longer permitted to publish, Darby by no means stopped writing. Over the next decade or so, she accrued a collection of manuscripts and drafts of stories, novels, and non-fiction, often focusing on local history and the Irish past more generally. But during the night of 30 July 1922, a party of anti-Treaty IRA fighters set fire to Leap Castle, one of many such acts of arson during the Civil War. In the conflagration all of her unpublished work was lost. Thus, though first suppressed by Jonathon's assertion of patriarchal might, her voice, once a strong vehicle for the Irish past, was now silenced permanently by the forces, ironically, of that very history.

The marginalisation of authors of Famine fiction, and particularly the neglect of female authors who wrote at length about the crisis and were often widely read, influences how we remember and conceptualise Ireland's history. Thus, in order to obtain a more diversified overview of this past, we must also assess and historicise the processes of inclusion and marginalisation that define which source material, and by extension which story, is granted visibility.

Sara Ahmed's *Living a Feminist Life* discusses the many ways a "citational practice" that excludes women's voices affects academic development and skews historical understanding (2017, 8). Actively including marginalised voices is not only important for the promotion of diversity as a goal in itself, but is in fact crucial for the epistemological authority of historiography. In the context of the Famine, too, such critical reappraisal of scholarly practices has considerable implications. "Methodological and theoretical renewal," David Lloyd argues, "finds its value in serving the purposes of a recollection whose meaning and value lies in giving to the past's untimely dead a memory that defies the repetition of their fate" (2014, 295). The project of reframing the story of the Famine to actively incorporate the voices of Mildred Darby, L. T. Meade, Emily Lawless, Jane Barlow, Katharine Tynan, Louise Field, and so many other women writers, thus harbours not just an academic but also an ethical imperative.

References

Ahmed, Sara. 2017. *Living a Feminist Life*. Durham, NC: Duke University Press.

Barlow, Jane. 1894. *Kerrigan's Quality*. London: Hodder and Stoughton.

——. 1897. "The Keys of the Chest." In *A Creel of Irish Stories*, 1–96. London: Methuen and Company.

Beatty, Aidan. 2016. *Masculinity and Power in Irish Nationalism, 1884–1938*. Basingstoke: Palgrave Macmillan.

Beiner, Guy. 2018. *Forgetful Remembrance: Social Forgetting and Vernacular Historiography of a Rebellion in Ulster*. Oxford: Oxford University Press.

Corporaal, Marguérite. 2017. *Relocated Memories: The Great Famine in Irish and Diaspora Fiction, 1846–1870*. Syracuse, NY: Syracuse University Press.

Cusack, Christopher. 2018. "Memory, History, and Identity in Irish and Irish-Diasporic Famine Fiction, 1892–1921." PhD Diss., Radboud University.

——. 2019. "Transformative Nationalism and Class Relations in Irish Famine Fiction, 1896–1909." In *The Great Irish Famine and Social Class: Conflicts, Responsibilities, Representations*, edited by Marguérite Corporaal and Peter Gray, 151–69. Oxford: Peter Lang.

Cusack, George, and Sarah Goss, eds. 2006. *Hungry Words: Images of Famine in the Irish Canon*. Dublin: Irish Academic Press.

Deane, Seamus. 1997. *Strange Country: Modernity and Nationhood in Irish Writing Since 1790*. Oxford: Clarendon Press.

Eagleton, Terry. 1995. *Heathcliff and the Great Hunger: Studies in Irish Culture*. London: Verso.

——. 1999. *Scholars and Rebels in Nineteenth-Century Ireland*. Oxford: Blackwell.

Fegan, Melissa. 2002. *Literature and the Irish Famine, 1845–1919*. Oxford: Clarendon Press.

Field, Louise. 1896. *Denis: A Study in Black and White*. London: Macmillan and Company.

Foster, John Wilson. 2008. *Irish Novels 1890–1940: New Bearings in Culture and Fiction*. Oxford: Oxford University Press.

"Gossip: On Miss Mildred Darby's New Book." 1910. *Irish Book Lover* 1 (May): 133.

Guinan, Joseph. 1908. *The Famine Years*. Dublin: Catholic Truth Society.

Gwynn, Stephen. 1897. "Novels of Irish Life in the Nineteenth Century." In *Irish Books and Irish People*, 7–23. New York: Frederick A. Stokes.

Janssen, Lindsay. 2016. "Famine Traces: Memory, Landscape, History and Identity in Irish and Irish-Diasporic Famine Fiction, 1871–91." PhD Diss., Radboud University.

Keary, Annie, 1875. *Castle Daly: The Story of an Irish Home Thirty Years Ago*. London, Macmillan.

Kelleher, Margaret. 1997. *The Feminization of Famine: Expressions of the Inexpressible?* Durham, NC: Duke University Press.

———. 2003. "*The Field Day Anthology* and Irish Women's Literary Studies." *Irish Review* 30: 82–94.

———. 2005. "'Wanted an Irish Novelist': The Critical Decline of the Nineteenth-Century Novel." In *The Irish Novel in the Nineteenth Century: Facts and Fictions*, edited by Jacqueline Bélanger, 187–201. Dublin: Four Courts Press.

Laird, Heather. 2018. *Commemoration*. Cork: Cork University Press.

Lawless, Emily. 1898. "After the Famine." In *Traits and Confidences*, 163–217. London: Methuen and Company.

Lloyd, David. 2014. "Afterword: The Afterlife of the Untimely Dead." In *Global Legacies of the Great Irish Famine: Transnational and Interdisciplinary Perspectives*, edited by Marguérite Corporaal, Christopher Cusack, Lindsay Janssen, and Ruud van den Beuken, 285–95. Oxford: Peter Lang.

McAleese, Mary. 2012. "Preface." In *Atlas of the Great Irish Famine*, edited by John Crowley, William J. Smyth, and Mike Murphy, ix. Cork: Cork University Press.

McCarthy, Justin. 1901. *Mononia: A Love Story of "Forty-Eight."* London: Chatto and Windus.

Meade, L. T. 1909. *The Stormy Petrel*. London: Hurst and Blackett.

Merry, Andrew [Mildred Darby]. 1910. *The Hunger: Being Realities of the Famine Years in Ireland 1845 to 1848*. London: Andrew Melrose.

Morash, Chris, ed. 1989. *The Hungry Voice: The Poetry of the Irish Famine*. Dublin: Irish Academic Press.

———. 1995. *Writing the Irish Famine*. Oxford: Clarendon Press.

———. 2012. "Literature and the Famine." In *Atlas of the Great Irish Famine*, edited by John Crowley, William J. Smyth, and Mike Murphy, 640–7. Cork: Cork University Press.

Murphy, James H. 1997. *Catholic Fiction and Social Reality in Ireland, 1873–1922*. Westport, CT: Greenwood Press.

——. 2011. *Irish Novelists and the Victorian Age*. Oxford: Oxford University Press.

Ní Chillín, Máire. 1917. "On the Bog Road." In *On Tiptoe: A Collection of Stories and Sketches by Irish Women*, 67–72. Dublin: M.H. Gill and Son.

O'Toole, Tina. 2013. *The Irish New Woman*. Basingstoke: Palgrave Macmillan.

——, Gillian McIntosh, and Muireann O'Cinnéide, eds. 2016. *Women Writing War: Ireland 1880–1922*. Cork: Cork University Press.

Pašeta, Senia. 2013. *Irish Nationalist Women, 1900–1918*. Cambridge: Cambridge University Press.

Reilly, Ciarán. 2018. "The Country House and the Great Famine: Mildred Darby's novel, *The Hunger*." In *Women and the Country House in Ireland and Britain*, edited by Terence Dooley, Maeve O'Riordan, and Christopher Ridgway, 200–210. Dublin: Four Courts.

Review of *The Stormy Petrel*. *The Academy* (30 January 1909): 736.

Reynolds, Paige. 2018. "Poetry, Drama and Prose, 1891–1920." In *A History of Modern Irish Women's Literature*, edited by Heather Ingman and Clíona Ó Gallchóir, 131–48. Cambridge: Cambridge University Press.

R. M. [Rosa Mulholland]. 1891. "Wanted an Irish Novelist." *Irish Monthly* 19, no. 217: 368–73.

Tynan, Katharine. 1908. *Father Mathew*. London: Macdonald and Evans.

Trollope, Anthony. 1860. *Castle Richmond: A Novel*. London, Chapman and Hall.

Whelan, Kevin. 2005. "The Cultural Effects of the Famine." In *The Cambridge Companion to Modern Irish Culture*, edited by Joe Cleary and Claire Connolly, 137–54. Cambridge: Cambridge University Press.

Yeats, W.B. 1895. "Best Irish Books." *Dublin Daily Express*, 27 February 1895. http://www.ricorso.net/rx/library/authors/classic/Yeats_WB/prose/Essays_Intros/Best_Books.htm.

4

"A Country of the Mind": Eva Gore-Booth and the 1916 Rising

Lia Mills

I n the early years of the Great War, Eva Gore-Booth—poet, suffragist, trade-union activist, campaigner for social justice and labour rights for women— was a committed, outspoken pacifist and proponent of non-violence.[1] After the 1916 Rising, however, she wrote extensively in support of its executed leaders and against the injustice and oppression that had motivated it. In her invaluable study *The Political Writings of Eva Gore-Booth*, Sonja Tiernan notes that Gore-Booth's post-Rising writing differs markedly from her writing about war more generally: "careful not to denigrate the Easter Rising … instead she focuses on the atrocities perpetrated by the British authorities" (2015, 183). Recent studies by scholars such as Maureen O'Connor (2016) and Marian Eide (2016) suggest an emerging consensus that Gore-Booth's belief in non-violence was suspended, or at least qualified, by events in Ireland. But was Gore-Booth an à la carte pacifist? It is true that she does not publicly criticise the Rising; nor does she refer to its extensive casualties during a week when more citizens of Dublin were killed than British soldiers and rebels combined. It is also true that she eulogises key figures of the Rising. This essay explores other possible readings of her public writing about Ireland at this critical time, suggesting that her emphasis on idealised qualities of Roger Casement, Francis Sheehy Skeffington, and the executed leaders served a different purpose. Gore-Booth was, in Judith Butler's terms, making those who had been executed *grievable*, in a bid to soften British attitudes to the Rising and to forestall the threatened introduction of conscription to Ireland. In *Frames of War*, Butler asks, "whose life, if extinguished, would be publicly grievable and whose life would leave either no public trace to grieve, or only a partial, mangled and enigmatic trace?" (2016, 75). It could be argued that in selectively assigning grievability rather

---

1   Biographical information is drawn from Roper (1929; 1934) and Tiernan (2012; 2015).

than acknowledging the scale of death and injury on all sides during the Rising, Gore-Booth does the principles of non-violence a disservice, but I propose her writing from this period as a deliberate strategy to win sympathy for the Irish desire for freedom and, more urgently, to prevent further killing. This does not equate with support for violent action. In the campaign for women's suffrage, Gore-Booth, a suffragist, was opposed to the militant, increasingly violent campaign of the suffragettes but that did not diminish her commitment to their shared goal, votes for women. I suggest that her writing about Ireland does not contradict her earlier pacifist position but sits comfortably on a continuum with broader humanitarian campaigns on both sides of the Irish Sea: to oppose conscription and support conscientious objectors, to improve prison conditions, and to abolish capital punishment altogether. Her writing in support of Ireland is mindful of the real dangers of anti-Irish feeling in Britain. Its focus deviates from her more general anti-war writing but it originates in the same principles of anti-imperialism, self-determination, and non-violence. Opening with reference to the spiritual dimension of Gore-Booth's literary work, the following discussion includes an account of her pacifist activism and her experience of the aftermath of the Rising, with particular attention to *The Death of Fionavar* (1916a) and *Broken Glory* (1918a).

Formative childhood experiences prefiguring Gore-Booth's lifelong dedication to literature, philosophy, and the study of world religions are evident in Esther Roper's biographical introduction to *Poems of Eva Gore-Booth: The Complete Edition* (1929). Most notable in this regard are observations made by her former governess, Miss Noel, and an autobiographical essay "The Inner Life of a Child" (Roper 1929, 49–61). As an adult, Gore-Booth belonged to many progressive philosophical groups, including the Theosophical Society, whose practice it is to hold study-groups based on esoteric and literary texts. She had a core belief that mankind was evolving towards a higher level of spiritual awareness and Being, based on principles of universal brotherhood and non-violence, which demanded individual effort and commitment. In her preface to the posthumously published *House with Three Windows* (1926), Evelyn Underhill observes that Gore-Booth's literary writing traces a chronology of her spiritual development, while both Sonja Tiernan (2018) and Paige Reynolds (2018) recognise and describe the philosophical underpinnings of her many collections of poetry.

In a 1917 lecture, "Rhythms of Art," Gore-Booth confirms this perception that her literary work has a philosophical dimension when she defines her conception of art (including poetry) as "the true expression in form of a human being's perception of one of the hidden rhythms of the Universe" (quoted in Tiernan 2015, 162). She argues that sensitivity to natural or artistic beauty are of the same order of experience as mysticism and religious feeling. In a late, major study of St John's gospel, she elaborates: "Most poets who have asserted that the individual soul (psyche) is one with the universal, have felt a 'soul' in 'nature' of which their 'souls' were part" (1923, 52). For her, poetic language is uniquely qualified to express what has been previously inexpressible. Furthermore, readers come to poetry equipped with a receptivity which opens them to esoteric understanding: "Those who have found thoughts that are precious and revealing to themselves must always offer them to others, in case someone else may be sensitive to receive them" (Gore-Booth 1923, xii). This suggests Gore-Booth's literary writing as a form of spiritual activism, despite her own recognition, that "we all know how easily a literature with a purpose ceases to be Art" (Tiernan 2015, 163). Although this spiritual dimension to her work can be problematic for secular readers, it must be considered in relation to her response to the Rising.

Gore-Booth's early poetry expresses a love of Ireland with occasional flares of political anger, as in "The Land to a Landlord," a poem which does not distinguish between English landlords and the Anglo-Irish class she was born into but rejected (Roper 1929, 238). She was drawn to the mythological material favoured by other Revival writers. Lauren Arrington observes that "[t]he Revival's focus on retelling, or inventing, myth and legend offered an ideal cast of characters which Gore-Booth could adapt to her purposes" (2016, 213). An anti-war play, *The Triumph of Maeve,* was published in 1905. Written in 1902, the year the Boer War ended, *Maeve* was almost certainly a response to that war. Maeve, warrior-queen of Connacht, is at war with Ulster. When she wins a battle, her sensitive, sheltered daughter Fionavar rushes to the battlefield to see her mother's "triumph" for herself. The shock of witnessing the devastations of war kills her. Fionavar's death is the hinge on which Gore-Booth's play turns. In grief, Maeve reflects on her roles, queen and warrior, and ultimately relinquishes both in favour of a life of contemplation.

In December 1914, at a meeting of the National Industrial and Professional Women's Suffrage Society (NIPWSS), Gore-Booth confronted "the intolerable and squalid horror of war" (1914, 4) and its consequent griefs. She noted that war, unlike natural disasters, accidents or plague, "is the deliberate and calculated result of human will power and intelligence, determined by some extraordinary paradoxical impulse on the destruction of everything that is of value to human life" (4). She decries the killing and mutilation of "brave people of all countries," because society needs heroic virtues in the struggle to develop a more ideal and equitable civilization. Gore-Booth's heroism was of a different order to the conventional militaristic version. It involved idealism, participation in the struggle for equality and social justice, and the courage to live according to one's own conscience, even when law and public opinion dictated otherwise—as can be seen in her later writing about Roger Casement and Francis Sheehy Skeffington. In a later speech, "Religious Aspects of Non-Resistance," she acknowledges that human beings are "fighters by nature," but not in a military context:

> The real battle is not against other human beings but the battle of evolution, by which the human race is seeking to wrest knowledge and unity, happiness and beauty out of a world of stubborn and adverse forces.
> To concentrate all our force and courage and heroism in this struggle is the opportunity that comes to those who refuse to use these qualities in a struggle against other living beings. (Quoted in Tiernan 2015, 150)

She believed that violence is only possible when we forget our true nature and lose touch with "the overwhelming inevitable purpose of all things, that spirit of unfaltering goodwill what we call God, the light and love that is also the deepest principle of our own minds" (154). Much of her pre-1916 anti-war writing is informed by such ideals but, as in her earlier work for suffrage and women's labour rights, she also relies on logic:

> Every war that has ever been fought, civil or international, has been fought for at least two good causes, one on each side, because naturally every cause is a good cause to its adherents. … whatever the cause of violence may be, its result is always the same, no amount of good motive makes any difference to the amount of pain, suffering and death brought into the world by violence. (Quoted in Tiernan 2015, 148–49)

Gore-Booth's belief in non-violence stems from Buddhist and non-ideological Christian principles, but the testimonies of her friends as given in Roper's biographical accounts (1929; 1934), suggest that violence was antithetical to her nature. Anti-vivisection and vegetarian, she was resolutely anti-imperialist, opposing the use of force in any circumstance. Her friend R. M. Fox writes that for Gore-Booth, "killing was even more horrible than suffering, because it degraded the men who killed, and, in its influence, debased society, brutalising those who condoned it" (Fox 1935, 24).

Gore-Booth wrote and spoke against the war from its beginning. Tiernan notes that she was at risk of being labelled a German sympathiser for the relief work she and Roper undertook from September 1914 in support of interned German citizens and their families (2012, 148). Later, Gore-Booth visited Conscientious Objectors (COs) in prison and campaigned for prison reform. In July 1915, she spoke at the Pacifist Philosophy of Life conference which led to the foundation of the League of Peace and Freedom, which she and Roper immediately joined. Gore-Booth also joined the No Conscription Fellowship (NCF) and campaigned against the introduction of conscription, which nevertheless came into effect in Britain in March, 1916. It was theoretically possible to gain an exemption from military service on grounds of conscience if a CO could convince a locally convened tribunal that his reasons were genuine. In practice this was extremely difficult. Penalties for continued refusal to fight included court-martial, imprisonment, and execution. While the latter penalty was never enforced in Britain, it did not need to be. As Gore-Booth notes in a January 2016 letter to the *Manchester Guardian*, offenders against military discipline could be dealt with at the front by firing squads (Tiernan 2012, 160–1). COs who agreed to undertake non-combat service were frequently sent to the Front as stretcher-bearers, a dangerous assignment.

As happened with the Land League in Ireland in the previous century, male members of the NCF were soon arrested, leaving the women to run the organisation (Parnell 1986). Gore-Booth was a "Watcher," one of many volunteers who attended CO tribunals throughout Britain, recording details to be collated and printed in the weekly NCF organ, *The Tribunal*. These activities were not without risk. The police raided offices, dismantled printing presses, made arrests. Gore-Booth's factional exposé, also entitled *The Tribunal* (1916b), describes the proceedings of a typical hearing, a series of hard-line rejections of legitimate appeals. Her account culminates in a scene between a Christ-like figure whose "conscience" is derided and dismissed by tribunal officials. The composed, gentle figure in the dock, unrecognised by his judges, resonates with her later portrayals of Casement.

Some NCF women served prison sentences for Fellowship activities. Writers such as Bertrand Russell were jailed for anti-war writing (Tiernan 2012, 160–3). Nevertheless, Gore-Booth continued her spoken and written opposition to militarism, using arguments primarily based on the principles of non-violent resistance and universal good fellowship common to many of the people she knew in the strikingly overlapping circles of Theosophy, pacifism, socialism, feminism, and campaigns for social justice at the time (Dixon 2003).

When news of the 1916 Easter Rising broke in England, one of the many rumours that spread in the absence of verifiable reports was that Constance Markievicz had been killed. In fact, along with her comrades-in-arms, Markievicz had been imprisoned, court-martialled and sentenced to death in a series of reprisal executions that was already underway. Her sentence was later commuted. Gore-Booth and Roper secured permission to travel to Ireland to visit her in prison (Roper 1934, 42). Gore-Booth opens her vivid account of that crossing and all that followed with a description of a glorious dawn, the sea and the mountains "transfigured with beauty and delight" as they sailed into Kingstown Harbour (now Dun Laoghaire). She continues: "The sea shifted and glittered and dreamed. It was hardly possible to believe that any man could look upon the vessel's shining track merely as the road to Empire and domination" (Roper 1934, 42). Disembarked, they were stunned by news-hoardings proclaiming the execution that morning of James Connolly, their friend and colleague in the trade-union movement. This forceful eruption of violence into the otherworldly transfiguration of land and sea crystallises Gore-Booth's idea that war and violence are inimical to everything that makes life worthwhile.

At Mountjoy prison, they were separated from Markievicz by a corridor and two sets of prison bars. They had to shout to each other across the stony space between them, where a wardress paced, listening to every word. Markievicz asked about Connolly. In her account of that visit, Roper writes that, although they had been forbidden to answer this question, "she must have seen the answer in our faces, for with tears running down her cheeks she said, 'You needn't tell me, I know. Why didn't they let me die with my friends?' It was a terrible moment" (1934, 54). They visited Hanna Sheehy Skeffington to hear about the murder of her husband, its immediate aftermath and subsequent actions by the military, who raided her house, shot out the windows and confiscated papers and other items in a futile effort to find some justification for killing him.[2] Francis Sheehy Skeffington had been a committed feminist, pacifist, and anti-conscription activist.

Dublin, a city they loved, had an atmosphere of mourning, dread and suspicion. They heard stories of atrocities, cruelty and "unspeakably insanitary conditions" in the prisons (Roper 1934, 50). Characteristically, Gore-Booth began to report on what they had witnessed as soon as she got back to London, in public talks and in print. She became an unofficial spokesperson for the case of Ireland in Britain, where many people were hostile to pacifist arguments *tout court* and many more were furious at the perceived treachery of the Rising. Roper claims that Gore-Booth never fully recovered from the strains and griefs of that terrible summer. She lost valued friends—James Connolly, Francis Sheehy Skeffington, and Roger Casement—to execution; she would have known many of the Rising's leaders, at least by reputation, or through their poetry. Dublin had been destroyed. Markievicz was still in the hands of the authorities who had so recently condemned her to death. Thousands of Irishmen and women were interned. Meanwhile, the war was escalating. Gore-Booth continued to campaign against conscription while supporting Hanna Sheehy Skeffington's demand for a commission of inquiry into the Portobello murders. More controversially still, she was a key member of the group working to secure a reprieve for Casement. Gore-Booth's arguments for leniency, along with other testimonies she compiled, were reviewed by Cabinet that July (Tiernan 2015, 203–8). She was one of a small group who met the King to plead for clemency the day before Casement's execution.

Patriotic feelings ran high in Britain at the time; it was not a small thing for someone living in England to defend Ireland and the leaders of the Rising as publicly as she did. Casement's execution had a devastating impact. The collective experiences of that summer would inform her continuing campaign against capital punishment. Meanwhile, she worked to support COs and to

---

2   For a first-person account of the Portobello murders, see Gibbon (1968).

prevent the introduction of conscription to Ireland. She also prepared a new book for publication that autumn, *The Death of Fionavar* from *The Triumph of Maeve* (1916a).

In her speech to the NIPWSS in 1914, Gore-Booth deconstructed a popular pro-war slogan of the time, "righteousness backed by force":

> What is this force that is the ally of righteousness? The most direct way to find out is to go to France or Belgium and see for yourself. …You will find that force means practically the power of killing, wounding and disabling masses of human beings. Now alter the phrase a little. Say 'righteousness backed by massacre and mutilation.' When you put it in plain words doesn't there seem something a little incongruous in such association? (1914, 5)

Visiting Dublin in 1916 was her version of going to the Front but, unlike Fionavar in *The Triumph of Maeve,* Gore-Booth came back fighting. She set to work on *The Death of Fionavar*, a publication that would include drawings by Markievicz. The script for the play, *Fionavar*, is a direct excerpt from the earlier *Maeve*, opening at Act 3 Scene 2 of the original; its text is otherwise unchanged. The addition of extraneous material—poetry and commentary, preceding and following the playscript —suggests that *Fionavar* was intended to be read for consideration of its pacifist argument in the context of the Rising. There is no evidence that either play was ever performed in public.

Fionavar's comparative brevity enhances its dramatic impact. Its tighter focus on Fionavar's rejection of violence and on Maeve's change of heart clarifies and strengthens the pacifist theme, as does the title's shift in emphasis from "triumph" to death. As the play opens, a vision of the crucifixion of Christ causes Fionavar to faint, indicating that State-sponsored killing is inimical to the human spirit. It introduces Christian values as Gore-Booth espoused them (forgiveness, mercy, brotherhood, equality) into her mythical world. As already noted, Gore-Booth avoids direct reference to the number of fatalities due to the Rising, concentrating instead on those who were executed by the British, but this emphasis on the shock of realisation that costs Fionavar her life is a clear comment on the effects of violence and what military-speak today would term collateral damage.

Markievicz's contribution is acknowledged on both cover and title page.[3] Placing the name of a convicted militant rebel alongside that of Gore-Booth, known pacifist, is a striking declaration of sisterly loyalty but it does not necessarily equate to support of violent action. The women's attitudes to violence were diametrically opposed but as sisters they were close. Local relief work in

---

3   For comprehensive discussions of Markievicz's contribution, see O'Connor (2016) and Eide (2016).

Sligo during years of famine is a likely source for their shared commitment to social justice. They also shared childhood memories of the intense beauty, mystery, and legends of Ireland's western seaboard. The countryside around Lissadell, where they grew up, is dominated by Knocknarea and the cairn on its summit, reputed to be Maeve's grave. The fighting role Markievicz adopted is reminiscent of the warrior-queen but Gore-Booth had a different sense of Maeve. In her "Interpretation," she explains that her character, Maeve, represents the struggle in the human mind "between the forces of dominance and pity, of peace and war" (1916a, 11–12). Maeve's attempt to force an entry to "Tirnanogue" failed because "force is a useless and futile weapon against the soul and its mysterious powers, and the ambitious fighter is forever an outcast from the country of the mind, which can only be entered by a pilgrim who has cast aside anger and power and worldly possessions" (12).

In *Maeve/Fionavar*, grief for her daughter's death causes Maeve to grow more reflective. Eventually, she discards her crown and golden robe. Rejecting the role assigned to her (as Gore-Booth rejected hers in life), she leaves the stage, turning her back on violence, wealth and power in favour of a personal search for inner peace:

> Now I will find the way
> to Tirnanogue [*sic*] – the way to my own soul,
> The way to the world's heart beyond night or day
> or love or hate or any golden goal of Empire. (1916a, 74)

Fionavar is dedicated "To the Memory of the Dead/The Many who died for Freedom and the One who died for Peace" (i.e. Francis Sheehy Skeffington). An epigrammatic poem name-checks several leaders of the Rising, characterised as "Poets, Utopians, bravest of the brave" (1916a, 9). The poem laments "Ireland of the coming time," which seems to allow but one service from its "true citizens": to die for it.[4] As Paige Reynolds (2018, 132) has also noted, this is reminiscent of Emily Lawless's poem, "After Aughrim," which characterises Ireland as insatiable in "her" demands of those who fight for her, indifferent to the bitter fate that awaits them (Lawless 1902, 3–5). Fionavar's final words, "Is this the triumph of Maeve?" (Gore-Booth 1916a, 51) challenge, not the soldiers, but the myth of glorious victory, a delusion invested in and perpetuated by a mother reminiscent of the Mother Ireland trope favoured by Gore-Booth's nationalist contemporaries. Both poems name the inevitable annihilation that attends patriots in the continuing tradition of violent uprising in Ireland. Gore-Booth's untitled poem ends:

> Dreamers turned fighters but to find a grave,
> Too great for victory, too brave for war

---

4   This line probably refers to Yeats' poem "To Ireland in the Coming Time" (1893).

Would you had dreamed the gentler dream of Maeve ...
Peace be with you, and love for evermore. (1916a, 9)

The poem praises the courage and idealism of those who fought, but fighting kills the dream; "victory" is beneath them; their courage, being born of individual conviction, is greater than the unquestioning obedience required of soldiers by war. Maureen O'Connor reads the tone of the poem as one of admiration, if not romanticisation (2016, 87). I would argue that it is elegiac, written in grief. O'Connor characterises the open-ended line "Would you had dreamed the gentler dream of Maeve ..." as "fairly wan regret ... trailing off into ellipses" (2016, 87). However, the poem comes to rest on eternal peace and love, prefiguring the play's movement from war to peace, from bloodbath to reflection and the pursuit of occult knowledge. *Fionavar*'s tighter focus clarifies *Maeve*'s pacifist stance, lending weight to the queen's decision to renounce violence. An epilogue gives an incomplete rendition of "Eineen's Song" from *Unseen Kings* (1904); its repetitive motif laments the grief and trouble wrought "for such a cause" as war (Gore-Booth 1916a, 83).

Gore-Booth's next collection, *Broken Glory* (1918a), is dedicated "In memory of August 3rd, 1916," the date of Roger Casement's execution. The opening section refers directly to the Rising, but through its after-effects: executions, graves, imprisonment. The epigrammatic "Poets, Utopians..." poem, featured so prominently in *Fionavar*, is absent, as it is from Roper's *Complete Edition* of Gore-Booth's poetry. Instead, a poem entitled "Utopia" deplores "Cruelty, bloodshed and hate" and suggests that war is overcome by friendship and love (1918a, 15). Apart from Markievicz, the only individuals named in the collection are Sheehy Skeffington and Casement, both non-combatants, and Dora Sigerson Shorter, who was rumoured to have died of grief caused by the Rising, a grief Gore-Booth shared. References to Casement recur throughout the collection, which includes some of Gore-Booth's best-known work, a series of poems written for her imprisoned sister. An eponymous poem eulogises Francis Sheehy Skeffington and his pacifist beliefs:

No green and poisonous laurel wreath shall shade
His brow, who dealt no death in any strife,
Crown him with olive who was not afraid
To join the desolate unarmed ranks of life.

Who did not fear to die, yet feared to slay. (14)

The laurel, enduring symbol of victory, glory, success and, significantly, honour, is "poisonous" in contrast with the olive, which also symbolises victory but is associated with peace and friendship. Gore-Booth links Sheehy Skeffington with Christ's agony in the Garden of Gethsemane. The characterisation of Sheehy Skeffington as one "who dealt no death in any strife," and "[w]ho did not fear to die, yet feared to slay," echo statements Sheehy Skeffington made, in print in his "Open Letter to Thomas MacDonagh" and verbally during a public debate with Markievicz in February 1916 (Sheehy Skeffington 1916; Mulhall 2016). Markievicz stated repeatedly that she would happily die for Ireland. Sheehy Skeffington replied that he was willing to die for Ireland but would not kill for it.

The poem "Easter Week" states Gore-Booth's position: admiration for idealism, and grief for all blood shed:

> Grief for the noble dead
> Of one who did not share their strife,
> And mourned that any blood was shed,
> Yet felt the broken glory of their state,
> Their strange heroic questioning of Fate
> Ribbon with gold the rags of this our life. (1918a, 9)

The poem that follows, "Heroic Death, 1916," alludes to the executions and the broken hearts and dreams of Ireland. Nevertheless, the lines, "Ah! ye who slay the body, how man's soul/Rises above your hatred and your scorns—" (9) apply to militant republicans and executioners alike, while "Utopia" proposes friendship and love as antidotes to "[c]ruelty, bloodshed and hate" (15). Tellingly, the collection moves on, past the poems associated with the Rising, through grief and loss to images of renewal and hope. A late poem, "1916," not directly associated with the Rising, laments the lost "dream of beauty" shattered by militarism. No one escapes its implications:

> The guns break forth with their insistent din,
> The dews of noon-day leave a crimson stain
> On grass, that all men's feet must wander in. (22)

"The Wood" describes a flight from "war's dark ugliness" to a rediscovered "Beauty, the world's lost peace" (25). The poet finds hope in nature, the persistence and courage of flowers emerging through that blood-soaked grass.

After the Rising, Gore-Booth published several letters, articles and pamphlets arguing forcefully against the executions and in favour of clemency for Casement. A letter of appeal in *The Manchester Guardian* reminded her readers that they cheered Kathleen Ni Houlihan and other representations of Irish national aspiration in theatrical performance: why could they not support that aspiration in real life? (Tiernan 2015, 209). An experienced strategist, she did not glorify the Rising so much as eulogise its principal figures and contrast their idealism and the dignity of their deaths with the repressive, punitive response of the British State. A comment on Casement offers a key to any apparent contradiction between her writing about the Rising and her non-violent convictions:

> People on this side of the Channel could not believe that an Irishman would rather be hung than state publicly that he had tried to stop the Sinn Féin Rising, and so seem to blame his fellow-countrymen in their failure and defeat. (Tiernan 2015, 211)

Gore-Booth would not blame them either. The struggle for freedom and self-rule in Ireland was unequal and, as ever, she sided with the disempowered. She did not write about the Rising to glamourise armed resistance, but to warn the authorities that glamour would result from violent reprisal and repression. Gore-Booth would continue to protest judicial executions, in any context, into the 1920s. A member of the Committee for the Abolition of the Death Penalty, she drew on her 1916 experiences in a speech given to a crucial meeting attended by members of the Labour Party, who would pass a resolution to abolish the death penalty two months later at their 1923 annual conference (Tiernan 2015, 225).

Eva Gore-Booth's commitment to non-violence was neither vague nor conditional. For her, non-violence was not a stance to be modified as the situation demanded; it was a core dimension of her character, founded on spiritual principles that were esoteric rather than ideological or institutional. Shortly after her return to London in 1916, she wrote to an unnamed friend: "Why will people not understand there is nothing worth having but good will, and nationality and patriotism are all illusion and sorrow?" (Unpublished letter, Eva Gore-Booth Papers).[5] Her Ireland was the "inner Ireland" of the poem she wrote "For Constance—In Prison" (1918a, 10), the Ireland of their shared childhood, a country of the mind. She did not believe in nations and was an outspoken critic of the mechanisms of states; her Ireland was a place she loved for its beauty, its stories and its otherworldly atmosphere. As a child, she experienced visions and an apprehension of elements beyond ordinary human understanding, a sensitivity she tried to share with others, but she was not a fantasist. She knew the effects of famine, poverty and exclusion and set herself against cruelty, oppression and injustice wherever she found them.

In her 1914 address to the NIPWSS Gore-Booth argued that "those who think that force is allowable in a good cause … though not in a bad one, have to face the fact that this theory would justify almost every violence in history" (Tiernan 2015, 148–9). In her last play, *The Sword of Justice* (1918b), justifications of violence are thoroughly deconstructed and overcome, confirming her consistent, continuing opposition. Similarly, in a 1924 letter to her friend T. P. Conwil-Evans, she asserts that "there's only one real alternative to violence and that's Christ. Because there is no *passive* alternative to violence, nothing but Love" (Roper 1929, 96, original emphasis). She writes about Sheehy

---

5   UCD Special Collections Library. Ref. IE/UCD/SC /GB item 7. Material quoted from the Eva Gore-Booth Papers is used with kind permission from the University College Dublin Special Collections Library.

Skeffington, absolute pacifist, in fighting terms, "on fire with hatred of violence and cruelty," defending workers, denouncing the war, "a greater danger to the authorities than many a more violent revolutionist" because his was "the voice of a new era, a terrible possibility, that nightmare of individual evolution and militant goodwill that shakes the dreams of militarism with a strange threat" (Tiernan 2015, 198–9). She could as easily have been writing about herself, attending the Tribunals, speaking and writing at every opportunity, public and private, against war, against execution, against repression. Pacifist, not at all passive, she stood her ground against injustice no matter how unpopular the cause.

References

Primary Sources

Gore-Booth, Eva. 1904. *Unseen Kings*. London: Longmans Green & Co.

——. 1905. *The Three Resurrections and the Triumph of Maeve*. London: Longmans Green & Co.

——. 1914. *Whence Come Wars?* London: Women's Printing Society.

——. (1915) 2015. "Religious Aspects of Non-Resistance." In *The Political Writings of Eva Gore Booth*, edited by Sonja Tiernan, 146–54. Manchester: Manchester University Press.

——. 1916a. *The Death of Fionavar* from *The Triumph of Maeve*. London: Erskine Macdonald.

——. 1916b *The Tribunal*. London: Labour Press.

——. 1916c. Unpublished letter to an unnamed friend. Eva Gore-Booth Papers. UCD Special Collections Library. Ref. IE/UCD/SC /GB item 7.

——. (1917) 2015. "Rhythms of Art." In *The Political Writings of Eva Gore Booth*, edited by Sonja Tiernan, 162–168. Manchester: Manchester University Press.

——. 1918a. *Broken Glory*. Dublin: Maunsel & Co.

——. 1918b. *The Sword of Justice*. London: Longmans Green & Co.

——. 1923. *A Psychological and Poetic Approach to the Study of Christ in the Fourth Gospel*. London: Longmans Green & Co.

——. 1926. *The House of Three Windows*. London: Longmans Green & Co.

——. 1929. "The Inner Life of a Child." In *Poems of Eva Gore-Booth: The Complete Edition*, edited by Esther Roper, 49–61. London: Longmans Green & Co.

——. 1930. *The Buried Life of Deirdre*. London: Longmans Green & Co.

Other Sources

Arrington, Lauren. 2016. "Poetics of Suffrage in Gore-Booth and Markievicz." In *Irish Women's Writing 1878–1922: Advancing the Cause of Liberty*, edited by Anna Pilz and Whitney Standlee, 209–26. Manchester: Manchester University Press.

Butler, Judith. 2016. *Frames of War: When is Life Grievable?* London: Verso Books.

Dixon, Joy. 2003. *The Divine Feminine: Theosophy and Feminism in England*. Maryland: John Hopkins University Press.

Eide, Marian. 2016. "Maeve's Legacy: Constance Markievicz, Eva Gore-Booth, and the Easter Rising." Éire-Ireland 51 (Fall/Winter): 80–103.

Fox, R.M. 1935. *Rebel Irishwomen*. Dublin: Talbot Press.

Gibbon, Monk. 1968. *Inglorious Soldier*. London: Hutchinson.

Mulhall, Ed. 2016. "'Shot Like a Dog': The murder of Francis Sheehy Skeffington and the search for truth." *Century Ireland*, September 2016. https://www.rte.ie/centuryireland/index.php/articles/shot-like-a-dog-the-murder-of-francis-sheehy-skeffington-and-the-search-for

O'Connor, Maureen. 2016. "Eva Gore-Booth's Queer Art of War." In *Women Writing War: Ireland 1880–1922*, edited by Tina O'Toole, Gillian McIntosh and Muireann O'Cinnéide, 85–102. Dublin: UCD Press.

Parnell, Anna. 1986. *The Tale of a Great Sham*. Dublin: Arlen House.

Reynolds, Paige. 2018. "Poetry, Drama and Prose, 1891–1920." In *A History of Modern Irish Women's Literature*, edited by Heather Ingman and Clíona Ó Gallchoir, 131–148. Cambridge: Cambridge University Press.

Roper, Esther, ed. 1929. *Poems of Eva Gore-Booth: The Complete Edition*. London: Longmans Green & Co.

——, ed. 1934. *Prison Letters of Countess Markievicz*. London: Longmans Green & Co.

Sheehy Skeffington, Francis. 1916. "An Open Letter to Thomas MacDonagh." www.irishtimes.com/opinion/francis-sheehy-skeffington-open-letter-to-thomas-macdonagh-1.2580899

Underhill, Evelyn. 1926. "Preface." In *The House of Three Windows* by Eva Gore-Booth. London: Longmans Green & Co.

Tiernan, Sonja. 2012. *Eva Gore-Booth: An image of such politics*. Manchester. Manchester University Press.

——, ed. 2018. *Eva Gore-Booth: Collected Poems*. Dublin: Arlen House.

——. 2015. *The Political Writings of Eva Gore Booth*. Manchester: Manchester University Press.

5

International Relations in the Writing and Artwork of Edith Œ. Somerville and Martin Ross: *French Leave* (1928) and the Académie Colarossi at the end of the Nineteenth Century

Julie Anne Stevens

One of the most important networking sites for women artists and writers at the end of the nineteenth century was Paris. Two women's private studios in particular, the Académie Julian and the Académie Colarossi, provided female artists with professional instruction and attracted an international clientele. Between 1873 and 1900 there were 1,076 foreign female artists admitted to the Paris Salon, a crucial marker of artistic success, and 10% of them worked in the Académie Julian (Bolloch 2017b, 263). Colarossi's records, however, were destroyed in a fire in the mid-twentieth century and so, unlike the Julian, fewer accounts of its student life are available. The Irish writer and artist Edith Somerville's novel, *French Leave* (1928), which recalls the *roman d'atelier* of the previous century, relies upon the author's diary accounts of study in Colarossi in the 1880s. As a result, the book provides a fictionalised account of Colarossi's vibrant studio culture. Indeed, the novel's manuscript draft in Harvard's Houghton Library shows clearly the source of that vibrancy and the author's awareness of its importance: the camaraderie and competition of an international student body.

Somerville did not write *French Leave* until she was sixty-eight years old. She selected 1884, the year that she arrived in Paris, as a kind of feminist *anno mundi*; however, her awareness of the female artist's predicament examined in the text had been informed by the intervening years and the artist/writer's numerous—if brief—study trips to Paris up until 1899. This essay thus considers Somerville's retrospective view of feminist thought in *French Leave*. It relies on Somerville and Ross's 1884–85 diaries in Queen's University Library, Somerville's 1885 sketchbook, and the novel's manuscript draft to show the author's examination of international relations in a central women's studio of the period.

In part, the novel and its extra-textual materials provide a means of examining the entangled lives and preoccupations of female artists in Colarossi's. Significantly, and in the manner of the atelier novel discussed below, Somerville includes at least one real life artist of the 1880s in her book: the Finnish artist, Venny Soldan. However, the diaries, sketchbook, and draft introduce many others, some who appear with altered names in the novel. Of these women artists certain groups or individuals stand out: the Nordic network of women artists, for instance, or the work of the French-Russian artist Marie Bashkirtseff. In this essay, I am as much interested in tracing the connections of these artists to each other as in examining the novel itself. At the same time—and perhaps more importantly—I want to show the text's response not just to European discourse on women and art but also to Irish art developments. *French Leave* explores an Irish gentlewoman's negotiation of the opportunities available to her in late nineteenth-century Paris while maintaining her Irish connection. Her struggle suggests a complex reality for the artist seeking to bring European ideas back home. Somerville's backward look gives a more comprehensive view of her situation and allows the author to incorporate arguments from across the century about women artists in both Europe *and* Ireland.

French Leave thus reflects an evolving art discourse over time. It also shows the overlapping of European and Irish discourse, and I examine the resulting tensions by considering two visual representations of female artists that provoked widespread response and to which Somerville's writing is indebted. A pair of portraits depicting the female artist at work stand out during in this period: Édouard Manet's 1870 portrait of Eva Gonzalès, which not only became significant in conversation about modern art in Paris but also served as a key painting in Irish art discourse, and Hanne Pauli's 1887 portrait of the aforementioned Venny Soldan, which came to represent the emerging woman artist of the time.

Somerville wrote her novel in 1926–27. As with other novels completed after her writing partner's death in 1915, she credited it to Somerville and Ross. Somerville and her second cousin, Martin Ross (Violet Martin), had joined forces in 1886. However, Somerville had a whole other life before Martin, and when writing *French Leave*, the deaths of two friends from earlier days in Paris occurred: the Danish artist, Johanne Krebs, in 1924, and the Austrian artist, Marianne Stokes, née Preindlsberger, in 1927. Somerville knew Stokes because of their shared Paris experience, and they worked together when Marianne and Adrian Stokes visited Cork in 1885.[1] Mrs. Stokes may have introduced

---

1   Marianne Preindlsberger contributed to the Irish Fine Art Society Exhibitions from 1882 onwards. After her marriage to Adrian Stokes, she and her husband visited the Somerville's in West Cork. For further discussion see Julie Anne Stevens, *Two Irish*

Somerville to the Finnish artist/writer, Helena Westermarck, whose picture appears in Somerville's sketchbook of the same year.[2] However, equally likely is that Somerville met the Finnish feminist at Colarossi's because Westermarck's childhood friend, the highly regarded artist Helene Schjerfbeck, enrolled in the studio the same year as Somerville (Bolloch 2017a, 254–5). Schjerfbeck also travelled and worked with Marianne Stokes, and so it seems likely that these women were part of a loose network of relations within which they operated. Johanne Krebs, then, might be linked to this group because when Somerville and Ross visited her women's studio in Copenhagen in 1895 as recorded in their travelogue, "In the State of Denmark," reference to a common background in Paris appears (Somerville and Ross 1920, 160–61).

Somerville's pencil sketch of Westermarck shows her standing and reading a book, as though so deeply absorbed in the material she cannot put it down to pose. Westermarck would go on to become an important critic of Nordic art. Her 1905 overview of Finnish female artists, "Some Finnish Women Painters," is seen as one of the first critical texts that positioned women artists as serious practitioners (Madeline 2017, 5). In her essay, Westermarck identifies three female principal artists: her friend Schjerfbeck, her teacher Marie Wiik, and Venny Soldan-Brofeldt (1905, 1976, 290–92). Venny Soldan, as she was known, worked in Colarossi's during Somerville's early visits and her portrait by the Swedish artist, Hanne Pauli née Hirsch, was undertaken at this time. It subsequently turned the Finlander into a figurehead for women artists in Paris. Soldan appears a number of times in Somerville's novel. And, as already mentioned, other characters in *French Leave* are based on real people Somerville knew, but most of their names are changed or altered. Soldan retains her own name.

By including artist characters based on real people in her work, Somerville recalls the atelier novel. In an overview of the late nineteenth-century *roman d'atelier*, Joy Newton points out that these books concentrated on bohemian male artists and sought to dignify their reputation, often including living artists as characters to increase the work's veracity. Novels such as Emile Zola's *L'Œuvre* (1886) not only show the male artist's dedication to the cause of modern art but also his resistance to women, one of the great distractions that may disturb his single-minded quest to create works that challenged traditional ideas and embraced modern urban life (Newton 1998, 173–89). Women were associated with the social sphere and served art best as muse or model. English-language versions of this kind of book, like George Moore's novella *Mildred Lawson* (1895), or W. Somerset Maugham's *Of Human Bondage* (1915), present female artists who practice so-called feminine art, in other words, inferior work, or

---

Girls in Bohemia: The Drawings and Writings of E. Œ. Somerville and Martin Ross, 90–91.
2   E. Œ. Somerville, pencil sketch of 'Frln Westermarck,' Paris April 1885 sketchbook, Edith Œ. Somerville Sketchbook Collection, 1881 – c.1912 (Private Collection).

who fail in their attempts to create modern art.

French Leave combines a feminist response to the atelier novel with an Irish country house story. Two young Irish artists of different classes, the daughter of an Anglo-Irish landowner, Patsey Kirwan, and the son of a Protestant lay-preacher, George Lester, leave the Cork countryside to study art in Paris, and the text moves back and forth between rural Ireland and urban France. The determining factor in both places is money. Patsey begs and borrows cash to travel, while George not only begs and borrows but also steals from his parents to fulfill his ambitions. In a study of Irish women writers and Paris, Matthew Reznicek argues that the book's interest in money reflects European discourse on developing metropolitan capitalism. He points out that the Ascendancy female heroine (who never appreciates the importance of cash flow) remains ensconced in her traditional private roles and returns home to marry, while the more fluid middle-class male character successfully enters the modern marketplace. Reznicek says that the text needs to be considered in a wider context than Ireland and alongside European metropolitan fiction (2017, 103–38). In fact, I suggest that *French Leave* needs to be examined in a wider context than fiction; materials other than books influenced the artist/writers Somerville and Ross. European visual discourse as revealed in both women's artwork and women artists' representation impacted on Somerville's study of art students in nineteenth-century Paris. Moreover, her manuscript draft marginalia—some of which lists artists from across the globe whom she knew in Paris—suggests the author's desire to write a novel that returns to her training in Colarossi's to explore female art education and to emphasise the international mix of students, both European *and* American, which helped to develop it. Nonetheless, and as Reznicek rightly notes, in the published work, Patsey Kirwan fails to enter the marketplace and retreats into an Irish marriage with a suitable husband of the same class. The question one faces with the novel is why Somerville selects such an ending to rebellious Patsey's Paris furlough.

By the time that Patsey begins studying in Monsieur Pianelli's *Atelier des Dames*, the fictional counterpart of Colarossi's women's studio, the novel is halfway over. The delay happens because of the struggle that she and George Lester face when trying to overcome their fathers' resistance to study abroad and then finding the means to travel. The extent of the patriarchs' suppression determines the courage and daring of the youngsters' revolt, and Somerville's manuscript marginalia, which on the first page includes a series of words suggesting escape, shows the writer's desire to emphasise the protagonists' rebellion.

Somerville's draft is written on a hardbound Signal Log of H.M.S. The notebook includes two loose-leaf pages with a list of chapters and a tentative title. "The Rebel" is written at the top of one of these pages and underneath is a further title, "The Runaway—'French Leave'." At the beginning of the draft and scribbled on its edges are a series of words: "Ferment—Revolt," "Equal Opportunity," "Clipped Wings," "Careering," "Fugitives," "Truants" (Somerville and Ross 1926–27). In addition to this emphasis on escape and rebellion is a careful attention to certain details in the story. Dates are listed, and Patsey's birthdate of 1863 makes her twenty-one when she first attends Pianelli's Studio (four years younger than Somerville when she first arrived in the French capital). Further notes at the end of the draft show a reckoning of the money needed by both characters to live in Paris, when various events occur, and the names of possible characters.

Somerville makes noticeable alterations as the narrative proceeds. Initially called Gavin Kirwan, the heroine eventually becomes Patricia Kirwan. Somerville clearly wanted a gender-neutral name, as indicated by Patsey's more frequent nomenclature of "Pat" in the final publication. Also, Somerville initially dates the Paris trip 1886 but in the course of writing changes it to September 1884. As mentioned, this date coincides with Somerville's arrival in Paris, but it is also just before the death of Marie Bashkirtseff, the painter greatly admired by Somerville and her contemporaries. When looking back over her diary entries that recorded her time in Paris, Somerville would have noted her response to Bashkirtseff's paintings displayed at the 1885 women's exhibition in Paris: "awfully clever" work, she had enthused (7 March 1885). Her writing partner Martin Ross would note six years later in her diary a gift of Bashkirtseff's journal from Warham St. Leger (3 November 1891).

For female artist-writers like Somerville and Ross, Marie Bashkirtseff exemplified the struggle for well-born women to professionalise their skills. Bashkirtseff worked in the Académie Julian in the late 1870s and depicted artistic endeavour in the women's studios in her painting, *In the Studio* (1881), and her writing, *The Journal of Marie Bashkirtseff* (1891). "I am jealous," wrote Bashkirtseff in her diary about a highly skilled fellow art student, Louise Breslau. "That is a good thing, because it is an incentive," she concludes (1985, 292). Bashkirtseff is acutely aware of female artists' limitations: "The gentlemen down-stairs have Robert Fleury, Boulanger, and someone else besides, whereas we have only Robert Fleury. It is not fair" (289). Art critics Rozsika Parker and Griselda Pollack note that the central conflict expressed in Bashkirtseff's journal lies between the longing for fame and the fact that renown for a female would cause "suspicion, jealousy and infamy." They say that the choice for Bashkirtseff appeared to her to be between solitary success and marriage to a great artist: "independence of mind or complete submission to another, solitary success or supportive subordination" (1981; 2013, 108–09). Bashkirtseff's death at twenty-five years from tuberculosis decided her in the end.

Like Bashkirtseff, Patsey Kirwan in Somerville's novel envies her new studio friends' artistic skill and is incentivised by a sense of competition she had never experienced before in Ireland. Her best friends, the German Hans (Henrietta) von Kapff and the American Mercy La Mont, are loosely based on Somerville's housemates in Paris, H. de Poncet and Marion Adams. At the end of her manuscript draft, Somerville lists other names culled from her memory and her diary:

> Names. Klein. Gallikoff. Kroupal (Amer.) Klahn. Lürich De Brémont. Blanchet. Foinet. Roget. Bouvier. Rennes La Croix 'Bozzeration.' Finn. Hellquist. Black Maria model who waved like a tree in the wind.— Peterson. Johannsen. ... Washed Ponce's head to cut her hair. (Somerville and Ross 1926–27)

Some of these names appear in the published work: "Bouvier" recalls Dagnan Bouveret who taught Somerville in Colarossi's; we also learn that "Fröken Hellquist headed the Northlanders" in the novel's studio (Somerville and Ross 1928, 187). One title in this group merits special attention. It appears simply as the "Finn." The appellation seems like a throwaway, but in *French Leave* the "big *Finlandaise*" in Pianelli's acquires a name taken from reality: Soldan (161). Patsey first meets the young Finn in the cheap crémerie in the Rue Bréa where the studio crowd gathers: "young girls, middle-aged girls, women of all ages, English and Americans, Germans and Scandinavians" (155). Patsey and her friends wonder if they might get the reasonably priced *tête de veau*, and Hans assures them that if anybody knows it will be Soldan:

> She [Hans] rose and went to a table at a little distance, at which a big fair Finlander was sucking an orange, with placid disregard of the fact that her mouth, though large, was not large enough to master the super-abundant juice.
>
> 'She says it was quite good—all but the eye of the calf. She said it looked so blue through ze sauce,' Hans reported seriously. (157)

Wendle Irene Soldan Brofeldt began working in Colarossi's in autumn, 1885, just after Somerville had finished her second visit. Soldan's other fellow student, Hanna Hirsch (better known by her married name, Pauli), painted Soldan during their time in the studio and exhibited the portrait in the 1887 Salon (Bolloch 2017a, 253). The significance of the portrait, *The Artist Venny-Soldan Brofeldt*, might be reckoned by its subsequent challenge to the arbiters of taste in the artists' home countries of Finland and Sweden. Both this painting and a contemporaneous picture of working women by Helena Westermarck called *An Important Question, or the Ironers* (1883), provoked negative reactions for displays of bohemian behavior and "nihilistic and overly direct" representation of women (Hansen 2017, 77).

Soldan's portrait stands out in women's art history as a representative work that displays the easy freedom and the artistic ambition of Nordic female artists in Paris at the end of the nineteenth century (Hansen 2017, 76). Its attention to woman's artwork rather than her toilette makes it significant during a time when there were few French depictions of artist women working. One well known picture of the woman artist that had appeared in the 1870 Paris Salon, Manet's *Portrait of Mlle E.G.*, provoked amusement because it concentrated more on the female artist's white gown than her work (Alsdorf 2017, 30). In Manet's painting, the artist sits in front of a floral study on an easel, her raised arm poised above the shimmering material of her dress and from under which a dainty foot emerges. She is apparently oblivious to the dangers that a splash of paint might cause.

Because Manet's picture of Gonzalès, purchased by Lady Gregory's nephew Sir Hugh Lane in 1904, became prominent in Irish conversation about art in the early twentieth century, as I discuss below, Somerville's treatment of the female artist at work in *French Leave* would have been informed not just by European developments but also by responses to art developments back home. I want to examine more closely Soldan's picture—in both Pauli's painting and Somerville's text—to consider its importance in terms of women's art and Irish art discourse. By considering the Nordic picture alongside Somerville's retrospective view in *French Leave*, we might consider a broader perspective of the development of feminist thought at the turn of the twentieth century.

Venny Soldan poses in a studio space in her portrait. Art implements surround her and she appears to have plonked herself onto the ground to work on a sketch. She looks up at the viewer, her mouth half open and her blue eyes distracted, as though she is still thinking about the drawing at hand. The Finnish artist wears a shapeless black dress and her sizeable foot juts out from underneath and towards the viewer. Because of the perspective, Soldan's foot, clad in a sturdy black walking shoe, looks larger than her head. The darkness of her dress emphasises the surrounding colours: the tawny brown of her scraped back hair repeats the browny-orange colour on the floor covering.

Somerville's inclusion of a textual sketch of Soldan in *French Leave* may deliberately allude to the Nordic network representative. Her description also suggests the uninhibited female artist whose pleasure in the senses overrides any need for feminine decorum. The orange she sucks drips juice down her face and she speaks openly of unpleasant things like a dead calf's eye. However, the Irish writer's appreciation of Soldan's casual disregard of feminine posturing which recalls Pauli's painting, gains in significance if we consider discussion about the visual representation of the female artist in Ireland in the intervening years and before Somerville wrote her book about women artists in Paris. One of the most talked about paintings in Dublin, the aforementioned painting of Gonzalès, took centre stage because it represented the need for good art in Ireland.

Somerville and Ross's familiarity with Manet's portrait would have been encouraged by George Moore singling out the work when lecturing on the need for new art in Dublin. Moore praised the painting and it became the signature picture of Hugh Lane's collection and an indicator of Ireland's lack of appreciation for fine art in the developing nation. William Orpen included the portrait of Gonzalès in his *Homage to Manet* (1909). In Orpen's painting George Moore sits at a table across from a group of male art critics and collectors. On the wall above them is Manet's painting of the female artist in her white gown, tiny foot peeping out from amongst its folds.

George Moore's lecture for Hugh Lane was aimed at encouraging the purchase of impressionist art for a Gallery of Modern Art in Dublin. The lecture not only reappeared as *Reminiscences of the Impressionist Painters* (1906) but also as a chapter in *Hail and Farewell* (1911), a copy of which Somerville owned and which she and Martin Ross read with close attention. Lady Gregory was Martin Ross's second cousin and Somerville and Ross contributed to her ultimately unsuccessful campaign to retain Hugh Lane's pictures in Ireland after his death on the Titanic in 1915. The co-authors would have been especially interested in Moore's discussion of the collection. In his lecture Moore draws attention to Gonzalès' portrait and, in particular, her foot. He admires it immensely. "Look at that girl's foot," he says, "it is stated without fear of offending or desire of pleasing anybody." The "rounded white arm" of the artist is equally a simple statement of fact and "entirely without sexual appeal" (1985, 652). The work demonstrates what George Moore saw as vital in good art: "'Be[ing] not ashamed of anything but to be ashamed'." Further, "the portrait of Mademoiselle Gonzalès is what Dublin needs. In Dublin everyone is afraid to confess himself. Is it not clear that whosoever paints like that confesses himself unashamed? He who admires that picture is already half free—the shackles are broken and will fall presently" (652).

Moore singles out Manet's portrait of the female artist not to encourage women artists but to chastise the viewing public for its prudery and to awaken it to modern development. What preoccupies Moore and others interested in art in Ireland was getting such material into Dublin's galleries. And even though Hugh Lane's collection never found a home in Ireland, the determined campaign of art enthusiasts (including Somerville and Ross) ensured that its contents became well known. Thus, Somerville's backward look at women artists in Paris at the end of the nineteenth century in *French Leave* would have been informed by arguments about modern art in Ireland as well as new ways of envisaging the female artist which had been taking place across the turn of the twentieth century and beyond. So, while *French Leave* celebrates the international mix of women student artists working in Paris and displays the freedom and authority of some women artists, it also asserts the importance of Irish realities that would have influenced someone like Patsey Kirwan. For instance, the character Soldan clearly represents the female professional at work in the manner of Pauli's portrait discussed earlier. Her authority in the women's studio is evidenced in her unashamed argument with M. Pianelli about the positioning of a nude female model. Patsey Kirwan, however, blushes at the sight of the nude and thus demonstrates the result of the social decorum that George Moore highlights when arguing against what he saw as false modesty found in Irish circles. And even though Patsey Kirwan and George Lester embrace wholeheartedly the studio system and live in an "ecstasy of effort, feeling as if they had come out of darkness into a growing glory of light" (187), Miss Kirwan of Kirwanscourt never really fits into this world; she stands out from the rest of the studio crowd throughout the novel.

Patsey's difference from her fellows lies in a rather unexpected source— her cleanliness, a characteristic for which Edith Somerville herself was not especially renowned.[3] Nonetheless, when Professor Bouvier first notices the new art student in Pianelli's he sees someone who is "tall and slim and clean" (170), and his tuition on art values leads him to compare Patsey's white collars to the highest value on the scale in colour theory: "absolute white" (278). When Patsey thinks of home and the "wind on the heath" she becomes aware of how "stale and stuffy" the studio is and "the greasy black-and-tan Italian model" begins to "remind her of a Kerry Beagle ('only it's an insult to dear Faithful and Fiddler to say so!')" (192). Patsey's dismissal of southern Europeans might be considered in relation to the text's appreciation of North European women artists. Moreover, her curious reference to a familiar term of 1920s Ireland— the Black and Tans—may not be deliberate, but it indicates how Somerville is considering the 1880s from the broader vantage point which time confers. Whatever the case, Patsey's need for order and cleanliness—as much as her artistic success—provokes envy amongst her peers: "Perhaps Pat's success with the professors had been too marked, her drawing had shown too rapid an improvement, her high linen collars too dazzling a standard of cleanliness" (278).

Somerville's emphasis on the low standards of cleanliness and order in Pianelli's not only serves to suggest Patsey's ladylike (and rather bourgeois) Irish modesty. More importantly it shows Somerville's awareness of some of the later developments in work spaces for women in Europe. Indeed, the international mix of women introduced in *French Leave* provides a clue as to the reason that Somerville draws attention to this aspect of Patsey's character.

As already noted, Somerville's novel, sketchbook, and manuscript, include references to the Nordic women's network in Paris, including Helena Westermarck, Venny Soldan, and Fröken Hellquist, "the grim champion of *les Scandinaves*" (Somerville and Ross 1928, 187). Somerville and Ross's ongoing connection with this network, as suggested by this cluster of materials, becomes evident in later writing. The co-writers' final travel article in a series of four

---

3   Gifford Lewis speaks of young Somerville's untidiness as indicated in one of her nicknames—"The Queen of Filth"—in *Edith Somerville, A Biography*, 74.

written from 1890 to 1895, "In the State of Denmark," pays particular attention to the Royal Danish Academy's new art school for women in Copenhagen, the Nordic capital which enjoyed closest relations with European art at this time (Gunnarsson 1998, 216–68). Somerville and Ross arrived in the city soon after a significant 1893 exhibition of extensive works by Paul Gauguin and Vincent Van Gogh. Their travelogue emphasises such new development when its female narrator points out with a mock scandalised tone that the "country's art is now in transition; there are heretics fresh from Paris schools; there are heretics of older standing, half ready to leave Denmark because of the narrowness that they find in it, there are those to whom the Parisian greens and mauves and majentas are the sin of witchcraft" (Somerville and Ross 1920, 160). However, the narrator's interest directs itself at women's art education rather than modern male artists. She describes how Johanne Krebs, the foremost figure in the founding of the women's department in the Royal Danish Academy in 1888, conducts the Irish visitors around the women's school, "a pattern to all others of its kind" (161). The narrator appreciates the "long and hardy efforts" of Fröken Krebbs in establishing this school as well as developing with others the Skagen artists' colony: "The school of the *pleinairistes* is strong in the North, and its reliance on Nature has a special fascination for the Northerners, whose passion for Nature is a wonderful exemplification of the principle of loving one's enemies" (160). Particularly praiseworthy attributes of the Copenhagen school are those we see in Patsey's character in *French Leave*: order and cleanliness. The narrator of "In the State of Denmark" says that superior craftsmanship results from good working conditions that are established by a cleanliness that is lacking in the Paris studios where Fröken Krebs (and Edith Somerville) had trained.

We might thus return to a question posed earlier in this essay and ask if Patsey's return to Ireland results from the limitations in the Paris studios, or if she runs back because of her inability to shake free of tradition and enter the modern marketplace. Perhaps the reason is more complex than either of these answers suggest. Indeed, in seeking an answer we might keep in mind that despite the various references to Northern artists in Somerville's sketches and diary and Somerville and Ross's writing, Somerville's position overall in relation to the Nordic network appears to have been peripheral. This is also the case for Patsey Kirwan in *French Leave*. When the Northlanders in Pianelli's oppose a rival group of British and Americans, Patsey and her friends take a neutral position and refuse to commit to either faction. Somerville seems to have adopted a similar stance in relation to the international links she forged in Colarossi's. The brevity of her study trips to Paris meant that Irish concerns dominated her life, as is the case with Patsey Kirwan who returns home readily—not just because her money has run out but also because her mother is ill. The text suggests further that Irish society lacks the support system necessary for women's artistic development. The implication is that the heroine's sense of order and fairness, as well as friendships forged in Paris, will enable her to embark on the work needed to create such support.

Despite Somerville's tangential relationship to the Nordic network, she appears to have retained her interest in this part of the world at different times in her life. For example, her letter to Douglas Hyde in later years includes the suggestion that Ireland might contribute to Finland's military resources in response to the Russo-Finnish war of the 1940s.[4] Somerville's outward perspective would have owed much to her time in Paris and her exposure to northern female women like the Finnish artists Venny Soldan and Helena Westermarck. After all, Nordic women and Finlanders in particular had played a prominent role in forging international networks in the 1880s. In 1888, the same year that Johanne Krebs founded a women's department in the Royal Danish Academy, the International Council of Women held in Washington D.C. included representatives from ten nations. The Finnish representative Alli Trygg-Helenius gave one of the final speeches of the meeting and spoke of a "golden cable of sympathy" amongst women of different nations, a cable not unlike the international transatlantic cables linking Finland to different parts of the world (McFadden 1999, 177).[5] In her study of international feminism, Margaret McFadden notes that the "number of international connections made by Nordic women was disproportionate to their population" (1999, 4). Finland in particular draws her attention because of the emphasis these women gave to connecting across countries, as so clearly shown with Trygg-Helenius's "golden cable" speech when she asserted that "'every victory you will win shall be ours; you work not only for the women of your country but for the women of the whole world'" (McFadden 1999, 171).

Somerville and Ross's *French Leave* pays tribute to the women artists who gave a presence to the female artist in picture and text at the end of the nineteenth century. It suggests the international network of women whose combined efforts established a platform for their work and whose sympathy of thought would go on to inform their work in their home countries. Glimpses of important feminist writers and artists in the range of material from the period of the novel's setting indicate how feminist discourse was established and the challenges which professionalization posed to young women. Edith Somerville brought new ideas about the female artist back home to Ireland, and her work with Martin Ross suggests that she aimed to introduce those ideas to Irish readers.

---

4   Edith Somerville, letter to Douglas Hyde, 20 January 1940 (L.B. 199.a–b), referred to in Otto Rauchbauer, *The Edith Œnone Somerville Archive in Drishane*, 185.
5   I am grateful to Heidi Hansson for drawing my attention to McFadden's work.

References

Alsdorf, Bridget. 2017. "Painting the *Femme Peintre*." In *Women Artists in Paris, 1850–1900*, curator Laurence Madeline, 24–39. New York: Yale University Press..

Bashkirtseff, Marie. (1891) 1985. *The Journal of Marie Bashkirtseff*. Translated by Mathilda Blind. London: Virago Press.

Bolloch, Joëlle. 2017a. "Artists Biographies." In *Women Artists in Paris, 1850–1900*, curator Laurence Madeline, 240–57. New York: Yale University Press.

———. 2017b. "Female Painters at the Paris Salon." In *Women Artists in Paris, 1850–1900*, curator Laurence Madeline, 258–65. New York: Yale University Press.

Gunnarsson, Torsten. 1998. *Nordic Landscape Painting in the Nineteenth Century*. New Haven and London: Yale University Press.

Hansen, Vibeke Waallann. 2017. "Female Artists in the Nordic Countries: Training and Professionalization." In *Women Artists in Paris, 1850–1900*, curator Laurence Madeline, 68–81. New York: Yale University Press.

Lewis, Gifford. 2005. *Edith Somerville, A Biography*. Dublin: Four Courts Press.

McFadden, Margaret. 1999. *Golden Cables of Sympathy: The Transatlantic Sources of Nineteenth-Century Feminism*. Lexington, Kentucky: University Press of Kentucky. ProquestEbook Central.

Madeline, Laurence. 2017. "Into the Light: Women Artists, 1850–1900." In *Women Artists in Paris, 1850–1900*, curator Laurence Madeline, 1–23. New York: Yale University Press.

Manet, Édouard. 1870. *Portrait of Mlle E.G.* Oil on canvas. The National Gallery of London, London.

Martin, Violet (Martin Ross). 1891. Diary. MS 17/874. Manuscripts, Queen's University Library, Belfast.

Moore, George. (1911) 1985. "Appendix A: Chapter VI of Vale." In *Hail and Farewell*, edited by Richard Allen Cave, 647–63. Gerrards Cross, Buckinghamshire: Colin Smythe.

Newton, Joy. 1998. "The Atelier Novel: Painters as Fictions." In *Impressions of French Modernity*, edited by Richard Hobbs, 173–89. Manchester: Manchester University Press.

Parker, Rozsika, and Griselda Pollack. (1981) 2013. *Old Mistresses, Women, Art and Ideology*. London: I.B. Tauris & Co.

Pauli, Hanne. 1887. *The Artist Venny-Soldan Brofeldt*. Oil on canvas. Gothenburg Museum of Art, Gothenburg.

Rauchbauer, Otto. 1995. *The Edith Œnone Somerville Archive in Drishane*. Dublin: Irish Manuscripts Commission.

Reznicek, Matthew. 2017. *The European Metropolis: Paris and Nineteenth-*

Century Irish Women Novelists. Clemson: Clemson University Press.

Somerville, E. Œ. 1885. Diary. MS 17/874. Manuscripts, Queen's University Library, Belfast.

———. April 1885. Pencil sketch of "Frln Westermarck." In *Paris Sketchbook*. Edith Œ. Somerville Sketchbook Collection, 1881–*c*.1912. Private Collection.

Somerville, E. Œ., and Martin Ross. (1895) 1920. "In the State of Denmark." In *Stray-Aways*, 83–183. London: Longmans, Green & Co.

———. 1926–27. Manuscript draft of *French Leave*. Somerville and Ross, MS 989. Houghton Library, Harvard University.

———. 1928. *French Leave*. London: Heinemann Ltd.

Stevens, Julie Anne. 2017. *Two Irish Girls in Bohemia: The Drawings and Writings of E. Œ. Somerville and Martin Ross*. Bantry, Co. Cork: Somerville Press.

Westermarck, Helena. (1905) 1976. "Some Finnish Women Painters." In *Women Painters of the New World from the Time of Caterina Vigni 1413–1463*, edited by Walter Shaw Sparrow, 290–2. New York: Hacker Art Books.

6

"Hunters in Red Coats": The Irish New Girl in Edith Somerville's "Little Red Riding-Hood in Kerry" (1934)

Anne Jamison

In her 1920 essay on women and hunting, "*Not* the Woman's Place," Edith Somerville argued that sport "played quite as potent a part as education" in the emancipation of women: "The playing-fields of Eton did not as surely win Waterloo as the hunting-fields and lawn-tennis grounds of the kingdom won the vote for women" (Somerville 1920, 230). Somerville here recognises the ways in which sport (especially hunting) in the late nineteenth and early twentieth centuries helped to create independent and empowered feminine identities that encouraged the broader campaign for women's rights. Indeed, Erika Munkwitz demonstrates how riding manuals for women peaked and "coincided with the appearance of the 'New Woman'" figure in the *fin-de-siècle* British media (Munkwitz 2012, 81). This essay will explore Somerville's use of traditional European fairy and folk tales for her own feminist purposes and, in the case of "Little Red Riding-Hood in Kerry" (1934), demonstrate how she revises a well-known tale to create a modern, equestrian Irish "New Girl" who exposes the economic exploitation of young women in early twentieth-century Ireland.

Embedded as it is in the renewed agitation for land under Ireland's 1933 Land Act, I will argue that the story explicitly subverts the commonly understood moral of "Little Red Riding-Hood" which was popularised in late Victorian and early twentieth-century Britain through the proliferation of Charles Perrault's and Jacob and Wilhelm Grimm's versions of the folk tale. Somerville's revision arguably rejects the folk story's (male-authored) warning to women against straying from the "right" path and, instead, proffers a biting criticism of contemporary Irish female social models, as well as the economic manipulation of young women in Ireland's early twentieth-century land-grab.

At the same time, the story of "Moira Cloca-dearg," or "Mary of the Red Cloak," clearly signals her author's ambivalent feelings over the rising Catholic, farming middle classes of De Valera's new Ireland in the 1930s (Somerville 1936, 61).[1] Moira's supposed social transgressions here become intertwined as her challenge to Catholic Ireland's gendered morality overlaps with her usurpation of the "hunters in red coats" and the Protestant ruling classes of old Ireland that they represent (1936, 61).

Much of Somerville's literary engagement with European fairy and folk tales stems from her writing for children, but while her co-authored short fiction and novels with her cousin, Martin Ross, have received detailed scholarly attention, her literature for children is, as Julie Anne Stevens recognises, a "neglected aspect of Somerville and Ross scholarship" (Stevens 2007, 41). Stevens' recent work begins to recuperate Somerville's children's writing for serious scholarly attention and, of particular relevance for this essay, suggests that Somerville recognised and leveraged the strong "feminist potential" of this genre (2007, 41). Stevens demonstrates how Somerville's unpublished picture book adaptation, *Growly-Wowly or the Story of the Three Little Pigs* (c. 1880), for example, turns the familiar fable story tale "on its head" with a plot in which "the youngest female pig gains the upper hand over the wolf" (Stevens 2007, 46). Similarly, Stevens identifies Somerville's unpublished drawings and plans for an illustrated adaptation of Robert Southey's poem, "The King of the Crocodiles" (1799), as an exploration of "how a children's book might convey a feminist message" (2017, 122). While Stevens rightly includes "Little Red Riding Hood in Kerry" in these discussions, Somerville's revisionary tale also distinguishes itself in several key ways from these other stories.

First and foremost, and unlike Somerville's more lavishly-illustrated children's literature, the tale's publishing history makes it clear that it was originally written for adults and not for children. Somerville's revision of "Little Red Riding Hood" first appeared in 1934 in a Christmas anthology of fairy tales, *The Fairies Return, or, New Tales for Old*, edited by the London publisher Peter Davies. As advertised on the inside cover of the anthology, the book was marketed as a collection of "well-known Fairy Stories retold for grown-ups in a modern setting" and penned by "several hands" (Davies 1934, iii). On completion, the story was enthusiastically received by Peter Davies, who thought it "magnificent" and was thoroughly "enchanted with Moira Cloca-dearg" (Somerville 1934). Somerville was less enthused by the final volume, however, and she subsequently requested permission to republish her story as a small booklet for private distribution to family members and printed 117 copies with Davies' printers in Edinburgh in December 1934, re-naming the

---

1 Somerville's story omits the síneadh fada (acute accent) in the correct Irish spelling of Moira's familiar name, Mary of the Red Cloak or Moira Clóca-dearg. This essay utilises Somerville's spelling of "Cloca-dearg" throughout.

story "Little Red Riding-Hood in Kerry." The story re-appeared in one last guise in 1936 as part of Somerville's collection of essays and fiction on hunting, *The Sweet Cry of Hounds*.

This manifold publishing history aligns Somerville's tale with her feminist literature on women and hunting in *The Sweet Cry of Hounds*, as well as groups it alongside her more adult short fiction. Its rural Irish setting, characters and idiolect further distinguish it from her other stories for children and explicitly transpose the politics of the original European folk tale to the contemporaneous land politics of Ireland in the 1930s. Little critical attention has been paid, however, to how the story straddles its traditional European folk origins as a warning tale, or *Warnmärchen*, for children, and its more localised adult anxieties over Irish land policy and the subsequent ramifications of these policies for Irish women. Indeed, aside from Stevens' recognition of the feminist impulses of the story, children's literature critics have largely ignored or trivialised the story's Irish context and gender concerns.

Contemporary critics have read the story in terms of its assumed delightful conventionality. Jack Zipes singles out Somerville's story as typical of the orthodox fairy tale revisions of the 1920s and 1930s in England and Ireland. His reading of the tale reduces it to a "charming Irish adaptation" and an "unusual blarney version" of the original European folk story, one which simply mirrors the traditional motif of taming a woman's sexual instincts and social autonomy (Zipes 1993, 56). Similarly, Maria Tatar pays little attention to the story's Irish context and reads "Little Red Riding-Hood in Kerry" in terms of sexual temptation and social initiatory rites (Tatar 2012, 20). I would argue, however, that while Somerville's story certainly reverberates with the more traditional and conservative morals of well-known versions of the original folk tale, "Little Red Riding-Hood in Kerry" delivers a far from conventional lesson for young women and significantly challenges the gendered Irish social and Catholic mores of its time.

Unlike *Growly-Wowly* and Somerville's illustrations for "The King of the Crocodiles," which either amplify or fashion anew empowered and triumphant female characters, "Little Red Riding-Hood in Kerry" concludes with its central female protagonist succumbing to her traditional fate. Moira Cloca-dearg is duly devoured by the wolf or, rather, the "divil's own play-boy" and farm neighbour, Cornelius "Curley" Wolfe (Somerville 1936, 67). The daughter of "a decent widow-woman" and owner of a "small handy little farm" (61), Moira is sent out on her eighteenth birthday in her "new red riding-coat" to visit her grandmother and pay her compliments with a basket of honey, eggs, butter and "a lovely soda loaf" (71). Knowing "old Mrs Dan Sheehan" to have "a power o' money," the Widow Sheehan suggests to Moira that "maybe yourself'd get a present from her" and warns her to "go straight there" (71). Encountering Curley on the way, however, Moira is enticed to join in the local foxhunt. She gets further waylaid by the "divilment of the fairies" who have a long held "spite" (66) against her for carrying off their favoured white pony, and who lead the hunters astray in pursuit of a "blagyard Fairy Fox" (80). Returning to Curley's farm where she left her basket, she finds Curley has gone ahead to deliver the basket himself and, on arriving at her grandmother's house, finds what she thinks is a "wicked fairy" disguised as her grandmother (82). Luring the girl closer, Curley reveals himself and (against her protestations) catches and "holds her tight" with a kiss and tells her that her grandmother has gone "to settle with the priest": "'I'll wait no longer … We'll be married to-night!' says he" (83–4).

As Zipes and Tatar point out, the story seems to echo—at least on a surface level—the established morality of popular Victorian and early twentieth-century British versions of the Red Riding Hood folk tale that circulated widely in the period. Zipes also observes that "the Perrault and Grimm versions remained dominant" during the first half of the twentieth century and it is likely that these two versions are the tales with which Somerville would have been most familiar both as a child and an adult (Zipes 1993, 49). "Little Red Riding-Hood in Kerry" certainly seems to contain elements of both the Perrault and Grimm versions and, in this sense, demands that the reader deduce and engage with its multiple intertexts and their interpretations. Ann Martin proposes that the "sheer variety" and multifaceted nature of fairy tales circulating in modernity suggests that they "were an almost inescapable source of reference" for early twentieth-century writers, invoking "an excess of meaning" (Martin 2007, 8–9). Within this context, Somerville's revised folk tale takes on a palimpsestic quality which both conjures up and, as I will go on to argue, undermines earlier variants of "Little Red Riding-Hood."

Somerville adopts the more gruesome (and less well known) ending of Perrault's "Little Red Riding Hood" (1697) whereby "the wicked wolf threw himself upon Little Red Riding Hood and ate her up" (Zipes 1993, 93), as opposed to the more popular saving of the young girl from the wolf's stomach by a male hunter in the Grimms' "Little Red Cap" (1812) (Zipes 1993, 137–38). Like the latter story, however, Somerville emphasises the Grimms' extended narrative of the mother's warning to Little Red Cap to not "tarry on your way … and stray from the path" and the girl's responding promise "to be very obedient" (Zipes 1993, 135). Critical interpretations of Perrault's and the Grimms' retellings of the Red Riding-Hood folk narrative note the different socio-historical contexts that governed their composition, as well as their authors' culturally-specific viewpoint. At the same time, there is a clear sense of how the tales both cohere around a sexually suggestive subtext and coded warnings of the self-discipline and restraint deemed necessary for a young girl's successful initiation into womanhood. Perrault's wolf, as Catherine Orenstein demonstrates, is "the dapper charmer of Parisian high society, seducer of young women and a threat to the family patrimony" and, symbolically, the young girl's own animal desires which need to be curtailed in order to enter adult society (Orenstein 2003, 38). While retaining some of the sexual suggestiveness of the French version, the Grimm brothers went some way in taming the implications of seduction in Perrault's story and shifted the focus to better suit the "social landscape of Victorian Europe" and the Victorian child, instituting a more domestic and "patriarchal lesson in female obedience" and a suitably heroic father figure (Orenstein 2003, 60). The focus of the Grimms' didacticism, suggests Martin, also signals a shift from Perrault's "sexually aware audience" of French adult court society to a "readership of primarily children" (Martin 2007, 14).

As critics have repeatedly demonstrated, both stories radically revise earlier oral versions of the tale which emphasised "the strength of the female protagonist and the empowerment that results from her brush with the wolf" (Martin 2007, 15). In so doing, the tale is transformed, as Zipes argues, from "a hopeful oral tale about the initiation of a young girl into a tragic one of violence in which the girl is blamed for her own violation" (Zipes 1993, 7). More pointedly, the literary tradition of "Little Red Riding-Hood" locks the protagonist into what Cristina Bacchilega terms a "gendered and constricting chamber":

> Whether she survives her journey into the outer world or not, the girl is *inside* when the tale ends—inside the wolf's belly for Perrault, or her grandmother's home for the Grimms. Devoured or domesticated, charged with sin or in charge of the feminine hearth ... Little Red Riding Hood is subjected to the laws of one deliberative masculine body. (Bacchilega 1999, 58–59)

At the end of "Little Red Riding-Hood in Kerry," Moira Cloca-dearg certainly finds herself inside an unwanted marriage and subject to the impatient sexual desire of her male pursuer and now lawful husband, Cornelius Wolfe. Somerville's folk tale here evokes the social and sexual messages of Perrault's and the Grimms' tales. In effect, and like her female precedents, Moira is symbolically punished for her deviancy from feminine norms of behaviour.

In Somerville's provision of a lengthy backstory to "Little Red Riding-Hood in Kerry," it is clear that Moira has several times transgressed multiple gendered social and class boundaries before setting off for her grandmother's house. Moira's riding to the hunt is perceived as a "strange thing and against nature" (Somerville 1936, 61), and her truancy from school sees her conversing with fairy folk despite her mother's cautions: "She had the fancy always to be going away by herself in lonely places ... she would stray away in the hills, and queer stories she would bring back with her to the Mother" (62). All of this takes place against Moira's burgeoning maturation which, as in Perrault and the Grimms, is symbolised by her red cloak, a sign of her predetermined fall into sin and lust, as well as the blood of menstruation and the story's closing sexual violence. Indeed, it is on the cusp of womanhood at thirteen years of age that she transgresses fairy lore and acquires the white pony, Lusmore, "as near and dear to her as the blood of her arm" (62). It is Lusmore that enables Moira to "follow the Hounds" and necessitates the "tasty red riding-coat" made for her by her mother (69). Moira is empowered by her acquisition of Lusmore and the weather-protective cloak to stray even further from home, but she is simultaneously bounded and judged by the behavioural standards and social status embodied in the community that names and claims her: "It was then the people put the name of Cloca-dearg on her" (69).

For centuries, notes Maria Pramaggiore, the horse has "functioned as a compelling symbol within Irish mythology, literature and visual culture" (Pramaggiore 2007, 141) and, linked as it is to "movement and mediation," has a "privileged relationship to temporal and spatial liminality" (142). Moira's liminal or transitional status, both in terms of her maturation and supernatural possession of "*the Sighth*," is thus heightened through her intimate connection to Lusmore (Somerville 1936, 74). Indeed, this connection further links the story and Moira's transgressions to a richly localised context of Irish oral narrative and fairy legend. Christened after the "fox-gloves" amidst which Moira finds her "pure white yearling pony"—"Lusmore is the name in Irish for it"—Moira's horse is a recurring reminder in the story of the little girl's flouting of traditional fairy lore and native morality (65).[2] Moira disregards resident knowledge of the fairy-occupied "old forts" in her rural domain when she flagrantly crosses into their territory (64), as well as flouts her mother's warning that she has "no business" keeping company with fairies (63). With further audacity, Moira encourages Lusmore out of the fairy fort and issues a bold rejoinder to the warning blow of the fairy horn: "I have her now and I'll keep her!" (66). In the context of early twentieth-century British and European children's fiction, the story's supernatural elements are taken as part of its accepted fantastical elements, but situated within what Angela Bourke terms the "highly coded" language of Irish oral fairy and folklore narrative, these same aspects take on an added resonance (Bourke 1995, 568). The casting of Moira as "Mary of the Red Cloak" and her habitual "going away" with the fairies (Somerville 1936, 61) carries with it an element of localised "social deviance and stigma" which constitutes a "highly coded" form of speech, a euphemistic means of referring to an array of women's alleged social and moral misdemeanours, or supposedly shameful mental and physical illnesses (Bourke 1995, 580, 571). Moira's participation in the hunt, as well as the independence Lusmore brings

---

2   Somerville's story utilises the English transliterated word, "Lusmore," rather than the Irish spelling, Lusmór. As with the spelling of Moira Clóca-dearg, this essay utilises Somerville's spelling of "Lusmore" throughout.

her, is further damned in this oral context which deems her headstrong nature as aberrant and corrupt and, possibly, the result of a changeling substitution.[3] Located in between childhood (nature) and adulthood (culture), as well as between reality and a land of fairies and Cluricaunes, Moira's liminal position is thus one of continual boundary-crossing and both actual and potential transgression on a number of formally sanctioned fronts. Unsurprisingly, the pony, like its new red-clad owner, is consequently associated with a fall from purity to sin when Curley, in mischievous jest, paints the white pony "with big patches of red" (68). Like Moira, Lusmore wears the red cloak, too.

If Moira's red riding cloak resonates with its earlier variants and their popular interpretations, however, it is also given a much more localised symbolism in Somerville's tale that is indicative of potential class and racial usurpation. Moira's red cloak is modelled on the "pictures in the town of hunters in red coats" and it is at her request that the Widow Sheehan makes her daughter a red hunting coat: "The world wouldn't content her without she'd get a red coat the same as she seen in the pictures" (62). More commonly associated with upper-class English hunters, Moira's sporting of a red hunting cloak takes on a somewhat mutinous air that potentially reminds us of both Anglo-Irish political decline and the rising Catholic middle classes of newly independent Ireland. Indeed, the reader's assumption that Moira's gender makes her participation in hunting an act "against nature" is slightly undercut by the narrator's emphasis on the social rather than gender implications of Moira's sporting activities (61). In so doing, the story also hits out at the new breed of Irish middle-class farmer-hunters by scornfully degrading their rank: "But sure these weren't grand English quality hounds at all. They were no more than only them big black dogs, Kerry Bagles they calls them, that the farmers' sons keeps to be hunting the foxes" (62). Moira's supposed political insubordination is here entangled with her broader social and gender transgressions.

Despite the ostensible alignment of Moira Cloca-dearg with the young girls who stray from the path in Perrault's and the Grimms' version of the tale,

---

3   A changeling in Irish folklore refers to the fairy or non-human substitute left in place after a fairy abduction of a human person, usually a woman or child. These women or children were sometimes rescued in the narrative by violent action against the changeling figure. Bourke argues that Irish fairy abduction stories often conceal a "coded aggression against women" and that "extreme violence ... is one of the most conspicuous features of changeling legends" (Bourke 1995, 571). There are distinctive similarities between Moira Cloca-dearg and the factual story of Bridget Cleary; a high-profile and sensationalised case of apparent fairy abduction that resulted in the death of Bridget by her husband's hand. Given its notoriety and media coverage, it is likely that Somerville would have known about the case. For example, Moira's empowered riding of the white pony, Lusmore, evokes details of Cleary's case; after her murder, her husband "spent three nights at the nearby 'fairy fort' ... apparently in the expectation of seeing his wife ride out on a white horse, cutting her free, and so rescuing her from the fairies" (Bourke 1995, 554).

however, "Little Red Riding-Hood in Kerry" does not seem to simply recall or echo the prevailing gender ideologies and patriarchal regulations instilled in those prior tales. Rather, it appears to elicit them in order to contest them, albeit tangentially. In adapting the fairy tale to the cultural and, in particular, linguistic landscape of Ireland, the "blarney" elements that Zipes finds so unusual in the tale are arguably utilised by Somerville to question the patriarchal social values imparted in earlier variants (Zipes 1993, 56). The narrator's Anglo-Irish and often blackly comic vernacular has the effect of undercutting the moralising, sober and often censorious tones associated with children's fairy tale literature and this, in turn, disrupts the conventional social and gender principles such tales attempt to inculcate. In this regard, the largely blithe Irish idiolect of Somerville's narrator, which lends an explicitly oral quality to the story, takes on a particularly irreverent tenor which arguably destabilises the authority of Perrault and the Grimms, as well as the broader didactic style of children's sermonizing literature. In terms of "Little Red Riding-Hood in Kerry," this destabilization is further apparent in the multiple shifts between different source texts and works to disrupt the dominance of these earlier patriarchal voices.

While the underlying narrative of the Perrault and Grimm variants orientates the reader's expectations in Somerville's revised tale, the narrator's meandering conversational style and Irish idiolect creates a powerful linguistic disruption of past "Little Red Riding-Hood" variants. It also creates additional textual space for an extended focus on Moira and a detailed characterisation that distinguishes her from the young female naïf of the Perrault and Grimm versions of the tale. Read in terms of its contemporaneous Irish contexts, opposed to its historical continental ones, Moira's red cloak, for example, overrides the purely negative symbolism with which it is traditionally associated and enables Moira to experiment with alternative and empowered female identities. First and foremost, her red cloak is a hunting coat and her ownership of both the cloak and the white pony, Lusmore, not only permits her to take part in the local farm hunts, but to *lead* them and the local farmer's sons who comprise the huntsmen. Moira is in "glory" as she rides to the hounds, "as proud as that she wouldn't call the King her cousin … Sure she had the boys all left behind, and the white pony under her ready to run to Cork!" (76). Moreover, her participation in hunting is one which consciously defies the domestic constraints with which her mother attempts to encumber her—"when the Mother wouldn't know, she'd pounce up on the pony, and away with her after the hunt!" (70)—and one which asserts a level of individual (as opposed to familial or communal) interest. While the Widow Sheehan views Lusmore as a familial asset that will contribute to the domestic and farm work—"in two years' time it'll be grown, and many a good basket o' turf it'll carry for us!" (66)—Moira considers her "darling little pony-een!" (65) as her own individual possession and one which facilitates her self-realisation beyond the domestic confines of hearth and home: "It's me it'll be

81

carrying, and not turf at all!" (66).

Through first-hand experience, Somerville certainly understood the liberatory potential of women's involvement in hunting as sport. She was Ireland's first female Master of Foxhounds (MFH) and, as Munkwitz demonstrates, "[h]er success was widely acknowledged" both in her local community, as well as in the pages of the sports and society press (2017, 409). As the *Polo Monthly* noted in 1920, "[a]s a true sportswoman, Miss Somerville has but few equals" (quoted in Munkwitz 2017, 409). Furthermore, as MFH, Somerville would have not only had to lead the hunt but would have had to achieve a high level of equestrian athleticism alongside a rigorous understanding of sport theory and hunting strategy. She also would have had to train and maintain horses and hounds, as well as exert both discipline and diplomacy in working with hunt servants, farmers and landowners. Moira's leading of the hunt is thus emblematic of the kind of "radical possibilities for female emancipation" that the role of MFH authorised (Munkwitz 2017, 396). In this role, Munkwitz shows how women "became leaders of not just sport but also community": "To be a master was certainly a tangible and visual demonstration of command, which had consequences in the social and political rights of women" (2017, 415). More potently, women authors of nineteenth-century riding manuals reminded their readers that to become knowledgeable and proficient in horsemanship required the ability to "guide and govern" the self and "learn inner strength and confidence," as well as craft "personal autonomy" (Munkwitz 2012, 78). Moira's confidence and ability on the hunting ground is here viewed in a very different light. Rather than a transgression "against nature," it is a means of self-governance and, according to Lady Violet Greville, author of *Ladies in the Field* (1894), a sign of the moral superiority required to support national "life and well-being" (quoted in Munkwitz 2012, 82). Through this perspective, the conventional symbolism of the red riding-hood is upended and instead of an indication of a young girl's unruly body which, without brute subjugation, will fall into sin and dishonour, signifies the ability of women to acculturate themselves by reimagining traditional gender roles. The communal aspect and sharing of knowledge of this acculturating process is also vital as it is through what Munkwitz terms women's "solidarity of leadership and mentorship" (413) that female equestrians found such public success and became an "important and necessary part" of the national character (Munkwitz 2012, 81).

However, "Little Red Riding-Hood in Kerry" makes it clear that the newly independent Irish nation at the time of the story's composition has no want of, or place for, this newly independent Irish girl. The socialising narratives available to her in the new Irish nation clearly continue to subject her to the same masculine body and masculine law of Perrault and the Grimms. On one hand, the "little old manneen" (Somerville 1936, 62) or "Cluricaune" who Moira finds such "good company" but who she knows "well enough" to avoid entrapment (63), wears the "neat red cap" of the Grimms' "Little Red Cap" and echoes the censuring narrative of domestic patriarchy with which that tale is coloured: "'Go home now,' he says, 'and do as your Mother bid ye'" (81). Moira several times rejects the Cluricaune's advice and the enchanted shoes with which he attempts to seduce and entrap her. On the other hand, there lies a trickier narrative to overcome. Curley Wolfe is the shape-shifting seducer of Perrault's text, the *loup doucereux* who is "as full of tricks as a fairy" and "the limb o' the divil" (68; 71). Akin to the fairies with which he is repeatedly associated, he eventually leads Moira to her near death, not in a bog-hole of "deep dark water … twenty feet and more wide" to which the fairies direct her, but in a *mariage de raison* which, to Moira, is a kind of death-in-life (80). Curley is significantly aided, however, by a community of women who betray the moral ideals and solidarity of mentorship that Somerville's experience in the hunt has signalled as essential to female emancipation. The violence of Curley's kiss in the closing scene of the story is not just redolent of the unwanted advances and sexual violence Moira will be subjected to in her marriage to Curley—"*I've* no wish for him, or the likes of him!" (72)—but the social and economic violence she has been subjected to as a hostage of Ireland's early twentieth-century land-grab. This violence again echoes the Irish changeling narrative; Moira's dominant and independent self (the headstrong changeling) is effectively killed off to reveal a tamed and morally corrected version of Moira.

If Curley is impatient for Moira's hand, then it seems her grandmother is only too happy to speed the marriage along and willingly goes "to settle with the Priest" and legitimate Curley's lewd sexual overture at the end of the tale: "Mrs. Wolfe … and the Grandmother, that was old Mrs. Dan Sheehan, were for making a match with Moira and Curley, for the farm being convenient that way" (82). The narrator also reveals earlier in the tale that Curley's father, John Wolfe, was "no patriot at all" and that "Wolfe Tone … had no call or claim to him" (67). Terence Dooley demonstrates that between 1923 and 1948, the reconstituted Irish Land Commission "became the principal agent of social engineering in modern Ireland" and that "its impact on Irish rural society was matched only by that of the Catholic church" (Dooley 2004, 182; 185). In addition, during the 1920s and 1930s "no other social issue was as important to political survival … as land division" and that "very few received land unless they were members of Fianna Fáil" (185). Without any political affiliation to lay claim to, John Wolfe's farm would have been unsparingly subject to the Land Act of 1933, a law which granted the Land Commission "draconian powers regarding the compulsory acquisition of land" for redistribution: "After 1933 farmers had to live with the fear that the Land Commission might resume their holding for the relief of local congestion, or if a land-hungry neighbour reported that it was not being worked in a satisfactory manner, or if a farmer fell on hard times and was unable to repay his annuities" (Dooley 2004, 192). The "matchmaking" in which Mrs. Wolfe and Mrs. Dan Sheehan engage is made all the more urgent by these economic concerns; the farms are not just "convenient" to each other, but necessary to each other's survival and Moira is, in effect, sold in marriage to Curley Wolfe as a means of securing the economic prosperity of the Wolfe and Sheehan farms into the future (Somerville 1936, 82). Somerville's tale twice reminds its readers that the "people" or the "neighbours put the name of Cloca-dearg on Moira" (61) and this appellation signifies Moira's broader commodification in the Irish marriage market. The complicity of Irish women in this patriarchal set-up is also brutally exposed.

Throughout the early 1930s, Somerville was greatly preoccupied with and depressed by Irish farming affairs, as well as deeply critical of De Valera's government and the "ruin" she feared was coming "on this miserable country" (Somerville, 1933). While her letters and diaries are replete with increasingly despondent farming news, "Little Red Riding-Hood in Kerry" demonstrates the gendered social concerns Somerville may have also harboured for the new Ireland. While there is some ambivalence over the tale's attitude towards the rising rural middle classes of independent Ireland, this essay has suggested that Somerville's concern for the position of Irish women in this new Ireland is more explicit. Like Moira, the nation is growing up and transitioning to independence, but Somerville's tale cautions that the new Ireland leaves no room for the independence of its women.

References

Bacchilega, Cristina. 1999. *Postmodern Fairy Tales. Gender and Narrative Strategies*. Pennsylvania: University of Pennsylvania Press.

Bourke, Angela. 1995. "Reading a Woman's Death: Colonial Text and Oral Tradition in Nineteenth-century Ireland." *Feminist Studies* 21, no. 3: 553–86. http://www.jstor.org/stable/3178199.

Davies, Peter, ed. 1934. *The Fairies Return, or, New Tales for Old*. London: Peter Davies Limited.

Dooley, Terence. 2004. "Land and Politics in Independent Ireland, 1923–48." *Irish Historical Studies* 34 no. 134: 175–97. http://www.jstor.org/stable/30008710.

Grimm, Jacob and Wilhelm. 1993. "Little Red Cap." In *The Trials and Tribulations of Little Red Riding Hood*, edited by Jack Zipes, 135-38. London: Routledge.

Martin, Ann. 2007. *Red Riding Hood and the Wolf in Bed: Modernism's Fairy Tales*. Toronto: University of Toronto Press.

Munkwitz, Erika. 2017. "'The Master is the Mistress': Women and Fox Hunting as Sports Coaching in Britain." *Sport in History* 37, no. 4: 395–422. doi

:10.1080/17460263.2016.1273846

——. 2012. "Vixens of Venery: Women, Sport, and Fox-Hunting in Britain, 1860–1914." *Critical Survey* 24, no.1: 74–87. doi:10.3167/cs.2012.240106.

Orenstein, Catherine. 2003. *Little Red Riding Hood Uncloaked: Sex, Morality, and the Evolution of a Fairy Tale.* New York: Basic Books.

Perrault, Charles. 1993. "Little Red Riding Hood." In *The Trials and Tribulations of Little Red Riding Hood,* edited by Jack Zipes, 91–93. London: Routledge.

Pramaggiore, Maria. 2007. "Animal Afterlives: Horses and Modernity." In *Modernist Afterlives in Irish Literature and Culture,* edited by Paige Reynolds, 141–52. New York: Anthem Press.

Somerville, Edith. 1933. Diary. MS17/874. Somerville and Ross Manuscripts. Special Collections Library, Queen's University Belfast.

——. 1934. Diary. MS17/874. Somerville and Ross Manuscripts. Special Collections Library, Queen's University Belfast.

Somerville, E. Œ. 1920. "*Not* the Woman's Place." In *Stray-Aways,* by E. Œ. Somerville and Martin Ross, 228–40. London: Longmans, Green and Co.

——. (1934) 1936. "Little Red Riding-Hood in Kerry." In *The Sweet Cry of Hounds,* by E. Œ. Somerville and Martin Ross, 61–84. London: Methuen.

Stevens, Julie Anne. 2007. "The Little Big House: Somerville and Ross's Works for Children." In *Divided Worlds. Studies in Children's Literature,* edited by Mary Shine Thompson and Valerie Coughlan, 41–49. Dublin: Four Courts Press.

——. 2017. *Two Irish Girls in Bohemia. The Drawings and Writings of E. Œ. Somerville and Martin Ross.* Bantry: Somerville Press.

Tatar, Maria. 2012. Introduction to *The Fairies Return, or, New Tales for Old,* edited by Peter Davies, 1–36. New Jersey: Princeton University Press.

Zipes, Jack, editor. 1993. *The Trials and Tribulations of Little Red Riding Hood.* London: Routledge.

7

A Thing of Possibilities:
The Railroad, Space, and Belonging in
Katherine Cecil Thurston's *Max*

Matthew L. Reznicek

" Space and place," argues Claire Norris, "play an integral role in both the creation of and rediscovery of identity, on both a personal and national level" (2004, 107). For Norris, the relationship between space and Irish fiction is determined by and determines the relationship between Irish identity and the nation-state of Ireland. If Irish literature is shaped by this Burkean order of space and nation, it offers the individual a constrained space of and a fixed mode of belonging. As feminist geographers have shown, however, the representation of belonging and the representation of territory are far from fixed in the way that Burke would suggest. Despite the associations that bind identity and nation in Irish literature, feminist geographer Catherine Nash has argued that Irish land "can symbolise the possibility of fluidity and openness," which allows for the "possibility of alternative configurations of identity that are open, changeable, and reworkable" (1994, 245). The question of the relationship between individual identity and space remains central to remapping Irish women's literature, as we re-locate it in a transnational framework.

In order to rework the relationship between Irish women's literature and space, we might look to the *fin-de-siècle* novels of Cork-born Irish writer Katherine Cecil Thurston. In her 1910 novel *Max*, the role of space, the construction of identity, and the mode of belonging attempt to provide an alternative to the "hegemonic, exclusionary power at the very heart of the identity structures" (Braidotti 2011, 9). This chapter argues for an analysis of Thurston's transgressive *Künstlerroman* that is attendant to the pressures and modes of resistance in feminist and nomadic geographies; such an analysis reveals an important and alternative answer to Norris's question about the "integral" relationship between space and identity in Irish women's literature at the *fin de siècle*. Instead of the fixed and stable identity that is demanded by a national identity, the novel's representation of the transnational European railroad as fluid destabilises heteronormative identities; as Tina O'Toole has argued, this "in-between space" is "deeply ambiguous" because of the ways its physical movement enables the protagonist's change in identity (2013, 118). This chapter expands O'Toole's important argument by arguing that the space of the railroad calls attention to the fissures, ruptures, and instabilities in the imbrication of national space and individual identity.

Max follows a young Russian woman who escapes a potentially disastrous second marriage by fleeing St. Petersburg, intending to pursue an artistic career in Paris. On the train, dressed as a man, she meets an Irishman who guides "him" through Bohemian Paris. Only later is it revealed that Max is actually Maxine, a Russian princess; when Blake sees Max's painting of this female self, his demands to meet her unravel the gendered performance that has dominated the novel, ultimately providing a heteronormative ending in which Maxine and Blake fall in love and move to Ireland. From the beginning, the narrator refers to the character as "Max" and presents him as a cis-male; as the performance becomes clear, the narrator uses the gendered pronoun corresponding to the gender the character embodies at that moment. Since Thurston shifts gendered pronouns to mirror the character's identity, I will use "Max" to refer to the male-presenting figure and "Maxine" to refer to the female-presenting. The relationship of these identities to the various spaces in which they are enacted complicates the supposed stability of the relationship between space and identity. Maxine follows Blake to Ireland not only as a cis-woman, but as an individual who chooses this one option from a panoply of alternatives, from an indefinite array of possibilities. Even though she chooses an identity as a cis-woman, the variability of identities throughout the novel, especially in its nomadic and interspace scenes, enables alternative constructions of identity and constructions of the relationship between identity and space.

The Towering Angel: Autocratic, Monumental Spaces and Gendered Violence

Max begins in a Russian space that carries the symbolic weight of the family and the state. The novel's Russian landscape resounds with the oppressive politics that characterise the representation of the home in much nineteenth- and twentieth-century Irish women's literature. The Russian spaces not only ensnare the protagonist in a space that compels heterosexuality, but also reveals the degree to which compulsory heterosexuality is premised upon the power and authority of men. By focusing on the representation of the Russian and domestic spaces, it becomes clear that the public spaces and the home in the novel's Russian geography share a sense of autocracy that insists on political authority and dominance.

While the earliest event in the narrative is located in the domestic sphere on the eve of Maxine's first marriage, the representation of the domestic in these flashbacks depend upon the autocratic nature of the Russian geography. Sleeping on the train somewhere between Cologne and Paris, Max dreams "he was standing again in the outer court of a house in Petersburg—a house to which he was debtor for one night's shelter" (Thurston 1910, 3). But here the dream of the momentary domestic shelter breaks up and the traveller "knew himself to be skimming down the Nevskiy Prospekt and across the Winter Palace Square, where the great angel towers upon its rose-granite monument. Forward, forward he was carried, along the bank of the frozen Neva and over the Troitskiy bridge" (3). This geography carries critical associations of power and authority that shape the type of belonging available within this landscape. Located within the grounds of St. Petersburg, the "fundamental symbol of imperial Russia," this escape route traces the symbolic tradition that centralises the "absolute" power of the monarch, the state, and the male figure of the Russian Tsar (Veidlé 1956, 213; Wortman 2013, 170).

St. Petersburg is "the emperor's city and the emperor ... a visible presence in its streets," especially in the central district around the Nevskiy Prospekt that is central to *Max*'s representation of the city. The Nevskiy Prospekt is a street "saturated with the emblems of empire" through its "grand displays of wealth, power, and glory, as well as [its] attention to the square's ensemble of palace and monument" (Wortman 2013, 171; Bowers 2017, 375.) "[G]randiose, overpowering at times, obsessed with rational design," the neoclassical architecture of central St. Petersburg and the Nevskiy Prospekt reflects, according to historian William Craft Brumfield, the imperial project and order of the Tsars through the urge "to measure, to build, to impose order at any cost" (2008, 1). This saturation of space with the symbols and order of imperial power reaches its apotheosis in the fleeting reference to "the Winter Palace Square, where the great angel towers upon its rose-granite monument" (Thurston 1910, 3). The Winter Palace reflects the shifting geography of power, following Ekaterina II's movement of the city's administrative center away from Vasilievskii island toward the area dominated by the navy, the Senate, the Sinod, and the Winter Palace (Gritsai and van der Wusten 2000, 35). A monument to the Russian Imperial Family, the Palace was meant "to maintain order and deepen their connection to the city that anchored their power" (McCaffray 2014, 65). Throughout the nineteenth century, the Palace "increasingly became an organic element of the city," shaping geography, commerce, and social events (67). It is impossible to understand the geography of St. Petersburg without understanding its dependent relationship with the structures of the Imperial Family, subordinating almost every aspect of the city and its citizens' lives to the Empire.

Enhancing this association between the palace and power, Thurston's narrator draws particular attention to the Alexander Column, "the great angel" over Palace Square. As a monument to Russian victory over Napoleon, the Alexander Column literally enacts the elevation of the Russian state over the individual. The language of towering replicates the verticality and hierarchy that characterises the politics of power the Imperial Family exerted over St. Petersburg, all the way up to and beyond the events of 1879 in which revolutionary terrorism threatened Alexander II's life. The subordinating relationship between the individual and the State, aestheticised in the Alexander Column, takes on a bloody reality in the exact space through which Max flees in 1905 when a procession of 150,000 workers and their families march on the Winter Palace to present a petition to the Tsar and are subsequently attacked by "squadrons of cavalry [that] prevent the demonstrators from getting close" (Smith 2017, 47). Of the 150,000 individuals marching on the Palace, 200 were killed outright and another 800 were wounded. Palace Square, the Alexander Column, the Winter Palace, and the entirety of Nevskiy Prospekt are all implicated in this geography of state-led violence, subordinating the individual to the Russian Empire and its Imperial Family.

Through the use of architecture and urban space to impose order, the Nevskiy Prospekt, the Winter Palace, and the Alexander Column all demonstrate the ways in which urban space in Petersburg was "crafted projections of the kind of power rulers sought to wield," meaning that the city itself functions as a type of "monumental space" that affords "each its proper place ... naturally, under the conditions of a generally accepted Power" (Lefebvre 1991, 220). Lefebvre's conception of "monumental space" is defined by its relationship to power; it remains unable to occlude or cover up its "element of repression" and its concomitant "will to power" (220-1). Thus, the Russian geography highlights a spatial politics of constraint, repression, and hegemonic power, which becomes evident through Max/ine's description of marriage and the domestic space in Russia. Indeed, these spaces enact a repressive form of belonging that mirrors Lefebvre's monumental space, revealing a key element of compulsion in the novel's politics of space and selfhood.

Lefebvre's monumental space reveals faint "traces of violence and death, negativity and aggressiveness," the monument also seeks to erase them and replace them "with a tranquil power and certitude which can encompass violence and terror" (1991, 222). These social spaces imply, contain, and replicate social relationships that are themselves revelatory of another form of violence. If the Russian monumental and public space offers a mode of belonging that is constrained by a violent hierarchy, *Max* depicts the violence of belonging in the representation of the Russian domestic space. Narrating Maxine's first marriage and her fear of the second, *Max* calls attention to the physical force that commands women's belonging by mirroring the violence that shapes the public role of the Winter Palace. Marriage, like Russian citizenship, "implies *violence*," to borrow from Lefebvre (112).

Following her father's death, Maxine "went to my aunt in Petersburg, and there she forgot both nature and art" when she married at eighteen to a "very callous, very profligate, very cruel" man (Thurston 1910, 201). The final emphasis on cruelty bears out in Max's detailed description of his "sister's" suffering. Love "snared her and its instrument crushed her," dragging her "down the sickening road of disillusionment—down that steep, steep road that is bitter as the Way of the Cross" (202). The images of suffering, entrapment, crushing, and crucifixion focus on the site of the body, highlighting a grammatically passive construction so that she is the victim of the husband, who is himself the instrument of violence. The grammar and the narrative implicate the institution of marriage as "an institution for policing women's obedience and enforcing patriarchal disciplinary power," blurring violence in intimacy (Lewis 2008, 107). The representation of the domestic violence functions as a replication of belonging to "the community and the nation," revealing the extent to which both the public and private form of community depends upon and enacts extreme forms of violence (106).

That Maxine's second marriage "was to be as the first" demonstrates the systemic nature of this violence embedded within the family and the nation (Thurston 1910, 204). After her first husband's suicide, Maxine "went back to the world" and, one night, her "*fiancé* begged the privilege of escorting her to her home" (204). On the ride, he "caught her in his arms, and his arms were like iron bands; his lips pressed hers, and they were like a flame" (204). The violence of this sexual assault, committed not only after an event at the Imperial Court of the Winter Palace but within the domestic space of the carriage ride home, reveals the "terror" and truth about marriage to the young woman (204). The violence, encoded in the geography of the Winter Palace, becomes undeniably real in the domestic space of the Russian household. Thus, the autocratic politics of Russia are replicated in the autocratic politics of the home and the marriage.

Away to Your Castle: Romance and Compulsory Heterosexuality

Despite its radical potentialities, its critique of the violence of marriage and heteronormative belonging, the ending of *Max* is a pastoral space that appears to replicate the same "compulsory heterosexuality" of Russia. I invoke Adrienne Rich's concept of "compulsory heterosexuality" because *Max* actually raises the question of "whether in a different context, or other things being equal, women would *choose* heterosexual coupling and marriage" (1980, 633). Despite the novel's potential for alternative imaginings of sexual and gendered identities, its resolution in the heteronormative and domestic space of marriage seems to affirm Rich's claims that heterosexuality is indeed "a *political institution*" (637). The spatial iconography of Maxine's and Blake's final scene evokes the established social order of a chivalric romance through the repeated evocation of a castle and pastoralism, naturalizing the political elements of heteronormativity.

After deciding to surrender her desire to achieve success as an artist, Maxine crosses the city of Paris from her apartment in the eighteenth arrondissement of Montmartre to Blake's apartment in the *Quartier Latin*, where she insists, "Ned! Ned! Take me! Take me and teach me! Take me away to your castle, like the princess of old. Show me the white sky and the opal sea, and the seaweed that smells like violets" (Thurston 1910, 315). This is hardly the first time that Blake's ancestral home in Ireland is associated with the imagery of the "castle." When they are formally introduced, Blake explains that he is "Edward Fitzgerald Blake, and I have an old barracks of a castle in County Clare. I have five aunts, seven uncles, and twenty-four cousins, every one of whom thinks me a lost soul" (65). Blake immediately associates Ireland with the iconography of the castle, the barracks, and the family, all of which embody social authority. The authority vested in these images and structures of ancestry, family, and the military associate Ireland with the type of "historicity" that characterises Bakhtin's chronotope of the castle (Bakhtin 1994, 246). The castle reveals its historicity through "various parts of its architecture, in furnishings, weapons, the ancestral portrait gallery, the family archives and in the particular human relationship involving dynastic primacy and the transfer of hereditary rights" (246). Bakhtin's emphasis on the primary role of the family's dynastic dominance over the past not only makes Maxine's return to the castle of Ireland feel regressive, but its feudal gendered identity recalls Moretti's claims that the "definitive stabilization of the individual" is only possible "in the world of 'closed social forms'" (2000, 27). The invocation of "princess" and the feudal elements of the castle suggest that Moretti's "definitive stabilization" is achieved by submission. Belonging in the feudal past is, as Lewis claims, "anchored in familial scripts," meaning "to belong as citizens, we have legitimate and 'natural' sexual roles to play" (2008, 107).

Through the feudal gendered imagery and the pastoral return to nature that emerges at the end of the novel, *Max* appears to affirm these heteronormative gendered relations as "natural," embedding within its discourse Rich's claim that heteronormativity compels the "disruption of women's creative aspirations" (1980, 640). Not only does Maxine actively opt for the "castle, like the princess of old," she describes this return to a feudal gender relation as a return to "the white sky and the opal sea, and the seaweed that smells like violets," echoing Blake's earlier description of Maxine as belonging to "the green groves" (Thurston 1910, 305, 315). The rejection of a sexualised space like Paris in favour of a pastoral and natural realm of "the green groves" affixes women in a spatial politics of purity in an innocent natural landscape. The relationship between women and a pastoral discourse, especially in Irish literature, depends upon this rejection of a sexualised modernity (see Nash 1994, 228-37).

The compulsive element seems obscure at first glance, especially since it is Maxine who expresses this desire, commanding Blake to take her to this space. However, this urging of a return to the feudal, ancestral estate in Ireland is actually an achievement of Blake's earlier description of Maxine as "Little Maxine, who could be taken in my arms this minute and carried away to my castle, like a princess of long ago" (305). The "world of 'closed social forms'" is premised in Blake's description upon an act of violence that mirrors the assault of Maxine's second engagement. The repetition of a passive construction positioning her as the victim is unmissable. That Maxine repeats this exact phrase but shifts it into the active voice attempts to erase the act of violence. This is where Rich's claim about the compulsive denial of women's creative capacity becomes central. Maxine is only able to submit to this feudal order when she willingly surrenders her desire to be an artist and commits fully to heteronormative forms of gender identity, resigning the artistic and male self of Max.

The return to Ireland, then, mirrors the authoritative and autocratic dynamics of Russia. In both, the threat of sexualised violence looms over Maxine. In both, art is denied her and she is fixed in the world of heteronormativity, especially considering that Max intends to use the painting "to strangle" and "to dismiss" the feminine self (Thurston 1910, 184).[1] Neither Russia nor Ireland provides her the opportunity to transcend the ineluctable choice between heteronormativity and creativity; whether it is Blake's ancestral castle or the Imperial Family's Winter Palace, neither Russia nor Ireland provides her the ability to construct an alternative form of belonging, beyond the compulsory, domestic, and autocratic spaces available.[2]

A Thing of Possibilities: Possible Future Selves and the Railway Space

Thurston's representation of the railroad, however, is different. It highlights a bifurcation in nineteenth-century discourse surrounding the train; it is both "mere transit, mere linking of experiences, ... a commonplace," and "a thing of

---

1   For further discussion of this painting, see Reznicek 2017, specifically 174-77.

2   While Ireland and Russia assert a form of heteronormativity, Blake's attraction to the masculine figure of Max on the rail journey and, especially, in the Place de la Concorde, suggests that Paris might offer an alternative to the compulsory heteronormativity that I am tracing.

possibilities ... romance in the very making" (Thurston 1910, 1). The apparent contradiction calls attention to competing rhetorics that shaped nineteenth-century thought about the advance of technology, the (dis)integration of space, and the impact on the individual. However, as the competing visions of the railroad suggest, the train can be both an everyday means of enforcing an emergent technological, national, and economic order, while simultaneously providing a "freedom through movement" that promises and achieves a form of cosmopolitical liberation from the disciplinary mechanisms of the local (Aguiar 2011, 29). In its ambivalent representation of the railroad, *Max* complicates the mode of belonging available to the individual, providing a stark contrast to the fixity of the novel's representation of patriarchal spaces in Russia and Ireland.

If it is "mere transit, mere linking of experiences," Thurston's railroad space clearly participates in the disciplinary rhetoric that shapes much nineteenth-century constructions of the railroad, particularly in the production of national spaces and markets (Thurston 1910, 1). As Marian Aguiar notes, the production of national spaces, markets, and modernity is closely connected to a rhetoric of movement and mobility. Movement "became a way of fulfilling and legitimizing the project of modernity undertaken in Europe, for, as James Clifford puts it, 'travel and contacts are crucial sites for an unfinished modernity'" (Aguiar 2011, 9). The railroad renders legible this division between modernity and those sites of "an unfinished modernity" through its spatialization. The train's demarcation between a completed, often Western European, modernity and an incomplete modernity associated with the East, functions as a form of discipline on a national and transnational basis.

The ability of the railway space to reveal a geographic division between the modern and the non-modern is particularly clear in *Max* through the disjointed nature of the narrative of travel. As the novel opens, the "powerful north express ... thunder[s] over the sleeping plains of Germany and France," but the narrative slips backward through a dream sequence to recount Max's departure from the Finland Station in Petersburg, where he awaits "a primitive, miniature train, white with frost and powdered with the ashes of its wood fuel" (Thurston 1910, 1). The primitivism and miniaturism depicts a non-modern rail system, revealing the degree to which the French and German railways are associated much more clearly than Russia with the concept of modernity itself. In contrast to the ease of the north express "thunder[ing] over the sleeping plains of Germany and France," where the two territories merge seamlessly into a fluid entity, the travel between Petersburg and Stockholm and ultimately Germany, where the young man boards the north express, involves multiple modes of travel, suggesting a failure of these territories to be integrated fully into the landscape of modernity. From the Finland Station, Max's "vision came and passed ... a suggestion of straight tracks" before "a shifting, a juggling of effects" produces memories of "the lonely sledge drive to the harbour [of Åbo]" and then "[h]e was on board a ship—a ship ploughing her way through the ice-fields as she neared Stockholm," before waking suddenly back on board the north express (3-4). By employing a modernist narrative of disjuncture to recreate the journey, Thurston's narrator implicitly highlights the fractured nature of travel between these spaces.

The fracture highlights the difficulty of producing a unified space of modernity through the railroad; it reflects the combined and uneven development of an integrated European railway space. According to William Siddall, "the European railroad network is remarkably uniform ... The high degree of industrialization and commercialization found in Europe certainly tended to bring about this uniformity," which, in turn, will "bring about economic integration" (1969, 48). Across most of continental Europe, "the gauge ... was originally 1.44 meters (about 4 feet 9 inches)," however in Russia the railroad was built on a five foot gauge because "the line [between Petersburg and Moscow] would not be connected to any other [line]" (40, 46). This technological decision, rooted in a sense of isolation from Western European railroads, both produces and maintains the Russian railroad space as distinct from its Western counterparts that makes Max's journey toward the potential liberation of modernity more difficult. Since the gauges are wedded to state decisions, the spatialization of the railroad and its production of national or transnational space reflects a mode of social, technological, and economic discipline.

While the railroad clearly enacts a form of discipline at the state- and transnational-level of space, it also asserts a disciplinary regime "on the micro-level" (de Certeau 1988, 111). This is most clearly felt within the interior space of the railway carriage, which Michel de Certeau has described as "[a] bubble of panoptic and classifying power, a module of imprisonment that makes possible the production of an order, a closed and autonomous insularity" (111). [D]e Certeau's disciplinary order is "the condition" of a railway car, enforced on the "traveller [who] is pigeonholed, numbered, and regulated" throughout the journey (111). The fixity of the railway carriage is fundamental to the narrative attempts to avoid fixity for Max in terms of gender. The maintenance of Max's "self-consciousness ... a need for caution" highlights the desire to evade and slip between the disciplinary mechanisms; this is, most suggestively, registered in the description of the protagonist as "the figure of a boy ... seen vaguely under a rough overcoat" (Thurston 1910, 2). The slippage between fixed genders connoted in the suggestive term "figure" highlights the need for Max's evasion of the disciplinary regime in a way that recalls Halberstam's theorization of "[a]mbiguous gender" in a space that traverses national boundaries (1998, 20). As Halberstam argues, the attempt to police "gender ... is intensified" in "travel hubs," which becomes increasingly clear through the various attempts to fix "the individuality" of various travellers (20-1). Halberstam's description of ambiguous gender in travel hubs demonstrates the macro- and micro-levels of discipline enacted in the railway space: just as the train dissolves the distinction between France and Germany, and as the narrative dissolves the distinction between parts of the journey from Petersburg to Stockholm, the disciplinary regime shifts from the production of space to the need to fix "the huddled figure" in a heteronormative regime (Thurston 1910, 6).

Despite the disciplinary regime of the train's tracks and carriage, it also remains a "thing of possibilities," a hopeful phrase that recalls Aguiar's claim that trains "creat[e] a forward-driven paradigm that rejects the immediate past and, perhaps more distinctively, propels the present towards a possible future" (2011, 1). Thus, while the railway clearly produces multiple spaces and modes of discipline, the "onrush of the train" remains a device of liberation, rejecting the patriarchal and authoritarian space of Petersburg and moving toward "the land of his desires," toward "the lights of Paris" (Thurston 1910, 6). Before his fellow passengers return to the carriage, Max stands at the window and "with a quick, exulting excitement he laugh[s]," a laugh that is "caught and scattered to the winds by the thunder of the engine" (6). The ambivalent relationship between the train and the passenger here is complex: on the one hand, it is a moment of joy as the protagonist moves speedily toward his desire for freedom, an association that seems to meld the individual and the technological together; on the other, there is the threat of dissolution because of the train's speed, catching and scattering that expression of joy. The train's ambivalence means it participates equally in the production of discipline and in the potential escape from that discipline.

It is in this ambivalence, sitting in-between fixity and freedom, that Susan Stanford Friedman identifies a new definition of selfhood that is clearly anticipated in this railway space of Thurston's novel. Friedman argues that a feminist "*geographics*" moves toward "a discourse of spatialised identities constantly on the move" and, as a result, emphasises "the ceaseless change of fluidity, the nomadic wandering of transnational diaspora," an identity that is "polyvocal and often contradictory" (1998, 18–9). A narrative of fluid change about nomadic wanderers that is often contradictory is ultimately the best summation of Thurston's *Max*. As a novel that begins in between Germany and France, but traces its narrative back to Petersburg and forward to Ireland, this *fin-de-siècle* novel disrupts an established narrative about the necessity of Irish places to an Irish identity. Indeed, in the words of Friedman, Thurston's *Max* produces "different discourses of identity and subjectivity" precisely because of its "movement through space" (19-20). By exploring the spaces and identities that shape Katherine Cecil Thurston's *Max*, it becomes clear that Irish women's writing understood not only Irish identity but Irish literature itself to be "a thing of possibilities" racing across the plains of Europe.

References

Aguiar, Marian. 2011. *Tracking Modernity: India's Railway and the Culture of Mobility*. Minneapolis: University of Minnesota Press.

Bakhtin, Mikhail. 1994. "Forms of Time and Chronotope in the Novel." In *The Dialogic Imagination: Four Essays*, edited by Michael Holquist, 84–258. Austin: University of Texas Press.

Bowers, Katherine. 2017. "Experiencing Information: An Early Nineteenth-Century Stroll Along Nevskii Prospekt." In *Information and Empire: Mechanisms of Communication in Russia, 1600–1850*, edited by Simon Franklin and Katherine Bowers, 369–407. Cambridge: Open Book Publishers.

Braidotti, Rosi. 2011. *Nomadic Subjects: Embodiment and Sexual Difference in Contemporary Feminist Theory*. New York: Columbia University Press.

Brumfield, William Craft. 2008. "St. Petersburg and the Art of Survival." In *Preserving Petersburg: History, Memory, Nostalgia*, edited by Helena Goscilo and Stephen M. Norris, 11–38. Bloomfield: Indiana University Press.

de Certeau, Michel. 1988. *The Practice of Everyday Life*. Translated by Steven Rendall. Berkeley: University of California Press.

Friedman, Susan Stanford. 1998. *Mappings: Feminism and the Cultural Geographies of Encounter*. Princeton: Princeton University Press.

Gritsai, Olga and Herman van der Wusten. 2000. "Moscow and Petersburg, a Sequence of Capitals, a Tale of Two Cities." *GeoJournal* 51, no.1–2: 33–45.

Halberstam, Jack. 1998. *Female Masculinity*. Durham, NC: Duke University Press.

Lefebvre, Henri. 1991. *The Production of Space*. Translated by Donald Nicholson-Smith. Malden, MA: Blackwell.

Lewis, Desiree. 2008. "Rethinking Nationalism in Relation to Foucault's *History of Sexuality* and Adrienne Rich's 'Compulsory Heterosexuality and Lesbian Existence'." *Sexualities* 11, no.1–2: 104–9.

McCaffray, Susan P. 2014. "Ordering the Tsar's Household: Winter Palace Servants in Nineteenth-Century St. Petersburg." *The Russian Review* 73: 64–82.

Moretti, Franco. 2000. *The Way of the World: The* Bildungsroman *in European Culture*. Translated by Albert Sbragia. New York: Verso.

Nash, Catherine. 1994. "Remapping the Body/Land: New Cartographies of Identity, Gender, and Landscape in Ireland." In *Writing Women and Space: Colonial and Postcolonial Geographies*, edited by Alison Blunt and Gillian Rose, 227–50. New York: Guilford Press.

Norris, Claire. 2004. "The Big House: Space, Place, and Identity in Irish

Fiction." *New Hibernia Review* 8, no.1: 107–21.

O'Toole, Tina, 2013. *The Irish New Woman*. Basingstoke: Palgrave Macmillan.

Rich, Adrienne. 1980. "Compulsory Heterosexuality and Lesbian Experience." *Signs* 5, no. 4: 631–60.

Reznicek, Matthew L. 2017. *The European Metropolis: Paris and Nineteenth-Century Irish Women Novelists*. Clemson: Clemson University Press.

Siddall, William. 1969. "Railroad Gauges and Spatial Interaction." *Geographical Review* 59, no.1: 29–57.

Smith, S.A. 2017. *Russia In Revolution: An Empire in Crisis, 1890–1928*. New York: Oxford University Press.

Thurston, Katherine Cecil. 1910. *Max: A Novel*. New York: Harper & Brothers.

Veidlé, Vladimir. 1956. *Zadacha Rossii*. New York: Chekhov Publishing.

Wortman, Richard. 2013. *Russian Monarchy: Representation and Rule*. Brighton, MA: Academic Studies Press.

8

"Morbid Deviations": Katherine Cecil Thurston, Degeneracy and the Unstable Masculine

Sinéad Mooney

T
he brief and brilliant career of Katherine Cecil Thurston (1875–1911) is in many ways an oddity. Although her writing career only spanned ten years from the period of her marriage in 1901 to her early death in 1911, her novels and their serialisations and adaptations were tremendously popular in the United Kingdom, Europe and the United States. Her very public divorce and the mysterious circumstances of her death in a Cork hotel only a matter of days before her anticipated second marriage both provoked public scandals which appear to have helped, rather than hindered, sales in the short term. Her work, however, fell out of favour soon after her death, as testified by the plummeting royalty statements among the papers of her literary executor in her archive at the National Library of Scotland.[1] Now long out of print, with the exception of a 1987 Virago edition of *The Fly on the Wheel* (1908) and excerpts included in *Field Day* (*Max*) and Colm Tóibín's 1999 *Penguin Book of Irish Fiction* (*The Fly on the Wheel*), Thurston's writing still frequently seems to elude or overrun the terms in which it has been critically framed by recent critical rehabilitations, which have been chiefly those of decadence and the Irish New Woman.

For Gerardine Meaney, Thurston's final novel *Max*, a *Künstlerroman* in which a runaway princess cross-dresses in order to claim the artistic and social freedoms denied her as a woman, epitomises "the particular achievement of decadents and New Women": namely "to make the artifice of identity, particularly sexual identity, into art, to counter the terrible pseudoscientific certainties of their age

---

1   See Standlee (2015, 147–48) for a discussion of Thurston's death, Copeland (2007, 167–70) for sales figures, and Lamond (2017) for an account of the success and reception of *John Chilcote, MP.*

with regard to gender and race with that art" (Meaney 2000, 173). Thurston's oeuvre as a whole is, however, more complex and contradictory than Meaney's reading of *Max* allows; many of her novels do not feature women in prominent roles, construct femininity only in relation to moments of male crisis, and in fact engage ambivalently with precisely those "pseudoscientific certainties." This essay will consider Thurston's engagement with two strands of late nineteenth-century medico-scientific discourses and offer readings of two of her texts, an unfinished, unpublished novel "The Healer of Men" (1906–7) and her 1904 bestseller *John Chilcote, MP*, for their interest, not in women's bodies or lives, but in male moral and physical ill-health, specifically her examinations of a "degenerate" or neurasthenic masculinity in crisis.[2] Drawing on the discourses of degeneracy, disease and Darwinism, these texts participate in late-Victorian cultural narratives about sickness and health, challenges to British national fitness and imperial dominance, while they both excite and manage anxieties about gendered bodies in the modern world.

As the Celtic Revival was concentrating on the recuperation of a pre-colonial Irish past, the turn of the twentieth century in British writing was particularly full of anxieties concerning "the collapse of culture, the weakening of national might, the possibly fatal decay —physical, moral, spiritual, creative—of the Anglo-Saxon 'race' as a whole" (Arata 1996, 1). If we set aside the realist, Irish-set *The Fly On the Wheel* (1908), the sensation novels of the London-based Thurston are a far better fit with the dark fantasies of decline characteristic of this eschatological late-Victorian impulse than with Irish cultural nationalism. Thurston is a writer who, despite the cultivatedly bland and inoffensive celebrity profile she repeatedly assumed in interviews, was obviously sharply aware of the cultural and intellectual climate of her times.

Her writing shows her conscious of the influence of the biological and physical sciences in creating a culture of unease around the issue of sexual equality; from prevalent theories of female inferiority, finite energy, and nervous degeneration it was not much of a leap to the prognosis of mental and physical debility levelled at those women who, in the last decade of the nineteenth century, sought educational and economic equality with men. As Jane Wood writes, "theories of biological determinism, together with the supposed greater susceptibility of women to neuroses, produced a climate in which women's nervous illnesses were increasingly seen as the physiological consequences of their reluctance to comply with social and sexual roles" (Wood 2001, 163).

If the gendered human body could register signs of cultural distress—

---

2   "The Healer of Men," unpublished MS, Box 5, Katherine Cecil Thurston archive, National Library of Scotland, Acc. 11378. All further quotations are from the typescript MS, henceforth "KCT papers."

whether through depleted nerves, muscular atrophy, or racial degeneration—and the interpretation of these, as Athena Vrettos argues, became an "important form of social cartography" in the late nineteenth and early twentieth century (Vrettos 1995, 8), then Thurston's private life and career would seem to encapsulate many of these issues. As a prominent New Woman author, she was indelibly associated by conservative commentators with a movement viewed as an example of "cultural, national and sexual degeneracy" (Meaney 2000, 157). Bolstering this association are the salacious press accounts of her 1910 divorce from the Anglo-Irish novelist Ernest Temple Thurston on the grounds of his desertion and adultery; these construct her as an all-conquering New Woman, whose novels out-earned her husband's, and whose personality "dominated" his in a manner incompatible with marital harmony, while, for Caroline Copeland, the Ernest Thurston who appears in the court reports "appears to embody the life and persona of a late Victorian rake" (Copeland 2007, 100). The brief, unhappy marriage thus seems to encapsulate many of the concerns of the New Woman novel in its anatomy of bourgeois matrimony.

Thurston's personal papers in her archive at the National Library of Scotland further manifest ample evidence of her own lifelong ill-health, and her preoccupation with ascertaining the realism of medical details in her work.[3] Particularly after the effective end of her marriage and the start of her relationship with a Scottish doctor, Alfred Thomas Bulkely Gavin, in 1908, her work also manifests a fascination with medicine and the figure of the medic as a form of *Übermensch*, confessor, moral arbiter and God-figure, and in general with scientific discourse as an interpellant of masculine power. The idea that a body contained narratives about that individual's habits, emotional life or heredity, and that doctors served, as Athena Vrettos notes, as "privileged interpreters" of those stories, gave the medical profession an overarching narrative structure for the investigation and revelation of social and scientific truths (Vrettos 1995, 8). Thurston's relationship with Gavin and her interest in doctors as powerful interpreters of bodily narratives appear to feed her sustained fascination with the figure of the male scientist as priest/confessor/artist-figure endowed with the power of life and death, which is manifest in several unpublished manuscripts in her archive.[4]

However, perhaps unexpectedly, Thurston appears uninterested in male

---

3   The NLS archive contains an undated note sheet where Thurston drafts questions about the symptoms Mark Coningsby in "The Healer of Men" should have, and a response from a doctor practising at an address at 20 South Mall, Cork, dated January 8th 1906. Box 5, Katherine Cecil Thurston archive, NLS.

4   Thurston's unproduced melodrama *The Crucible /The Day After Tomorrow* hinges on a surgeon acting as confessor to an adulterous couple who make a suicide pact when he saves the life of the husband they are betraying, while her short story, "The Hand," has a sceptical scientist paying a large sum to possess a "cursed" relic purported to be the hand of John the Baptist. Box 5, NLS.

medical "readings" of the afflicted bodies of female patients. If the New Woman novelist negotiates a narrative both inside and outside the scientific narrative dominating public culture at the *fin de siècle*, then the Irish New Woman, demoted by both "race" and sex according to the late nineteenth-century Darwinian hierarchies used to legitimate oppression, is doubly "othered." Yet, when Thurston's surgeon Victor Ansell in "The Healer of Men" characterises a patient on whom he is about to operate as "my subject—the block on which I exercise my craft," the "subject" in question is not a nervous or debilitated New Woman, but another prevalent cultural stereotype, a "degenerate" man. Thurston is less interested in refuting the terms in which women's bodies are pathologised than, in these texts, in constructing all-male fictional case histories which recreate the diseased male body as its symptoms are inspected, categorised and isolated, then diagnosed by male medics, albeit in relationships triangulated by women. Male bodies are in these texts the prime candidates for medical scrutiny, and it is male bodies around which they construct conflicting theories of the normal and the pathological, and cultural apprehensions about "fit" and "unfit" masculinity. Arguably, these both obliquely serve Thurston's feminist project and serve as a riposte to the warnings of Darwinian discourses against unsexed intellectual women.

The powerfully ambivalent scientist-genius and his opposite, the "degenerate" man, are central to Thurston's unpublished and unfinished novel "The Healer of Men." She worked on this after *The Gambler* (1906) and before *The Fly on the Wheel* (1908) at the beginning of her relationship with Gavin; it exists in two forms in the NLS archive, a partial handwritten manuscript and a typescript of the early part of the handwritten draft, with some scenes formatted as a play, suggesting a certain amount of genre instability during the composition process. The text exhibits a self-conscious engagement with the physical and medical sciences, and with the widespread social and cultural anxieties which extended Darwinian theories into ideas about the exhaustion of evolutionary energy, degeneration, and regression from a once-healthy standard. First aired in scientific journals in the 1860s, such theories suggested that evolution, "far from being a progressive process which necessarily involved the development of an organism to a higher state of complexity, could just as easily involve degeneration, or a diminution in the complexity of an organism" (Pykett 1996, 13). Bénédict-Augustin Morel's 1857 *Treatise on Degeneration* had drawn attention to the apparent mental and physical deterioration of subsequent generations within families, arguing that these become a

> new sub-species, which, like all others, possesses the capacity of transmitting to its offspring, in a continuously increasing degree, its peculiarities, these being morbid deviations from the normal form—gaps in development, malformations and infirmities. (Quoted in Greenslade 1994, 2–3)

Subsequently, Max Nordau's *Degeneration*, first published in 1892, exercised a pervasive and insidious influence by claiming a connection between hereditary degeneration and the spiritual and moral decadence he perceived in contemporary art and literature (Nordau 1892).

As Jane Wood points out, the term "degeneration" was never free of moral connotations, and it became a central concern in *fin-de-siècle* literature, particularly New Woman writing, whose plots dealt with perceived crises in the institution of the family, marriage, sex roles, and female emancipation (Wood 2001, 177). "National efficiency" and its relation to the tasks of empire remained pressing issues, and degenerationism offered the writer a rich field of sensational subjects and effects, of which many of Thurston's works take full advantage.

In both manuscripts of "The Healer of Men," Helen Gunning, an obvious New Woman with her "self-possessed, independent air," "athletic carriage of the body" and an impatience with gendered social rules, is sidelined. Instead, Thurston puts in place a triangular set of confrontations between a eugenicist surgeon-scientist, Victor Ansell; the patient he kills, the degenerate "moral monster" Mark Coningsby; and finally Coningsby's devoutly Catholic young widow, with whom Ansell unwittingly falls in love and later marries. Initially, Ansell resembles a less obviously grotesque version of Wells's hubristic vivisectionist Dr Moreau in his scientific fable *The Island of Dr Moreau* (1896). Autocratic, ascetic, hyper-masculine and atheist, Ansell is a magnificent physical specimen, but a remorseless man who feels no emotion other than an all-engrossing faith in progress and intellect constructed in the text as the acme of progressive masculinity: "[t]he man within the man; the light, the power, the governing faculty from which science, invention, all the marvels of this later age glanced forth" (KCT papers).

At the beginning of the manuscript, he is consumed by work on his "magnum opus," which argues for the suppression of the degenerate, according to tropes which continued to permeate public thought long after the scientific basis for Lombroso or Nordau's arguments had been debunked. As the vigorous history of the eugenics movement in Britain indicates (a movement with which the New Woman writers had considerable involvement), fears of racial decay and of the unfit hordes continued to motivate scientific research well into the twentieth century. "The intelligent physician does not permit the physically monstrous to burden the earth," writes Ansell; "why then, it may be asked, does he not rid it of the morally monstrous?" (KCT papers).

The "moral monster" he kills as a form of eugenicist experiment is first encountered falling drunkenly out of a pub on the Tottenham Court Road in the company of a frightened teenage boy. This man, Mark Coningsby, is conceived of in familiar terms from Lombroso and Nordau and the practitioners of positivism and psychiatric Darwinism—degenerate, animalistic, "inefficient":

It was a face on which the marks of vice were legibly written; a face possessed of a certain peculiarity, but cruel and animal in all its essential. The skin had the pallor of lengthened dissipation and the eyes had a leaden look while the mouth, relaxed by the conditions of the moment, betrayed in gross completeness the character behind. (KCT papers)

His is a textbook case of degeneracy, arisen "almost as an illustration to Ansell's own thoughts [on] the problem of the moral wreck, the inefficient man" (KCT papers). It is as though Ansell has conjured up a suitably "unclean" subject upon which to exercise his craft. The spectre of the Wilde trials and illicit male–male desire detectably underlie this encounter. The decipherable body of the "social brigand" Mark Coningsby and his accompanying wraith, the "weak, scared boy, whose feet he was so evidently guiding into the downward road," are legible in terms similar to the way in which Wilde himself was read alongside his novel *Dorian Gray* as morbid, unnatural and unhealthy. The homosexual body is viewed as "bearing on its surface the marks of an underlying nature that is at once revealed and hidden by its stigmata," the purport of the "decoding" clear without being stated (Arata 1996, 66). Coningsby, while well-dressed and conventional in appearance, is described as "noxious and unclean," exuding "something subtle and repellent ... at once difficult to analyse and impossible to express," but "filling the beholder with an uneasy sense of things repulsive and obscure" (KCT papers). In the best Foucauldian fashion, the identification— or, as Foucault argues, the *production*—of deviance is instrumental in the construction of "normal" bourgeois identities.

There is a clear and anxious imperial subtext in this confrontation of "types." Mark Coningsby has worked in India, and Ansell is told by Rufus Coningsby that his brother, despite knowing he was infected with a venereal disease he caught in India, returned and married the woman Rufus loved. The fear of "going native" and atavism which dominates imperial Gothic of the period conceals worries about Britain itself relapsing into barbarism, and the diseased Mark Coningsby, a returned son of Empire further characterised as a "black sheep"—"there was never a time you could call him white; even as a boy"— has actualised such fears by bringing contagion and regression back home into the heart of London and of the bourgeois family (KCT papers). If, as David Punter does, we read Stephenson's *Dr Jekyll and Mr Hyde* as "an urban version of going native" which served as a model for later writers of more explicit imperial Gothic, then it is not hard to see, in the repelled fascination of Ansell's encounter with Coningsby, the mechanism by which Jekyll's moral superiority produces Hyde's morbidity (1980, 241). However, if Jekyll's science releases the apelike barbarian who lurks beneath the civilised skin, then Ansell's science views it as a medical duty to excise it.

When this man is coincidentally delivered into Ansell's hands as a patient, the surgeon views his illness as more moral than physical and deliberately allows Coningsby to haemorrhage to death after the surgery. By dehumanising or abhumanising the degenerate, the normative male subject re-humanises itself, moving from the initial shudder at the uncleanly spectacle to complete excision of the "inefficient wreck" out of the body politic. However, Thurston's delineation of her eugenicist is pointedly ironic. The "healthy," ascetic Ansell is in some sense a double of the "unclean" Mark Coningsby—a high-minded, ascetic Jekyll to his repellent Hyde, both men successively husbands of the same woman—and while the brilliant doctor may represent the apex of human intellectual evolution, he is fully as inhuman as his grotesque victim, bereft of the civilising human emotions of compassion and pity. Lack of "fitness" in the patient is paralleled by an equivalent lack of fitness in the surgeon. In this, Thurston is drawing on another strand of psychiatric Darwinism—that of the French neurologist Jacques Joseph Moreau. His *Morbid Psychology* (1859) places the genius on the same "family tree" as the criminal, the lunatic, and a variety of other pathologues and "nervous sufferers" (Moreau 1959, 468). Here the scientific genius descends into criminality.

Like Wells' Moreau, Ansell moves beyond the hermeneutic interpretation of somatic narratives, to become a personification of post-Darwinian Nature itself, a nature whose idle experiments on living flesh are as wanton, aimless and cruel as Moreau's creation of "beast men" (KCT papers). And yet the work of the scientist and Nature alike is subject to undoing; Thurston's Ansell moves from a position of arrogant and murderous metaphysical certainty towards an uneasy, hesitant attraction towards the Catholicism of Phyllis Coningsby. At this point the comparatively fluent typescript ends, and the text devolves into brief handwritten notes for the section of the plot detailing Ansell's courtship of and marriage to Phyllis Coningsby, which is in part fuelled by his reluctant fascination with her religious belief. These notes break off in their turn with Ansell thrown into a metaphysical crisis by his pregnant wife's sudden death in a carriage crash. We are left only with the suggestion that Helen Gunning, the New Woman in love with Ansell at the start of the novel, will somehow be the one to pick up the pieces. Ultimately, different types of masculinity are found wanting in this fragment, not independent-minded women. If, at the turn of the twentieth century, British culture was in the grip of paranoid fantasies of degeneration and regression in large part because of anxieties surrounding women newly entering the public sphere, Thurston's "The Healer of Men" turns its focus away from the pathologisation of women's biological functions, and instead turns men's bodies into somatically-encoded and medically-legible texts which are deciphered by other men, with both finally found deficient.

As Sally Ledger has noted of the crises that permeate and are mediated by New Woman fiction, the crisis in gender definitions was accompanied by, and inextricably linked with, a crisis within the politics of empire, a link that must inform any reading of the work of Irish women writers (Ledger 1995, 31). Though an implicit imperial-racial subtext informs the representation of the "black" Coningsby in "The Healer of Men," male neurasthenia and drug addiction meets a more explicitly imperial narrative in *John Chilcote, MP* (1904), Thurston's first bestseller. The novel is another of her sensational parables concerning the moral incapacity of privileged masculinity. Losing the figure of the God-surgeon from "Healer" but retaining a comparatively marginal female figure as a form of moral arbiter, the novel also hinges on the mutual confrontation of doubles. A drug-addicted Conservative MP, John Chilcote, substitutes himself with his exact physical double, the "manly," ambitious but impoverished John Loder, who, while impersonating Chilcote, emerges as a strong pair of hands in the House of Commons at a moment of imperial crisis. If Loder's "masquerade" foreshadows that of the Princess Davorska's cross-gendered performance in Thurston's own *Max* (1910), the novel is also a knowing reworking of *Jekyll and Hyde*—Loder remarks to Chilcote's unwitting secretary "I'm a sort of Jekyll and Hyde affair" (Thurston 1904, 57) to explain the abrupt changes in manner when he and Chilcote swap places—and *The Picture of Dorian Gray*, and focuses like both its predecessors on the carefully-concealed depravity of Victorian manhood.[5]

Like "The Healer of Men," a medical taxonomy of evolutionary experiment is actively at play when the two men swap identities: "Like all other experiments, this showed unlooked-for features when put to a working test" (69). This time, however, the chief medico-scientific discourse engaged is that of another late Victorian disease, that of neurasthenia, a nervous malady which came to be both causally and symbolically linked to the period. Neurasthenia, or nervous exhaustion, excited a deal of medical controversy centring in the main on the disputed contributory roles of heredity, gender and modern life stress in its causation (Wood 2001, 163). Most medical case studies focused on male stress and exhaustion, while fictional representations concentrated on women; Hardy's *Jude the Obscure* is typical in situating a narrative of female nervous breakdown at the problematic intersection of biological theories of determinism, gender and cultural anxieties about the alleged deleterious effects of modern life. However, it is not *John Chilcote, MP*'s frustrated New Woman, Eve Chilcote, who is neurasthenic, but her husband.

John Chilcote under the influence of morphia might be one of Nordau's male hysterics, the typically enervated, nervous and ineffectual modern gentleman, subject to fits of petulance, hysteria and morbid indecisiveness. His retreat from

---

5   A 1905 review in Pearson's *Novel Magazine* further suggested that *John Chilcote, MP* bore a strong resemblance to Israel Zangwill's 1889 novel *The Premier and the Painter*, an accusation Thurston fought successfully via the Society of Authors. See Copeland, 161 and following.

the business of the House of Commons to taking morphia in Loder's obscure lodgings in Clifford's Inn strongly resembles a satiric version of the gendered "rest cure" devised by Silas Weir Mitchell for female neurasthenics, and attacked on feminist grounds by Charlotte Perkins Gilman in *The Yellow Wallpaper* (1892). Of course, the desiring economies found within *fin-de-siècle* Gothic are highly unstable ones, throwing into confusion such essentialist constructs as normal masculinity and normal femininity in ways which also foreshadow Thurston's *Max*. Eve Chilcote, the MP's wife, is an obvious New Woman, composedly negotiating an apparently celibate marriage with her degenerate, drug-addict husband. Politically-engaged, on close terms with the Conservative leader, and as likely to be found in the corridors of the House of Commons as at home, she is at times openly resentful of male privilege: "'You will always despise your opportunities, and I suppose I shall always envy them,' she said. 'That's the way with men and women'" (1905, 62). "'How splendid it must be to be a man!'" she cries when a telegram arrives telling of the Russian incursion into Persian territory and brings the novel's imperial narrative to the fore (127).

Chilcote under the "tyranny" of morphia on the other hand, is depicted as feminised—passive, resistless, voiceless and inert, bereft of volition and rationality, traditionally the special prerogative of the male subject. While he publicly blames his "nerves" for what we are to understand are the symptoms of his addiction, in fact Chilcote incarnates many of the symptoms of nervous disorders previously associated with the hysterical woman, and which so troubled late Victorian diagnostic categories because they muddled the category of what constituted appropriate masculine behaviour in a climate which set a premium on bodily vigour and mental toughness in the service of empire. Emotionally labile, easily excited, Chilcote's movements and speech are continually described as "nervous" and "agitated." His "manly" double Loder, impatiently rejecting the ineffectuality of modern masculinity in Chilcote, nods in his masquerade towards the hyper-masculine, ultra-jingoistic heroes of G. A. Henty's novels, identified in terms of self-possession, reason and knowledge. In attempting to erase his "feminised" other self, a man he considers "a weakness in human form," he strongly resembles a less murderous version of Victor Ansell (117).

As an Irishwoman from a nationalist background, Thurston would have been particularly sensitive to the issues raised by British imperial conquest and domination, and the masquerade in *John Chilcote, MP* is framed fore and aft with a Russian incursion into Persian territory to subdue rebellious tribesmen, the murder of the British Consul-General, and Loder, the "fake" MP, making his political name with a great imperial speech from the back benches. In *Empire and Efficiency* (1901), the imperial propagandist Arnold White warned that "the Empire will not be maintained by a nation of outpatients" (White 1901, 27). While it would not be strictly accurate to see the novel as a critique of imperialism, though numerous contemporary reviews saw parallels between Chilcote and Charles Stewart Parnell at the height of his political success in the early 1890s—a gifted orator with a private life which would at some point prove his political and personal undoing—it nonetheless depicts the beginnings of degeneration at the heart of the British government and the Empire, rather than in the masses of the urban poor.[6] Chilcote's drug use, which Thurston's archive shows she researched by reading De Quincey's *Confessions of an Opium Eater*, does not take place in the East End opium dens on the edge of the city but in its political and social heart, and Chilcote is no social outsider, but an up and coming Tory MP specifically connected with the empire and imperial trade. Neither is Chilcote's morphia use represented in terms of the kind of pleasurable lifestyle commodity of Dorian Gray and Lord Henry Wotton's use of opium and hashish cigarettes, a form of "New Hedonism"; on the contrary, he is far gone in addiction. As in "The Healer of Men," Thurston indicts establishment masculinity, which is found wanting, though she is ambivalent about its vigorous replacement.

The boundaries between norm and deviant are always surprisingly permeable in Thurston. Each man adapts to his new life in a consciously Darwinian naturalism, to the point where the novel's imperial frame turns into a kind of inner colonisation reimagined as a form of survival of the fittest. The weak MP is supplanted by an interloper because the interloper has a stronger personality, and the interloper kills off the host and steals his identity with the eventual collusion of the host's wife. Chilcote muses that "[t]he lay figure he had set in his place ... had usurped his life, his position, his very personality, by sheer right of strength" (214), while Loder, the "usurper," is conceived of in explicitly Darwinian terms:

> To trample out Chilcote's footmarks with his own had been his tacit instinct from the first; now that instinct rose paramount. It was the whole theory of creation—this survival of the fittest—this deep egotistical certainty that he was the better man. (1905, 255)

Fin-de-siècle empire-identified "manly" masculinity anxiously denies its own shadow side, in line with the Darwinian narrative of the evolution of species, within which any combination of morphic traits, any transfiguration of bodily form, was possible. Again, Thurston's apparent championing of imperialist ideologies leaves gaps through which critique may enter. Though the novel explicitly portrays Loder as one of the great defenders of Empire, his position performs its own bankruptcy in terms of political self-interest, and is undercut

6   See Bergin (2014, 159–60) for a discussion of Thurston's references to her father, Paul Madden, and his association with Parnell in interviews around the time of publication of *John Chilcote, MP*, and reviewers' perception that Loder/Chilcote was a disguised portrait of Parnell.

by what many critics have seen as a resemblance between the composite character of Chilcote/Loder and Parnell, and Thurston's dedication of the novel to her father, Paul Madden, a nationalist mayor of Cork, and a convinced associate of Parnell (Bergin 2014, 159–60).

It is also the case that Empire acts as an alibi and enabler for deviance. If, by the latter stages of the novel, Eve Chilcote is largely relegated to the sidelines as a politically well-informed domestic angel, her moral imprimatur is nonetheless needed to grant legitimacy to John Loder permanently becoming John Chilcote after the real Chilcote's death from an overdose. By her voice, the needs of empire are interpellated as a mechanism by which deviance is rendered acceptable for the sake of the national interest. It is because, as she urges, "your country needs you" that the interloper remains in place, ends the novel poised to benefit from his borrowed name by becoming Under-Secretary for Foreign Affairs, and a wife forms a "legitimate" sexual relationship with a man who is not her husband. The true MP for East Wark will be laid to rest under another man's name in a pauper's grave.

If on the one hand, Loder's illegitimate rise to power on merit could be regarded a form of allegory for the suppressed political ambitions of Eve Chilcote, who continually expresses the wish to be a man, it is also ultimately, a parable of political hollowness, mendacity and duplicity at the heart of the establishment and empire. Normality is never re-established in the text, as American reviewers in particular noted; the *New York Times* ran several weeks of correspondence with readers complaining about the immorality of the ending, which sees Eve Chilcote conniving at the permanent replacement of her dead husband by his substitute, even though he has proved himself in Darwinian terms the "fitter" man.

For those few critics who have re-evaluated Thurston's work, *John Chilcote, MP* is of interest only insofar as its successful reinvention of identity foreshadows the cross-gender masquerade of *Max*; in fact, this was the tagline used to publicise *Max* on its publication six years after the earlier novel's success, having become something of a trademark in Thurston's fiction. However, if read together with "The Healer of Men," the two texts constitute a searching examination of various forms of male power—political, economic, domestic, scientific—and competing varieties of monstrous masculinity within the medical and political establishment, as if to counter the ways in which New Women in her other novels manage to transcend social and sexual boundaries. On the surface, both "Healer" and *John Chilcote, MP* focus on a pair of male doubles, one half purportedly an upright corrective to the "unfit" other half, but, in Thurston, the line between deviance and norm is surprisingly porous; the dividing line between the "good" and "bad" halves of the double cannot be sustained in these strongly homosocial texts, in which male identities are without integrity or stability. If anxieties about social and sexual non-compliance reached a crisis at the turn of the twentieth century in Britain in the context of increased threats from discomposing forces such as suffragettes, socialists, homosexuals, Fenians and others, then Thurston's fictional landscape, peopled by male deviants, inadequates and monsters, insists instead on an already-extant central rottenness and neurasthenic hollowness at the heart of the British medical and political establishmens. The beast is within.

References

Arata, Stephen. 1996. *Fictions of Loss in the Victorian Fin de Siècle*. Cambridge: Cambridge University Press.

Bergin, Alan. 2014. "Masquerade, Self-Invention and the Nation: Uncovering the Fiction of Katherine Cecil Thurston." PhD Diss., National University of Ireland, Galway.

Copeland, Caroline. 2007. "The Sensational Katherine Cecil Thurston: An Investigation into the Life and Publishing History of a New Woman Author." PhD Diss., Napier University, Edinburgh. https://www.napier.ac.uk/~/media/worktribe/output-239836/copelandpdf.pdf

Greenslade, William. 1994. *Degeneration, Culture and the Novel, 1880–1940*. Cambridge: Cambridge University Press.

Hardy, Thomas. (1895) 1999. *Jude the Obscure*. London and New York: Norton.

Harvey, Alison. 2014. "Irish Aestheticism in Fin-de-Siècle Women's Writing: Art, Realism, and the Nation." *Modernism/ Modernity* 21, no. 3: 805–26.

Lamond, Julieanne. 2017. "Katherine Cecil Thurston's *John Chilcote, M.P.*: Popularity and Literary Value in the Early Twentieth Century." *Book History*, 20: 330–50.

Ledger, Sally. 1995. "The New Woman and the Crisis of Victorianism." In *Cultural Politics at the Fin de Siècle*, edited by Sally Ledger and Scott McCracken. 22–44. Cambridge: Cambridge University Press.

Meaney, Gerardine. 2000. "Decadence, Degeneration and Revolting Aesthetics: The Fiction of Emily Lawless and Katherine Cecil Thurston." *Colby Quarterly* 36, no. 2: 157–75.

Moreau, Jacques-Joseph. 1959. *La psychologie morbide*. Paris: Victor Masson.

Nordau, Max. (1892) 1913. *Degeneration*. London: Heinemann.

Punter, David. 1980. *The Literature of Terror: A History of Gothic Fictions from 1765 to the Present Day*. London: Longman.

Pykett, Lyn, ed. 1996. *Reading Fin de Siècle Fictions*. London and New York: Longman.

Standlee, Whitney. 2015. *Power To Observe: Irish Women Novelists in Britain. 1890–1916*. Bern: Peter Lang.

Thurston, Katherine Cecil. 1905. *John Chilcote, MP.* Edinburgh: Blackwood.

———. "The Healer of Men." Unpublished MS, Box 5, Katherine Cecil Thurston archive, National Library of Scotland, Acc. 11378.

Tóibín, Colm. 1999. *The Penguin Book of Irish Fiction*. London: Viking.

White, Arnold. 1901. *Empire and Efficiency*. London: Methuen.

Wood, Jane. 2001. *Passion and Pathology in Victorian Fiction*. Oxford: Oxford University Press.

Vrettos, Athena. 1995. *Somatic Fictions: Imagining Illness in Victorian Culture*. Stanford, California: Stanford University Press.

9

"Modernist Silence" in Irish New Woman Fiction

Aintzane Legarreta Mentxaka

Virginia Woolf once suggested that "when you make a character speak directly, you're in a different state of mind from that in which you describe him indirectly":

> I think the great Victorians ... created their characters mainly through dialogue. Then I think the novelist became aware of something that can't be said by the character himself ... *Middlemarch* I should say is the transition novel: Mr Brooke done directly by dialogue: Dorothea indirectly. Hence its great interest—the first modern novel. Henry James of course receded further and further from the spoken word. (Letter to George Rylands, 27 September 1934; 2008, 354)

If Woolf's hypothesis is correct, and dialogue receded at this point in fiction, what kind of indirect methods were developed in its place? I argue that the deployment of silence may be one such strategy. The "inward turn" in narrative has been associated with a slow and progressive "stretching of consciousness" in fiction (Kahler 1973, 5), and in this essay, I consider how silence is a concern of writers attuned to psychology in the late nineteenth century, focusing on two Irish New Woman authors, George Egerton (Mary Chavelita Dunne) and Emily Lawless. The two stories I discuss here are not set in Ireland or concerned with explicitly Irish characters or issues of national identity, but they focus on women's experience, which, significantly, is treated in a similar way to Irishness in their work.

"[I]n silent contemplation ... thinking and thinking"

Early modernist writing by New Woman writers is often at home in silence. This is unsurprising, as self-effacement and compliance have been desirable attributes for Western women, and their silence has been enforced by law since the sixteenth century, when gossiping and "flyting" women were punished by wearing a brank over their heads with a spiked mouthpiece "to depress the tongue, keeping the mouth open and the offender silent" (King 1978, 4). Silence has long standing in English-language fiction as a survival strategy for dependent women with a modicum of education, so that Fanny Price's "I feel more than I can express" is the mantra of countless women (Austen 1996, 216), for whom being a "*silent* angel" like Frances Burney's Evelina Anville, is quite simply the only option (Burney 1997, 80). Silence, therefore, acquires a specific, gendered meaning when endured or wielded by a woman. While it has been often expected and imposed, silence has also been managed and deployed to serve the interests of the underprivileged.

Within the British empire, this historical silence was spectacularly breached by the flood of New Woman writing in the late nineteenth century. Irish authors were so important to the movement that Tina O'Toole has described their contribution as "foundational" (2013, 2). The very term "New Woman" sprang from an 1894 essay by Irish writer Sarah Grand, a call to activism explaining that: "the new woman ... has been sitting apart in silent contemplation all these years, thinking and thinking" (2001, 142). What had she been thinking about? She had been reconsidering the dictum that "Home-is-the-Woman's-Sphere," and had decided to explode it (142). There is an interesting tension in this image, because quiet reflection is a regular feature in New Woman authors, not just as the springboard to action, but as itself constituting *action*. Action versus stasis, or public engagement versus domesticity, have traditionally been aligned with man and woman respectively, and, as posited by de Beauvoir, to transcendence and immanence, with women representing "the static ... closed in on itself" (2011, 108). New Woman heroines, in the very act of questioning, arguably become transcendent beings.

The work of Egerton and Lawless is representative of New Woman writing in some respects, anomalous in others. The movement tends to be seen as part of a "rebellion" starting in the 1890s against the "social and economic restrictions" on women, with a focus on "women's gaining parliamentary suffrage" (Nelson 2001, xi). In fact, Lawless and Egerton both distanced themselves from the suffrage campaign—Lawless deplored its violent methods, and initially saw suffrage and professional politics as something unrelated to the female domain and belonging to the male sphere, although later she changed her views (see Prunty 2009, 168–9, and O'Neill 1995, 137), and Egerton disliked the authoritarian tendencies of the leaders of the movement, and believed, like the heroine of her 1893 short story "A Cross Line," that "[a]t heart we [women] care nothing for laws, nothing for systems" (2003, 11). It is beyond question, however, that Lawless and Egerton sought to further female autonomy and curtail structural inequality, and in this respect they are typical of the New

Woman movement. Something less common within the movement is that they both present modernist stylistic strategies and thematic concerns, particularly related to psychology. Sally Ledger has made it clear that not all New Woman writing was progressive, either politically or stylistically, and has cautioned against placing it "*en masse*" in a proto-modernist canon (1997, 118–19). Yet Ledger herself has claimed that "it is in [Egerton's] work that an incipient modernism can most clearly be identified" (2003, xvi), with Emily Lawless highlighted by other scholars as another clear precursor of modernism (see Fogarty 2014, 147–60). I argue that the use of silence in Egerton and Lawless is partly a stylistic strategy to make thought visible, which places them in the modernist avant garde as much as in the New Woman movement.

In a review of 1886, Oscar Wilde declared that: "[o]ur ordinary English novelists ... fail ... in concentration of style. Their characters are far too eloquent and talk themselves to tatters. What we want is a little more reality and a little less rhetoric ... we wish that they would talk less and think more" (5). Rather than the novel, as Ledger has shown, New Woman short stories were to be the forge of "a fully-fledged modernist aesthetic," because of their focus on psychology (2003, xv). George Egerton herself explained that when she began to write fiction, "[i]f I did not know the technical jargon current today of Freud and his psycho-analysts, I did know something of complexes and inhibitions, repressions and the subconscious impulses that determine actions and reactions. I used them in my stories" (quoted in Showalter 1993, 13). The field of psychology was developed by nineteenth-century thinkers such as Ernst Weber, Franz Brentano, and William James, whose "pragmatic" or "philosophical" psychology has been described by Judith Ryan as "a lost element" in the alchemy of modernist studies (1991, 5). This early psychology made an impact on New Woman writers, who often aligned consciousness and silence, as we will see below in two examples, Egerton's "An Empty Frame" (1893), and Lawless' "Plain Frances Mowbray" (1886).

In canonical high modernist fiction, the representation of consciousness is regularly aligned with silence. Patricia Ondek Laurence has investigated this link in Woolf's fiction, identifying several valences of silence: "what is 'unsaid,' something one may have felt but does not say; the 'unspoken,' something not yet formulated or expressed in voiced words; and the 'unsayable,' something not sayable based on the social taboos of Victorian propriety or something about life that is ineffable" (1991, 1). By contrast, Joanne Winning has analysed the "reification" of silence in Dorothy Richardson's encoded "signification of [lesbian] sexual desire" (2000, 137, 150). Annika Linskog associates modernist silence with "the unsayable," defining it as those "aspects of human experience and the 'real' that are difficult to convey concretely in words" (2017, 12), and has traced it in Richardson, Woolf, and Joyce. In "An Empty Frame" and "Plain Frances Mowbray," silence is most obviously linked to the unspoken. As a concern, it is also more significant in short stories, because in a concentrated narrative such as the short story, silence becomes more "visible" and its consequences are magnified.

Lawless: "locked up, swathed, unexpressed"

Emily Lawless' short story "Plain Frances Mowbray," first published in 1886 and subsequently included by Lawless in a book collection of 1889, is set in Venice, where an expatriate English upper-middle class spinster and her bachelor colonel brother are spending the winter, as is their custom. The protagonist, Frances, is "grotesquely" and "irredeemably ugly" (1889, 13, 11), as well as socially retiring, frugal in habits, and self-contained in her demeanour, but she has a fulfilling inner life, in the sense that she finds the simple routines she shares with her brother Henry the perfect scaffolding for her enjoyment of life. When a serious love interest materialises for Henry, he begins to slip out of her orderly life, and Frances undergoes a crisis. Her customary silence is broken by an outburst expressing her feeling of panic and her sense of betrayal. In a postscript, we learn of Frances's painful adjustment to a new life on her own.

Venice is famous for the quality of its light and for its beauty, but Frances loves it for "that peculiar Venetian silence which is unlike any other silence in the world" (16). Silence is Frances' emblem: "A momentary ray of benevolence ... was about the only manifestation of the inner woman which ever succeeded in finding its way through that impenetrable husk of ugliness behind which all her finer and better qualities lay shrouded. Everything else was locked up, swathed, unexpressed" (38). As with Jane Eyre, Frances' ugliness is associated with a rich inner life, because beauty is gendered, as Frances notes (9–10). Significantly, she is financially independent—via an inheritance—and a spinster. In Western women, silence is often associated with chastity, and verbosity with promiscuity—think of Becky Sharp, Nana, Mary Crawford, or the "fluent" Jinny in *The Waves* (Woolf 2015, 59). Frances does not need to talk, because she does not seek a husband or a lover. She and her brother have a "quasi-matrimonial" arrangement rooted in "friendship," which is seen by others as "unnatural" (69, 81). Monique Wittig famously contended that the term *woman* "has meaning only in heterosexual systems of thought and heterosexual economic systems" (1980, 32). Seen in this way, Frances is not a woman, either. She has sidestepped into an ungendered position—a position that is muted, or rather, inaudible.

In Lawless' work, through the treatment of silence, the non-normative is embraced and promoted, while the normative, in the form of sociability and chattering, is rejected. A "gift for sociability," as we see in her story "Borroughdale of Borroughdale" (1889, 223), is a beautifully wrapped but empty package, whereas an "incapacity for small talk" is invariably associated with an "absorption ... in larger interests" (250). If Frances spends most of this one-hundred-page-long story sitting and thinking, what does she think about? She remembers, invents, and surmises, and she notes what she sees. In other words, hers is an *active* silence. Frances takes "to thinking, dreaming rather, open-eyed, over scenes, bygone scenes" (Lawless 1889, 16), or makes up stories about strangers, "a fashion of composing fiction," we are told, which is more satisfactory than writing (15). Frances is so often and so conspicuously silent that when dialogue is recorded, it is unnerving to realise that even the narrative conspires to silence her, when her contribution is often reported by the interlocutor. If we were to judge Frances by her dialogue or her actions, she would simply disappear.

In Lawless' stories the silence of a character is often *misread* by other characters, for example as ignorance ("Namesakes"), as substance ("A Ligurian Story"), as character trait ("Quin Lough"), or as stupidity ("Borroughdale"). Frances' silence opens up like a box at various points to show the reader the contents of her mind, via third-person indirect speech or stream of consciousness, revealing increasing fury and mental anguish. As the crisis reaches a crescendo, Frances' mind explodes on the page in three full uninterrupted, jumbled-up pages of thoughts: "Lady Frances gave an inward groan. So that was the way of it, was it?—*that* was the way! How extraordinary! How incredible!" (74). At the peak of the crisis, brother and sister eventually talk, standing on adjacent balconies in their lodgings (outside and inside at once, like their words), and Frances *speaks* her mind at last. Henry's marriage will affect, she explains, "her life, her home, her whole heart, her very existence, everything she cares for" (79). But the decision has been made, and soon after Frances is forced to "accep[t] defeat" (101). In the epilogue, after a period of "exile" in London, Frances returns to Venice, and we learn that she is "sufficiently occupied," and has settled into a "very peaceful, very quiet" life (105). Silence, embraced once more, proves her most constant, most reliable companion.

Egerton: "truth-telling hours of quiet scrutiny"

George Egerton was deeply concerned with the "truth-telling hours of quiet self-scrutiny" in women. I will look here at her short story "An Empty Frame," of 1893, which begins with one such moment (2003, 9). Stillness can be seen as a "kinetic" form of silence, as Adam Jaworski has suggested (1997, 4), which reverts us to Sarah Grand's image of the New Woman sitting "thinking and thinking" (2001, 142). We can speculate that the limited mobility of educated Victorian women—in terms of access to public spaces and opportunities for travel—may have resulted, in literature, in a "functional" emphasis on inner life, together with a valuing of the quotidian object or the unremarkable occurrence, inducing the private epiphanies which would become a distinctive feature of modernism. Late-Victorian women in fact availed of increased mobility, thanks to affordable bicycles, the normalisation of omnibuses, the expansion of the railway system, and faster transatlantic journeys. Emily Lawless and George Egerton were well travelled, and while their stories showcase an almost frantic array of locations, these are far from glamorous: inaccessible rural Irish homes, Dublin slums, remote Italian villages, Basque woodland hamlets, or Norwegian fjords; even Frances' Venice is the Venice of San Raffaele rather than San Marco. While suggesting mobility, these international dis-locations invoke withdrawal, suitably enough for the reflexive, static protagonists in the stories. But in "An Empty Frame," the world has been evacuated from the page, and no reference is given to location or period—the story is set in a room, an ordinary room with a thinking being in it, and the reader is shown that this apparently ordinary mind contains a universe.

In "An Empty Frame," a woman sits in her bedroom by the fire, in her nightclothes, contemplating a small portrait frame on the mantel-board, an empty frame which once held the portrait of the man she loved. In a reverie, she recalls how they parted because he did not believe in marriage, and she chose not to defy society by living together. As she cries quietly, her husband comes in, undresses, and gets into his nightclothes, prompting her to reflect he is "an unlovely object" (Egerton 2003, 42). Her unattractive husband is not honourable either: while she has disposed of her beau's portrait, he has not returned his previous lover's letters. She blurts out that she is a failure, that her husband would have been content marrying any available girl, while she herself could only have been a great woman in a match to a great man. The husband goes to bed, and she throws the frame into the fire. She falls asleep, and dreams she is "a fiery globe rolling away into space," and that "[t]he inside [of the ball] is one vast hollow" (43).

In this way, the sustained silence in "An Empty Frame" is followed by an outpouring where the protagonist speaks her mind, a narrative structure which we saw in "Plain Frances Mowbray," and which we find in many Egerton stories. For example, in "Her Share" and in "A Psychological Moment," two women "sit in silence" (2003, 89, 97), until one of them launches into a revelatory monologue. Conversely, in Egerton listening quietly is an active, transformative experience. For example, in "Regeneration of Two," a reserved lady listens to a homeless man and undergoes a Tolstoyan politico-moral transformation, or in "The Spell of the White Elf," a woman realises that her female interlocutor is clarifying "most of the things that had puzzled me for a long time; questions that arise in silent hours; that one speculates over, and to which one finds no answer in textbooks" (2003, 27). In Egerton, the talk tends to reveal the background to a "fallen" woman, pushed into a moral *cul de sac* by an unscrupulous man. When the talk is not confessional, it reaches far and wide, as in "Now Spring has Come" (1893): "Did we not talk about anything? Of course we did. Tolstoi [sic] and his doctrine of celibacy. Ibsen's Hedda. Strindberg's view of the female animal. And one agreed that Friedrich Nietzsche appealed to us immensely" (2003, 22).

Outspokenness, as this quotation makes clear, extends to sexuality. According to Egerton's biographer Terence de Vere White, it is in her work that "for the first time in English the heroine admits to sexual feeling" (1958, 10). It is worth noting that two other Irish New Woman writers have been highlighted as pioneers in "directness in writing about sexual matters": "Iota" and Mona Caird (O'Toole 2000, 148). The marketing strategy of Egerton's publisher aligned her with the sexually-provocative Decadents, which meant that the popularity of her work rose and fell in conjunction with the movement in the aftermath of the Wilde trials (see Ledger 2003, xi). Interestingly, Egerton's writing style changed over time in terms of its levels of directness and circumvention. In her short stories, after the reflective *Keynotes* of 1893, characters break into lengthy monologues in *Discords* (1894), spelling out grievances and launching manifestos; by 1897, in *Symphonies*, the characters have retreated into the unexpressed, while the 1898 *Fantasias* adopts the distancing code of fairy tales; and in *Flies in Amber*, in 1905, she is again matter-of-factly discussing women pushed beyond the pale of morality, such as Dublin "hetairai" (41).

The suppressed is one of Egerton's *leitmotifs*. In "An Empty Frame" the scooped-out possibilities refer to the negation of intellectual and sexual fulfilment. The directionless, empty ball is also a visual translation of the woman's skull, recalling the depressed wife in the story "Pan" (1897), who feels "almost restful" when she is finally "thought-free" (241). The frame also suggests externals, and it is significant that the unnamed protagonist's face "is more characteristic than beautiful" (40), which recalls Frances Mowbray, and is also a common trait in Egerton's unconventional, hard-thinking heroines.

The pre-ordered orbit of the ball is in contrast with the organic shooting out of consciousness in various directions. One of Egerton's characters explains: "Study yourself, and what will you find? Just what I did; the weak, the inconsistent, the irresponsible" (2003, 16). In "Under Northern Sky" (1893), a woman sits communing with her "inner self," and "[h]er thoughts ... flash past as the landscape seen from a mail train" (60). In "Now Spring has Come" (1893), the protagonist ponders on "how dazzlingly swift our thought can travel; like light" (23), demonstrating how "some trivial thing will jog a link in a chain of association, and set it vibrating until it brings one face to face with scenes and people long forgotten in some prison cell in one's brain" (15). As these dynamic descriptions indicate, thinking is action. Typically, the protagonist of New Woman fiction, "having her consciousness raised by feminist ideas, gains confidence in her ability to voice her rights, and is ultimately willing to fight for them" (O'Toole 2013, 2). When a New Woman thinks, she activates herself, and her very autonomy challenges the status quo—each female *res cogitans* is a new Descartes, with the power to recalibrate the universe.

"[A]wful, unwonted silence"

Heather Ingman has investigated how "the emergence of Irish short fiction in the nineteenth century was entangled in the rise of national consciousness" (2011, 55), and Michael McAteer has discussed the links between "silence as a form of psychological disturbance ... and silence as a mark of violent political change in Ireland" (2017, 5). Critics have tended to side-step Egerton and Lawless' Irishness. In 1926 Egerton declared that "I am intensely Irish" (quoted in White 1958, 14), and her biographer Terence de Vere White once pointed out that "anyone alive to the niceties of syntax might have recognised that the author [of *Keynotes*] was Irish" (9). Born in Melbourne (of Irish and Scottish parents), and having lived in several countries for long periods, Egerton can be seen as an example of a transnational Irish identity, drawing "on her Irish diasporic experience to posit a range of different subject positions beyond normative nineteenth-century codes relating to gender, class, and nation" (O'Toole 2013, 130). A comparable claim has been made for Lawless who, Heidi Hansson has contended, dwelled in an interspace "between male and female, English and Irish, rational and fantastic positions," interrogating both "the nature of gender definitions [and] national identity" (2007, 8).

In the case of Lawless, we hear little about her "patriotism" towards "the country to which I belonged, and which I certainly ... loved" (1898, 37, 219), her insistence that "I am not English," or her recollection that as a young woman, England was "mine ancient enemy," synonymous with "War, Famine, Massacre," which "stood visibly out as the Great Bully, the Supreme Tyrant, red with the blood of Ireland and Irish heroes" (2010, 68–70). Lawless was born in Ireland into an Ascendancy family, and critics tend to mention her evicting landlord brother rather than her United Irishmen grandfather. Against this, Brendan Prunty has argued that "Lawless is by far the most articulate and accomplished representative of a unionist [Irish] nationalism" in the nineteenth century (2009, 289). She is one of the "New Irishwomen" writers in their "creative and commercial success" (O'Toole, 2018, 125, 127), and yet, in the words of Whitney Standlee (which equally apply to Egerton): "She may have found abundant room in her fiction for Ireland. She could not, however, find abundant room in Ireland for those such as herself" (2015, 63).

The two stories discussed above are concerned with middle- or upper-class women whose material needs are not at stake, but whose limited options as women have placed them in a psychologically dislocated position. I would argue that Irishness plays a part in Egerton and Lawless' awareness of historical and structural inequality, such as that suffered by women. In stories about the rural dispossessed, Egerton and Lawless' natives, generally silent, penniless women (Irish, Italian, Norwegian, Basque), tend to be seen through the eyes of non-natives, generally talkative English males who are wealthy, educated, and self-aggrandising. If the silence of the disempowered can be "an essential survival strategy," and we can see "work with voice ... as another kind of power" (Parpart and Parashar 2019, 5–6), Lawless' silent peasants measure survival against self-respect. Egerton's laconic wild rural women are often driven—to perdition or to joy—by the need to conjugate their sexuality; their inarticulacy may be related to an "untameable quality" in women, which as Egerton puts it in the story "A Cross Line" (1893) is "never eradicated by culture" and is in fact a woman's "keynote" (2003, 9).

In modernist studies, we are accustomed to the association of fiction with the public, material, and sonic chaos of urban centres. Egerton and Lawless' use of silence invites a revision of that trope. Lawless' treatment of post-Famine rural Ireland is particularly interesting. In addition to the human catastrophe, in Lawless' words, "whole modes of existence and ways of thought passed away ... The entire fabric of the country was torn to pieces" (1896, 308). George Petrie, writing in 1855, referred to the "*awful, unwonted silence*" which "struck more fearfully upon th[e] imaginations [of the famine survivors], and gave them a deeper feeling of ... desolation ... than any other circumstance" (emphasis added, 2003, viii). In "Namesakes," a powerful post-Famine parable by Lawless, a homeless peasant's stony silence, when dealing with an English visitor, ends when she can state her case in her own language and "a torrent" of Irish pours from her (1889, 305). In Lawless' "After the Famine," an allegory of Ireland in 1848, silence is multivalent: a sign of trauma in an impoverished young noble-woman, and a political rebuttal in a peasant. When the narrator tells his affable driver of his work for an English company seeking cheap land, he turns away "as if I had been a leper, and our journey was continued in absolute silence" (1898, 168). A similar scene takes place in "Quin Lough" (1889), where another traveller from England in the West of Ireland tries to break the entrenched reserve of his driver, and when he asks about famine relief, the silence breaks like a dam:

> "Did no money come from England?"
> "From *Ingland!*" in a tone of withering sarcasm. "'Tis so loikely they'd be sendin' it from there! 'Tis out of this counthry they do be takin' it, and have been since the beginnin' of the warld, but begorra they won't do it much longer. There's a toime comin'." (Lawless 1889, 115–16)

The use of dialect here is an authenticating strategy, rather than a stereotyping trope, because the peasant has the moral backing of the story. We find a similar authenticating use of dialect in Egerton, for example in a reference to the privation caused by the Land Wars on the Cork–Kerry border:

> "Have you any more 'colouring' [i.e. milk], Honora? . . . "
> "No'a, then, I had to squeeze out all I cud to make up the quantity for

the cramery; we had none in our tay afore aither; there's enough there for yerself an' me Da!"

"Faith, it was betther livin' we had before them separators started. I hate them; no butther, nor crame, nor even a drain o' butther-milk, nor feedin' for the pigs." (1897, 124)

Egerton and Lawless were polyglots, and had some knowledge of Irish (see for example Egerton's use of Irish in "Oony," in *Symphonies* (1897), or Lawless' referring to Connemara as Iar Connaught in "Famine Roads and Famine Memories" in *Traits and Confidences*, 1898, 146). Lawless is particularly interested in heteroglosia, while Egerton pointedly incorporates snippets of Maori, Roma, Chilean Spanish, Norwegian, Irish, or Basque into her stories (visibilising the cultural silences on which anglocentrism depends), and treats music as yet another alternative language, notably used as carrier of erotic meaning.

Thus, the silence of the individual affluent female protagonists in "Plain Frances Mowbray" and "An Empty Frame," as symptomatic of the silencing of women, is on a continuum with the treatment of silence in impoverished post-Famine and Land Wars survivors, as related to the silencing of the dispossessed Irish in official records. In Egerton, Catholic morality is another suppressor and "killer" in Ireland, as we see in "Mammy" or "Oony." The silence of Oony, a child whose Catholic father and Presbyterian mother have been murdered (after he engages in "emergency work" and is "boycotted" (1898, 116)), is set against the chatter of Oony's abusive and Protestant-phobic Catholic foster family, and aligned with an inarticulate and physically-deformed but musically-gifted neo-pagan "fairy" boy. In Lawless' "After the Famine" (1898), the silence of the aristocratic young woman is equivalent to that of the peasant man; in the first section of the story, nothing happens except the gigantic silence of the local cart driver, which swallows up the page, including the "notions" of the educated English businessman he is paid to drive. O'Toole has contended that the "revolutionary Irish context" covering "the period from the Land Wars to partition, *c.* 1880–1922," was "an important constituent of the discursive nexus that produced the literary New Woman" (2013, 3–4). An alternative history of New Woman literature's engagement with silence would have to go back, via Egerton and Lawless, to the discursive, moral, and structural rupture of the Great Famine. Some critics have suggested that the Famine's "pulverisation of society" is a crucial background to Irish modernism (Cleary 2014, 9), and the short stories of Egerton and Lawless support the suggestion.

In their short stories, both Lawless and Egerton focus on what we could call the "deep realism" of psychological modernist fiction. As English-language fiction readied itself to investigate thought, these late nineteenth-century writers opened up silence like an archaeologist's trench, and began to systematically document and extract fears, grievances, wants, ecstasy, logic, or ethics, together with "the inconsistent [and] the irresponsible" (Egerton 2003, 16). As modernism developed, this strategic use of silence would not be superseded, but it would coexist with other techniques dealing with the mental operations of characters, such as *oratio obliqua* and stream of consciousness. In Egerton and Lawless' short stories, silence tends to be associated with intelligence and with women, which is effectively a rebuttal to the Western attribution of reason to Man. Interestingly, in some of their short stories silence is also aligned to the aftermath of catastrophe and rebellion in Ireland, as we see in their treatment of the upheaval of the Land Wars and of post-Famine shock and fury. Ultimately, Lawless' and Egerton's use of silence is a utopian invitation to listen to oneself and others without prejudice, paying particular attention to individual and group experiences which have been suppressed. That is, their focus on silence is an invitation to fine-tune our inner ear, like the traveller in Egerton's fairytale "The Star-Worshipper," so that we can begin to learn to "registe[r] the continuance of all the air waves—called, for convenience, sound—of every vibration since the beginning of the world" (1898, 55).

References

Austen, Jane. (1814) 1996. *Mansfield Park*. Harmondsworth: Penguin.

de Beauvoir, Simone. (1949) 2011. *The Second Sex*. Translated by Constance Borde and Sheila Malovany-Chevallier. London: Vintage.

Cleary, Joe. 2014. "Introduction." In *The Cambridge Companion to Irish Modernism* edited by Joe Cleary. 1–20. Cambridge: Cambridge University Press.

Burney, Frances. (1778) 1997. *Evelina*. Boston: Bedford Books.

Egerton, George. 1897. *Symphonies*. The Bodley Head.

———. 1898. *Fantasias*. London and New York: John Lane, The Bodley Head.

———. 1905. *Flies in Amber*. London: Hutchinson.

———. (*Keynotes* 1893; *Discords* 1894) 2003. *Keynotes and Discords*, edited by Sally Ledger. London: Continuum.

Fogarty, Anne. 2014. "Women and Modernisms." In *The Cambridge Companion to Irish Modernism*, edited by Joe Cleary. 147–60. Cambridge: Cambridge University Press.

Grand, Sarah. (1894) 2001. "The New Aspect of the Woman Question." In *A New Woman Reader: Fiction, Articles, Drama of the 1890*, edited by Carolyn Christensen Nelson. 141–52. Ontario: Broadview Press.

Hansson, Heidi. 2007. *Emily Lawless 1845–1913: Writing the Interspace*. Cork: Cork University Press.

Ingman, Heather. 2011. *A History of the Irish Short Story*. Cambridge: Cambridge University Press.

Jaworski, Adam. 1997. "Introduction." In *Silence: Interdisciplinary Perspectives*, edited by Adam Jaworski. 3–14. Berlin and New York: Mouton de Gruyter.

Kahler, Erich. 1973. *The Inward Turn of Narrative*. Princeton, NJ: Princeton University Press.

King, Elspeth. 1978. *The Scottish Women's Suffrage Movement. "Right to Vote" Exhibition.* Glasgow: People's Palace Museum.

Laurence, Patricia Ondek. 1991. *The Reading of Silence: Virginia Woolf in the English Tradition.* Stanford, California: Stanford University Press.

Lawless, Emily. (1886) 1889. "Plain Frances Mowbray." *Plain Frances Mowbray, and Other Tales.* 2–105. London: John Murray.

——, with Mrs Arthur Bronson. 1896. *The Story of Ireland.* New York: G.P. Putnam and Sons.

——. 1898. *Traits and Confidences*, London: Methuen.

——. (1901) 2010. *A Garden Diary: September 1899—September 1900.* Cambridge: Cambridge University Press.

Ledger, Sally ed. 1997. *The New Woman. Fiction and Feminism at the Fin de Siècle.* Manchester: Manchester University Press.

——. 2003. "Introduction." In George Egerton, *Keynotes and Discords.* ix–xxvi. London: Continuum.

Linskog, Annika J. 2017. *Silent Modernism: Soundscapes and the Unsayable in Richardson, Joyce, and Woolf.* Lund: Lund University Press.

McAteer, Michael. 2017. "Introduction." In *Silence in Modern Irish Literature*, edited by Michael McAteer. 1–20. Leiden and Boston: Brill.

Nelson, Carolyn Christensen. 2001. "Introduction [to 'Short Stories by New Woman Writers']." In *A New Woman Reader: Fiction, Articles, Drama of the 1890*, edited by Carolyn Christensen Nelson. ix–xiv. Ontario: Broadview Press.

O'Neill, Marie. 1995. "Emily Lawless." *Dublin Historical Record* XL VIII, no. 2 (Autumn): 125–41.

O'Toole, Tina. 2000. "*Keynotes* from Millstreet, Co. Cork: George Egerton's Transgressive Fictions." *Colby Quarterly.* Special Issue *Irish Women Novelists: 1800–1940.* XXXVI, no. 2 (June):145–56.

——. 2013. *The Irish New Woman.* London: Palgrave McMillan.

——. 2018. "New Woman Writers." In *A History of Modern Irish Women's Literature*, edited by Heather Ingman and Clíona Ó Gallchoir. 114–30. Cambridge: Cambridge University Press.

Parpart, Jane L. and Swati Parashar. 2019. "Rethinking the Power of Silence in Insecure and Gendered Sites." In *Rethinking Silence: Voice and Agency in Contested Gendered Terrains*, edited by Jane L. Parpart and Swati Parashar. 1–15. London: Routledge.

Petrie, George, ed. (1902–5) 2003. "Introduction." In *Petrie's Complete Irish Music.* i–xiii. Mineola, NY: Dover.

Prunty, Brendan. 2009. "The Irish Fiction of Emily Lawless: A Narrative Analysis." PhD Diss., National University of Ireland, Maynooth.

Ryan, Judith. 1991. *The Vanishing Subject: Early Psychology and Literary Modernism.* Chicago and London: University of Chicago Press.

Showalter, Elaine, ed. 1993. "Introduction." In *Daughters of Decadence: Stories by Women of the Fin-de-Siècle.* 7–20. London: Virago.

Standlee, Whitney. 2015. *"Power to Observe": Irish Women Novelists in Britain, 1890–1916.* Oxford and Bern: Peter Lang.

White, Terence de Vere, ed. 1958. "The Author of *Keynotes.*" In *A Leaf from the Yellow Book: The Correspondence of George Egerton,* edited by Terence de Vere White. 7–98. London: Richards Press.

Wilde, Oscar. 1886. "Pleasing and Prattling." *Pall Mall Gazette,* XLIV, no. 6672, (August): 5.

Winning, Joanne. 2000. *The Pilgrimage of Dorothy Richardson.* Madison, WI: University of Wisconsin Press.

Wittig, Monique. 1980. "The Straight Mind." In *The Straight Mind and Other Essays.* 21–32. New York and London: Harvester Wheatsheaf.

Woolf, Virginia. (1934) 2008. "Letter 2936: To George Rylands," 27 September 1934. In *Virginia Woolf, Selected Letters,* edited by Joanne Trautmann Banks. London: Vintage.

———. (1931) 2015. *The Waves.* Oxford: Oxford University Press.

Recoveries

10

Intellectual Journals and the Irish Woman Writer: The Example of the *Nineteenth Century*

Heidi Hansson

Apart from providing novelists, dramatists and poets with additional outlets for their work, nineteenth-century periodicals attracted professional journalists, opinion-makers and occasional writers who only or primarily wrote for journals. Partly because of the tendency in criticism to privilege fiction before other prose work and partly because of the comparative neglect of periodical literature as a genre of its own, these writers' importance for the development of a female literary voice in Ireland risks being lost. Women who published in high-brow, non-Irish journals like the *Nineteenth Century* are particularly easily overlooked, unless their contributions can be integrated in the larger political discourses of the time, like women's suffrage or Irish Home Rule. A further cause for neglect is that those who appear in print mainly belong to the social elite, not always representative for Irish women and occasionally not even identifying themselves as such. Nora Moroney's article in the *Victorian Periodicals Review* 2018 goes some way towards remedying the lack of attention to Irish women periodicalists, but as a case study of Charlotte Grace O'Brien and Alice Stopford Green, it is primarily concerned with the individual pieces (Moroney 2018, 504–20). Taken as a whole, the submissions of Irish women writers to the first fifty volumes of the prestigious journal the *Nineteenth Century* provide information about contributors and topics on a more general level. In many of the texts, the conventional modesty topos is present, manifested as an insistence on eye-witness knowledge, as appeals to external political or cultural authority or as semi-fictional or literary style. In terms of content, the majority of the Irish women writers adhere to the original vision for the *Nineteenth Century* as a forum for debate, while they widen its scope in terms of genre and form. The journal's first quarter-century was however a transitional period, not least regarding the status and comparative influence of women in public affairs, and the publication moreover changed over time, gradually allowing for differences in subject matter and style that its initial declaration of purpose would seem to exclude.

The Nineteenth Century

The Nineteenth Century was launched in 1877 by James Knowles, founder of the Metaphysical Society, and began as a platform for the society's members, a distinguished group of (male) scholars, politicians, theologians, authors and opinion-makers that included W. E. Gladstone, Alfred Lord Tennyson, Cardinal Manning, John Ruskin, Leslie Stephen, and T. H. Huxley. As a *Monthly Review* at the fairly steep price of half a crown, the journal was set apart from the more popular magazines which were flooding the market at the time. It was aimed at the educated and affluent classes, and the style was intended to be intellectual as well as readerly. In its early years, the periodical had a circulation of 10,000 copies, which translates into five times as many readers (Houghton 1972, 624). Since both contributors and presumably many readers were among the political and cultural arbiters of the day, the journal had a significant influence on current debate.

The Metaphysical Society was characterised by an open exchange of opinion between people with different sets of convictions, and the emphasis on diversity was carried forward into the *Nineteenth Century*. The publication was intended to reflect its moment in time in all its variety rather than to advocate a particular political or ideological position. It was an integral part of this intention that the readers as well as any future respondent should know who had expressed a certain opinion. By the last quarter of the nineteenth century, signature had become an important factor in ensuring the respectability of journalism, with *Macmillan's Magazine* and the *Fortnightly Review* pioneering the policy in the 1860s. The principle was meant to signal moral accountability and the contributor's independence in relation to the editor: if a writer expressed opinions or offered criticism, he—because the generic writer was still perceived as male—should be willing to personally account for his views if challenged (Nash 2010, 58). From the start, Knowles insisted that all contributions to the *Nineteenth Century* should be signed, and in the Index of the first fifty volumes he compares unsigned contributions to anonymous letters:

> No man can make an anonymous speech with his tongue, and no brave man should desire to make one with his pen, but, having the courage of his opinions, should be ready to face personally all the consequences of all his utterances. Anonymous letters are everywhere justly discredited in private life, and the tone of public life would be raised in proportion to the disappearance of their equivalent anonymous articles from public controversy. (n. d., 2)

As Hao Li notes, the practice of signature "promised to promote honesty and seriousness" but it also made contributors "self-conscious about their public identities" (2018, 175). Signature, and by implication the creation of a public identity, was the very opposite of the modesty ideal that had characterised women's publishing from the seventeenth century onwards, and in this respect, the insistence on signed contributions may have affected women's inclination to seek publication in the journal.

In the first four years, more than a quarter of the articles in the *Nineteenth Century* were written by members of the Metaphysical Society (Brown 1947, 187). As Laurel Brake notes, the primary topics of science, politics and religion were intimately connected to nineteenth-century institutions that denied access to women, like the government, the church and the universities (1994, 56). Thus, when Knowles solicited contributions from renowned experts in these fields, or "stars" whose opinions would carry weight and whose names would ensure sales, they were almost invariably men.[1]

The notorious appeal against women's suffrage in June 1889 indicates the periodical's conservative stance towards the woman question. It was signed by many of the most influential women of the day, among them the Irish writers Emily Lawless and Alice Stopford Green (786). The "Appeal" is given a prominent place as the introductory item in the June number and Knowles supplies an opportunity for women readers to show their support by inserting a detachable page to be signed and sent to the editor. In addition, he adds a rare editorial comment, in deviation from his practice to present both sides of an argument: "The deliberate opinion of the women readers of the *Nineteenth Century* might certainly be taken as a fair sample of the judgement of the educated women of the country, and would probably receive the sympathy and support of the overwhelming majority of their countrywomen" (1889, 788). The issue contains no articles in dialogue with or opposition to the "Appeal," and it seems indisputable that Knowles is in favour of the protest, not least, perhaps, since his wife is among the signatories.[2] Although the journal's anti-suffrage position was in itself no reason for women to avoid publishing in the *Nineteenth Century*, the periodical remained an unlikely channel for women writers in general and perhaps even more so for Irish women writers for at least its first few decades. The few women writers who began to appear after the first fifteen months were most of them little known, partly because a reputation as a novelist or a poet was no particular motive for inclusion. Their contributions are significant and worthy of scholarly interest, however, not least since they

---

1   A female "star" would be Florence Nightingale who contributed an article on the people of India in August 1878.

2   It should be noted that the *Nineteenth Century* also included articles arguing for women's suffrage, although not in the number containing the "Appeal." A reply to the "Appeal" by Millicent Garrett Fawcett was published in the *Nineteenth Century* 26 (1889): 86–96.

reveal that the declared rationale of the journal was not all-encompassing.

Irish Women Writers in the *Nineteenth Century*

Given the insistence on signature, it is logical to assume that the security of class might be a factor for the women published in the *Nineteenth Century*. Possibly high social rank also counted as an equivalent to the star rating of the male contributors within the economy of the journal. Accordingly, the first woman contributor was not unexpectedly an aristocrat, Lady Juliet Creed Pollock, wife of the Law Professor William Frederick Pollock who was one of the members of the Metaphysical Society. Lady Pollock's article appeared in the June number of the first volume, in 1877, but it was to be another year before the next articles by women writers were published and two and a half years before the first piece by an Irishwoman, Charlotte Grace O'Brien's article on "The Irish 'Poor Man'" in December 1880.

Lady Pollock had made a name for herself as a theatre critic, and in her first contribution to the *Nineteenth Century* she uses the semi-fictional form of the dialogue to debate the beneficial and detrimental effects of play-going (1877, 611–22). This plasticity of format characterises many of the early items and is typical of literature in transition. In their study of the gendered facets of Victorian periodical literature, Hilary Fraser et al. suggest that such textual instability "articulates the unevenness and reciprocities of evolving gender ideologies in the periodical press" as the "material realisation, generically and formally, of that dynamic and relational cultural process" (2003, 2). Even so, the dialogic arrangement of Lady Pollock's article should not be understood as stylistically feminine, but was used by several of the recurring male contributors to great effect, among them the political writer Henry Duff Traill, the Scottish academic William Minto and, most frequently, the Catholic sociologist William Hurrell Mallock. The dialogue form was obviously well-suited to the *Nineteenth Century*'s aim of presenting different perspectives since it can accommodate opposing views without privileging either position.

Dialogue can also be encouraged by editorial design, however. The editor's introduction or the placement of a contribution in a particular section, on the page or adjacent to other material modifies or even subverts the message. Thus, Charlotte O'Brien's first article on "The Irish 'Poor Man'" (1880) was sandwiched between a piece by the anti-Parnellite politician Justin McCarthy entitled "Ireland in '48 and Ireland Now," and an article on "The Irish Land Question" by the pro-landlord House of Lords representative James Hewitt, 4th Viscount Lifford, which makes it part of a debate where the outcome is not given. Although the innate meaning of the piece is not affected, the placing introduces a sense of controversy that may well have influenced contemporary readers.

O'Brien treats subjects where her Irishness and perhaps the fact that she was the daughter of the Young Irelander William Smith O'Brien are sources of reliability and authority, and her three articles in the *Nineteenth Century* are all strongly critical of the Union with England. In "Eighty Years" she makes claims for a free Ireland on the basis that management from London has harmed Irish interests from 1801 onwards: "I would have all local affairs managed by the province, all public affairs managed by the council. I would have at the head of the executive an Irishman appointed by the Crown, permanent and unconnected with English party" (1881, 413). Self-government, not Home Rule, is her demand, with Lord Dufferin in charge (1881, 412, 414). In comparison with her confident censure of English misrule in the first two contributions, it seems an anomaly that her passionate condemnation of so-called assisted emigration in 1884 should be introduced with a conventional modesty declaration: "What I have to say myself is a sketch—a mere sketch from my personal experience; I do not know enough to piece it in or combine it to the larger whole. It must be accepted, as all such sketches should be, as drawn from very limited premises: therefore necessarily one-sided, imperfect, and perhaps mistaken" (1884, 530). Unlike in the first two articles where she speaks from lived experience, "The Emigrant in New York" is based on observation and interviews, but her conclusions are equally forceful, despite the initial reservation, and again, her solution is autonomy for Ireland. Her articles in the *Nineteenth Century* convey a consistent political message, describing different negative effects of English mismanagement and proposing Irish self-rule as the answer to the resultant problems, inside and outside Ireland.

Based on a broad definition of Irishness that includes self-identification, being born in Ireland, or being married to an Irish person and residing for long stretches of time in the country, fourteen Irish women writers can be identified in the *Nineteenth Century* between 1877 and 1901, mainly from a privileged background.[3] With eight articles, one of them in two parts, Emily Lawless is the most prolific contributor, and like Lady Gregory and Alice Stopford Green, she has an established reputation as a writer in her own right. Most of the Irish women in the *Nineteenth Century* appear with one to three pieces, and for some of them, like Lady Edith Blake, the Countess of Meath and Lady Eva Wyndham-Quin, social position may have been an important factor for solicitation or acceptance.

An unexpected piece is the supposedly authentic diary account "A Young

---

3   In *The Wellesley Index to Victorian Periodicals 1824–1900* vol 2, the article "The Humours of Ter-na-nog" is ascribed to Lina Orman Cooper, the wife of Reverend Jonathan Sisson Cooper, Rector at Coolock, County Dublin. In the Index to the *Nineteenth Century* covering the first fifty volumes, the author is also identified as "Mrs Orman Cooper" (34). Internal evidence in the text however suggests that this is a misidentification and that the actual writer is a male medical doctor. I have therefore not included the article in my sample.

Lady's Journey from Dublin to London in 1791" by Jane Hester Reilly, a detailed description of the diarist's experiences and impressions of London society reprinted with original style and punctuation (1898, 795–808). In its focus on material objects and the social whirl of the time, it is remarkably similar to the recollections of Emily Charlotte Boyle, Countess of Cork and Orrery, describing London society over the past fifty years since 1892 (1892, 465–73). For an Irishwoman looking back to the 1840s, a mention of the Great Hunger might be expected, but the author is entirely concerned with social events and personages. As basically society gossip, these two articles are exceptional, however, and most of the Irish women writers publishing in the journal take part in public debate and address the same or similar issues as the male contributors, although they frequently use different genres and forms to do so.

Regardless of the true or underlying topic of the article, the choice of genre is crucial to the way in which the writers frame their claims of authority. The majority of the articles can be loosely categorised as travelogues or accounts of life and circumstances in foreign or non-metropolitan parts of the world based on their first-hand experiences. The description of the Allgemeines Krankenhaus in Vienna by Charlotte O'Conor-Eccles is a particularly illustrative example. The article gives a severely critical overview of patient care at the Viennese hospital, making unfavourable comparisons between the sloppy procedures and inhumane practices at the Krankenhaus and the well-trained nurses and ordered systems in the large London hospitals. It is an early example of investigative journalism, containing detailed information leading up to a number of conclusions and recommendations. Yet, the value of the account is ostensibly compromised by O'Conor-Eccles' declaration that "I can therefore only answer for what came under my notice as a visitor, and for what I gathered by questioning the various doctors and students that showed me round" (1899, 593). In actual effect, her avowed inability to vouch for the truth of a particular story (O'Conor-Eccles 1899, 594) or the purported limitations of her survey instead foreground her eye-witness authority. In travel writing, credibility proceeds from the circumstance of having seen and visited the place, and although the article—like Charlotte O'Brien's account of Irish emigrants in New York—can only nominally be categorised as a travelogue, the information it contains is validated by the remark that it was collected "during a recent visit to Vienna" (O'Conor-Eccles 1899, 591).

O'Conor-Eccles is the only professional journalist of the Irish women contributors in the first quarter-century of the journal. For her, the generous payment offered by Knowles may have been one incentive to seek publication in the *Nineteenth Century,* together with the status it offered to be included in the illustrious list of contributors. For some of the other Irish women, like Charlotte Grace O'Brien or the pro-Boer historians Elisabeth Lecky and Alice

Stopford Green, the journal's function as a non-sectarian political platform was probably more important. Just as O'Brien traces the early expressions of the Land War to insensitive British policies over the preceding eighty years (1881, 397–414), Lecky and Green connect the Boer War to British imperial politics. Nora Moroney finds it "significant that all of O'Brien's and Green's *Nineteenth Century* pieces focus on topics of a social and political bent" (2018, 507). As a matter of fact, these topics should be expected, considering the publication channel, and with a few, significant exceptions, the majority of the contributions by Irish women can be seen as social or political interventions, albeit more or less overt. An example is the article by Augusta, Lady Gregory which professes to be a comparison of English presumptions about Irish life and the real situation, but transforms into a three-part discussion of economic politics, represented by Horace Plunkett and the agricultural movement, cultural politics, as represented by Douglas Hyde and the Gaelic League and cultural politics in the form of folk literature (1898, 769–82).

Gendered Writing?

The idea of gendered writing and gendered topics was very much alive at the end of the nineteenth century, and an opinion held also by writers today considered as proto-feminist or literary foremothers. In an essay in June 1897 described as "startlingly anguished" by Helen Kingstone (2014, 442), Alice Stopford Green claims that women have remained comparatively aloof from "theological, metaphysical, and political speculation" (968), or in other words those topics most clearly associated with the public arena. She identifies what she defines as a feminine style that is detrimental to the messages women want and need to disseminate: "For even in her literary venture woman remains essentially mysterious. It is as though some inherent diffidence, some overmastering self-distrust, had made her fear to venture out into the open unprotected and bare to attack" (1897, 965).

Green's argument is difficult to penetrate, since she employs a meandering, poetical style, embellished with simile, imagery and literary references remarkably similar to the feminine mode she appears to reject. The picture is even more complicated if the article is juxtaposed with her 1900 argument against votes for women where she proposes a kind of difference feminism in many ways corresponding to what she seems to criticise in the earlier text: "It is possible, indeed I think certain, that what is most needed in us for the service of the State is divergence, not similarity" (1900, 840). In 1897, Green advocates learning before emotion and the cultivation of a rational style of discourse that epitomises the similarity she dismisses three years later:

> These, however, are the first conditions for discovering the contribution which woman has to make to human thought. If she is to deliver her

true message, or to be the apostle of a new era, she must throw aside the curiosity of the stranger and the license of the anarchist. The history and philosophy of man must be the very alphabet of her studies, and she must speak the language of the world to which she is the high ambassador, not as a barbarian or foreigner, but as a skilled and fine interpreter. (1897, 974)

In 1900, she instead argues against women throwing themselves "on the dull old beaten track, for the sake of proving they could walk in it as well as the men" (841). In her rejection of female suffrage, Green cautions against a complicity with a political system that has stagnated into bureaucracy and urges women to change the nature of public and political institutions. Nevertheless, although both pieces are argumentative, they are characterised by a flowery circuitousness that threatens to defy the purpose and is far from the straightforward approach she advises.

Three of Green's articles are directly or indirectly concerned with the Second Boer War, the first a historical overview of Dutch-English relation, the only piece that clearly relates to her work as a historian and written in the dispassionate, objective style she recommends (1899, 891–904). Her first intervention on behalf of the Boer prisoners of war employs a considerably more personal tone, with a slow build-up to a veiled critique of English camp management (1900, 982–83). Like O'Brien and O'Conor-Eccles, she begins by limiting her claims, stating that she wishes "simply to tell a few incidents which I saw for myself, and of which I speak only because they came within my personal knowledge" (1900, 972). The article is introduced with an impressionistic description of St. Helena, suggesting that nature itself, like the prisoners, has been relocated to the island: "The Kaffir thorn, the African palm, the Indian banyan, the Scotch fir, the Port Jackson willow, are not at home, but transported as it were to a friendless inn" (1900, 974). Whereas nature is "tattered and battered, ignoble, dingy, vulgar and unashamed" (1900, 974), the Boer prisoners come across as dignified, pious and committed to democratic principles. The second article about Deadwood Camp falls into two parts, with the first half based on the prisoners' stories and appealing to the readers' emotions, while the second half appeals to reason and calls for better camp administration and preparation for the Boers' eventual return to South Africa (1901, 755–71). As a group, Stopford Green's *Nineteenth Century* articles demonstrate how periodical writing—perhaps particularly by women—was a genre in flux at the turn of the twentieth century.

Only a few of the articles by Irish women writers in the *Nineteenth Century* follow Alice Stopford Green's 1897 edict to adopt a direct style of argument—including her own. The clearest example is the Marchioness of Londonderry's attack on the Workmen's Compensation Act in 1897, where she draws on her position as political hostess and member of the Primrose League Grand Council (Finley-Bowman 2003, 16). Using a strong, unapologetic, political voice and using the collective "we," Lady Londonderry argues for voluntary associations and against public compensation for workers who have accidents: "It is obvious that no employer will, after the Bill becomes law, continue to find work for any except able-bodied, strong men in the prime of life, and, if possible, without dependents, so as to lessen the chance of accident and consequent compensation" (1897, 351). The article resembles a political speech, and in both tone and approach it is atypical of the Irish women represented in the journal.

Travel Writing as Pretext and Purpose

In contrast to O'Brien's New York article which could be characterised as political pamphleteering framed as travel writing, Emily Lawless's travel texts contain few descriptions of people and consequently no political or social dimension, unless the much later idea of ecopolitics is included. Her solid reputation as a writer enables her to create her own niche, and she describes Irish or foreign scenery from the point of view of a natural historian, without politicising what she sees. In her first contribution to the *Nineteenth Century*, "A Dredging Ground" from 1881, she gives a personal, naturalist account of Killary Bay between Mayo and Galway and "North Clare—Leaves from a Diary" is focused on the special characteristics of the landscape as "an interspace between land and water" that does not "strictly belong either to the one or to the other" (1899b, 604). Even her description of Florence (1899a, 327–35) is concentrated on the gardens and flowers of city, and there is little sense of Italian life or culture. Her travel accounts mix precise botanical and zoological information with descriptions of emotional and aesthetic pleasures, from an intensely private point of view that makes them unusual in the context of the journal. Essayistic writing in the final decades of the nineteenth century sometimes bordered on fiction as illustrated by her tales from Irish history in the *Nineteenth Century* (Hansson 2015, 61–81). Thus, a personal-fictional approach characterises her travelogues as well as the more argumentative pieces, "A Note on the Ethics of Literary Forgery" (1897, 84–95) and "Of the Personal Element in History" (1901, 790–98), where she obliquely comments on her own literary work.

There are similarities between Lawless' 1901 discussion of history as best transmitted through colourful personages from the past and Elisabeth Lecky's narrative "A Visit to the Grande Chartreuse" from March 1891, a detailed history of the Carthusian Order introduced as travel writing. In contrast to most travel writers, Lecky does not begin by establishing her own eye-witness authority, but by employing the point of view of the order's founder St Bruno. The self-narrative element usually found in a travelogue is down-played and occasionally absent, and the scattered anecdotes place the text in the semi-fictional camp, the illusion only occasionally broken by a mention of the travelling company. A similar leakage between genres is discernible in Lecky's article about "The House in the Wood" where the 1899 Peace Conference initiated by Tsar Nicholas II took place. The conference is primarily a pretext for a description of women in Dutch royal history, particularly Amalia de Solms who erected the house as a memorial to her husband. In the piece, Lecky draws on her knowledge of Dutch history as born in the Netherlands, although married to the historian William Edward Hartpole Lecky, and a long-time Irish resident. In a similar manner, she makes use of her knowledge of the Dutch settlers in the Transvaal in her outspoken criticism of British inability to see to anything except their own interests during the period of unrest leading up to the second Boer War (1896, 19–26). While her articles are not travelogues in the strict sense of the word, she quotes first-hand sources to give a sense of immediacy.

Lady Edith Blake's contributions are more traditional examples of travel writing. Like Emily Lawless, she was an ardent student of botany and entomology, as well as an accomplished illustrator, but unlike Lawless she combines naturalist information with local history and ethnography in her accounts of the Bahamas and Newfoundland where her husband served as Governor. Despite her considerable work as a writer and an artist she has received scant interest from scholars, possibly because she neither conforms to the stereotype of the "intrepid woman traveller" or the national-minded Irishwoman.

The Blakes resided in the Bahamas between 1884 and 1887, and Edith Blake's article describes plants, animals and the population of the islands, occasionally making generalising comments about "the darkies" (Blake 1888a, 683). The description of the indigenous Beothuks of Newfoundland in her next article is considerably more empathetic, blaming the colonisers for the extinction of the people: "The wrongs of the Beothuks had been too many and too deep for them ever again to trust the white man" (1888b, 918), a conclusion she does not draw in connection with the former slaves in the West Indies. Her final piece, "On Seals and Savages" concerns seal hunting, with the savages of the title referring to the Newfoundland sealers whose dirty habits and cruel hunting practices are condemned in the text. Although she finds the "intellectual faculties" of the local population "decidedly in abeyance" (1889, 515), Blake does not blame what she sees as barbarity on any inherent flaws in the sealers or on a lack of civilising influence, but on commercialism: "Now-a-day trading interests are supposed to override all other considerations, and to the Moloch of Commerce the health, morality, and happiness of millions of human beings are too often ruthlessly sacrificed" (1889, 525). Unusually for her time and class, she directs her moral message towards the commercial actors as the cause for what in her eyes appears as a degrading lifestyle.

The racism typical of its period that emerges particularly in Edith Blake's account of the Bahamas is considerably more flagrant in Lady Eva Wyndham-Quin's articles about tiger hunting in Nepal (1889, 60–64) and bison hunting in India which display little or no sensitivity to local life. India appears as a hunting preserve for the rich in her articles and she assumes an unapologetically superior position in relation to the Indian people who are either troublesome "coolies" (1892, 259) or quarrelsome Nairs in need of British control (1892, 256). There is no sense of the intellectual rigour or powers of observation evident in many of the other articles by the Irish women contributors, nor of the political ardour of some of the writers. The articles are primarily to be seen as diary entries, and it is difficult to understand their inclusion in the *Nineteenth Century* given the otherwise lofty aims of the journal, except for the celebrity status of the writer.

In contrast to Wyndham-Quin's imperial superiority, Hariot Dufferin's essay about the medical needs of Indian women is informed by imperial responsibility and social pathos. In 1885, during her husband's term as Viceroy of India, Hariot Hamilton-Temple-Blackwood, Marchioness of Dufferin and Ava, set up the National Association for Supplying Female Medical Aid to the Women of India, and the article is intended to promote the association's work to train women doctors and midwives. It is certainly true that, "Lady Dufferin's efforts and her writings are deeply inscribed by colonial paradigms," as Daniel Sanjiv Roberts states (2006, 453), but at least in the *Nineteenth Century* essay, she shows an awareness of imperial prejudice and acknowledges Indian resentment of Western ignorance. Giving out school prizes, she notes that the dolls presented to Indian children are "intensely European" (1891, 362) which makes her deeply uncomfortable, and she is careful to qualify prevalent views of female seclusion as a kind of imprisonment (1891, 361, 363). In the opening paragraph of the article Hariot Dufferin declares that there is "no statement one can make from personal observation of one part of India which is not open to flat contradiction from good authorities in another" (1891, 359). The declaration may be read as a conventional expression of modesty, but in the political-philosophical context of the *Nineteenth Century*, there is also an undercurrent of imperial critique, as well as a questioning of the truth-claims of travel writing.

Although primarily a brief travel episode, the article about the first female hospital in Morocco by Mary Jane Brabazon, Countess of Meath, follows along similar lines as Lady Dufferin's article, insisting on sensitivity to local culture (1898, 1002). The final medically oriented piece is "Nursing the Poor in their Homes" by Lady Mabel Howard, daughter of the Earl of Antrim, describing the situation in the Irish countryside which for some of the metropolitan readers of the *Nineteenth Century* may have been as exotic as India or Morocco. The article is introduced and concluded with an emotional plea to provide medical relief for the very poor but the substance of the argument concerns the inflexible rules of Queen Victoria's Institute for Nurses in relation to the county associations affiliated with it. As social interventions, all three articles remain within the bounds of the gendered public sphere of caring and humanitarian work, and to some extent, they obviously exemplify a superior aristocratic approach to people who are not given the opportunity to speak for themselves. At the same time, they take part in consolidating a public platform for Irish women, albeit an initially exclusive one.

Privileged Position, Diverse Opinion

On the whole, the Irish women writers published in the first fifty volumes of the *Nineteenth Century* are connected by class, education and social networks. Their contributions demonstrate that they negotiated a public space where a female perspective was neither invited nor necessarily encouraged. Accordingly, none of them is represented in Michael Goodwin's anthology of extracts from the periodical's first twenty-five years, despite the fact that his selection includes a fair number of women contributors. One reason may be the uncertain genre designation of the Irish pieces, which makes it difficult to group them into Goodwin's categories even though they actually address the questions he identifies. Elisabeth Lecky's and Alice Stopford Green's articles, for example, offer forceful critiques of British imperial politics, but only male writers are listed under the rubric "British Imperialism" (Goodwin, 1951, table of contents). Lady Gregory's and Charlotte Grace O'Brien's articles could have been included under the heading "The Idea of Government" (Goodwin, 1951, table of contents), but their articles are particular rather than general, which makes them less exemplary, and again, only male writers appear in the category. The Irish pieces that touch on the woman question do so obliquely rather than directly, which reduces their usefulness as examples of current debate. In many cases, the writers utilised the Victorian audience's fascination with travel, enclosing their political and social messages in the popular format of the travelogue. In other cases, they addressed philosophical and moral questions in an idiosyncratic, personal manner or in semi-fictional form. There is no evidence of any particular feminine technique, however, and certainly no consensus of opinion, neither regarding Irish or gender politics. Studying them as a collective and foregrounding the publication channel rather than the thematic or political content, nevertheless, highlights some of their unconscious strategies as well as their diversity of outlook and style, broadening the understanding of how women fashioned their public roles.

References

"An Appeal Against Female Suffrage." 1889. *Nineteenth Century* 25: 782–88.

Blake, Edith, Lady. 1888a. "In the Bahamas." *Nineteenth Century* 23: 682–92.

———. 1888b. "The Beothuks of Newfoundland." *Nineteenth Century* 24: 899–918.

———. 1889. "On Seals and Savages." *Nineteenth Century* 25: 513–26.

Boyle, Emily Charlotte, Countess of Cork and Orrery [Emily Cork]. 1892. "Some Social Changes in Fifty Years." *Nineteenth Century* 31: 465–73.

Brabazon, Mary Jane, Countess of Meath. 1898. "The First Woman's Hospital in Morocco." *Nineteenth Century* 43: 1002–7.

Brake, Laurel. 1994. *Subjugated Knowledges: Journalism, Gender and Literature in the Nineteenth Century*. Houndmills, Basingstoke and London: Macmillan.

Brown, Alan Willard. 1947. *The Metaphysical Society: Victorian Minds in Crisis, 1869–1880*. New York: Columbia University Press.

Dufferin and Ava, Hariot Hamilton-Temple-Blackwood, Marchioness. 1891. "The Women of India." *Nineteenth Century* 29: 359–66.

Finley-Bowman, Rachel E. 2003. "An Ideal Unionist: The Political Career of Theresa, Marchioness of Londonderry, 1911–1919." *Journal of International Women's Studies* 4 no. 3: 15–29. http://vc.bridgew.edu/jiws/vol4/iss3/2

Fraser, Hilary, Stephanie Green and Judith Johnston, eds. 2003. *Gender and the Victorian Periodical*. Cambridge: Cambridge University Press.

Garrett Fawcett, Millicent. 1889. "The Appeal against Female Suffrage: A Reply I." *Nineteenth Century* 26: 86–96.

Goodwin, Michael, ed. and comp. 1951. *Nineteenth Century Opinion: An Anthology of Extracts from the First Fifty Volumes of* The Nineteenth Century *1877–1901*. Harmondsworth: Penguin.

Green, Alice Stopford. 1897. "Woman's Place in the World of Letters." *Nineteenth Century* 41: 964–74.

———. 1899. "English and Dutch in the Past." *Nineteenth Century* 46: 891–904.

———. 1900. "A Visit to the Boer Prisoners at St. Helena." *Nineteenth Century* 48: 972–83.

———. 1901. "Our Boer Prisoners—A Suggested Object-Lesson." *Nineteenth Century* 49: 755–71.

Gregory, Augusta, Lady. 1898. "Ireland, Real and Ideal." *Nineteenth Century* 44: 769–82.

Hansson, Heidi. 2015. "Emily Lawless and History as Story." In *The Irish Short Story: Tradition and Trends*, edited by Elke D'hoker and Stephanie Eggermont, 61–81. Oxford: Peter Lang.

Houghton, Walter. 1972. "The Nineteenth Century, 1877–1900." *The Wellesley Index to Victorian Periodicals 1824–1900* vol 2, 621–26. Toronto: University of Toronto Press.

Howard, Mabel. 1898. "Nursing the Poor in Their Homes." *Nineteenth Century* 44: 835–39.

Kingstone, Helen. 2014. "Feminism, Nationalism, Separatism: The Case of Alice Stopford Green." *Journal of Victorian Culture* 19, no. 4: 442–56.

Knowles, James. n.d. Preface. *The Nineteenth Century and After Catalogue: Contributors and Contributions from March 1877 to December 1901.* 1–2. *The Nineteenth Century and After* vols. 19–20.

Lawless, Emily. 1881. "A Dredging Ground." *Nineteenth Century* 10: 131–41.

———. 1897. "A Note on the Ethics of Literary Forgery." *Nineteenth Century* 41: 84–95.

———. 1899a. "Florentine Gardens in March." *Nineteenth Century* 45: 327–35.

———. 1899b. "North Clare—Leaves from a Diary." *Nineteenth Century* 46: 603–12.

———. 1901. "Of the Personal Element in History." *Nineteenth Century* 50: 790–98.

Lecky, Elisabeth. 1891. "A Visit to the Grande Chartreuse." *Nineteenth Century* 29: 405–14.

———. 1896. "A Warning to Imperialists." *Nineteenth Century* 40: 19–26.

———. 1899. "The House in the Wood." *Nineteenth Century* 45: 795–801.

Li, Hao. 2018. "Victorian Periodical Publishing and Ethical Debates: Subjectivity, Evidence, and the Formation of Ethos." *Victorian Periodicals Review* 51, no. 1: 168–85.

Londonderry, Theresa Vane-Tempest-Stewart, Lady. 1897. "The 'Conservative' Compensation (Workmen's) Bill of 1897." *Nineteenth Century* 42: 349–52.

Moroney, Nora. 2018. "Gendering an International Outlook: Irish Women Writers in the *Nineteenth Century*." *Victorian Periodicals Review* 51, no. 3: 504–20.

Nash, Sarah. 2010. "What's in a Name?: Signature, Criticism, and Authority in *The Fortnightly Review*." *Victorian Periodicals Review* 43, no.1: 57–82.

"The Nineteenth Century. A Monthly Review." 1877. Rev. of the *Nineteenth Century*, edited by James Knowles. *North American Review* 125 (257): 172–73.

O'Brien, Charlotte Grace. 1880. "The Irish 'Poor Man'." *Nineteenth Century* 8: 876–87.

———. 1881. "Eighty Years." *Nineteenth Century* 9: 397–414.

———. 1884. "The Emigrant in New York." *Nineteenth Century* 16: 530–49.

O'Conor-Eccles, Charlotte. 1899. "The Hospital where the Plague Broke Out." *Nineteenth Century* 46: 591–602.

Pollock, Juliet. 1877. "For and Against the Play: A Dialogue." *Nineteenth Century* 1: 611–22.

Reilly, Jane Hester. 1898. "A Young Lady's Journey from Dublin to London in 1791." *Nineteenth Century* 43: 795–808.

Roberts, Daniel Sanjiv. 2006. "'Merely Birds of Passage': Lady Hariot Dufferin's Travel Writings and Medical Work in India, 1884–1888." *Women's History Review* 15, no. 3: 443–57.

Wyndham-Quin, Eva, Lady. 1889. "Sport in Nepal." *Nineteenth Century* 26: 60–64.

———. 1892. "A Trip to Travancore." *Nineteenth Century* 31: 255–62.

11

Daughters, Death and Despair in Ethel Colburn Mayne's Short Stories

Elke D'hoker

Although many late nineteenth-century Irish women writers have benefited from recovery projects seeking to reclaim a lost tradition, Ethel Colburn Mayne, who was born in Johnstown, Co. Kilkenny in 1865, is not one of them. If she is remembered at all, it is through her association with *The Yellow Book*, as a contributor and sub-editor in the 1890s.[1] Her name—or the pseudonym she used for these early stories, Frances E. Huntley—thus crops up in studies of *The Yellow Book* (Hanson 1989, 17; Chan 2007, 64) as well as in O'Toole's *The Irish New Woman* (2013, 4), where she is mentioned alongside writers such as Sarah Grand, George Egerton, L. T. Meade and Katherine Cecil Thurston. Even in her own lifetime, it may have seemed as though Mayne's association with the more celebrated men of *The Yellow Book* was her main claim to fame. It earned her praise in Ford Madox Ford's 1920 overview of modern English literature,[2] sparked off a heated discussion about James and literary aesthetics with A.R. Orage in *The New Age*,[3] and led a New York professor to ask for her "Reminiscences of Henry Harland" in the 1930s (Lasner 2006,

---

1   From her home in Cork, Mayne submitted a story to the newly founded *Yellow Book*, which was published in the July 1895 issue, together with stories by James and Egerton. Harland subsequently invited her to London in December 1895 to become sub-editor at *The Yellow Book* (see Lasner 2006).

2   Ford has great praise for Mayne in this essay, both for her work for *The Yellow Book*—"the real motive power of this very important movement came from Miss Ethel Colburn Mayne"—and as a "great, or, at any rate, a consummate, artist" in her own right (Hueffer 1920, 10).

3   In *The New Age* of 3 October 1918, A. R. Orage responded to an article Mayne had published about Henry James in *The Little Review* (Mayne 1918). His off-hand dismissal of *The Yellow Book* provoked a letter from Mayne, published in *The New Age* of 17 October, together with Orage's reply. This led to a further letter and reply in *The New Age* of 31 October.

18–26). Yet, Mayne's literary production did not end with her impressionist stories for *The Yellow Book*. After her London experience, she returned to her parents' home in Cork, where her father was resident magistrate, and wrote the stories for her first collection, *The Clearer Vision*, which was published by Fisher Unwin in 1898. It was the start of Mayne's quite successful literary career as a novelist, short story writer, biographer, critic and translator.[4] When her father retired in 1905, the family relocated to London. Mayne found a close friend in the flamboyant English writer, Violet Hunt, and became acquainted with many of the well-known writers of the day. She never married, but cared for her father and invalid sister. During the London Blitz, their home in Twickenham was bombed and, after some weeks in a nursing home, Mayne and her sister moved to Torquay. They never fully recovered, however, and died within weeks of each other in 1941 (Waterman 1999, 201).

In her 1945 essay, "The Short Story in England," Elizabeth Bowen refers to Mayne as "another woman short-storyist" who had come "into greater prominence" in the 1920s and 1930s, following the success of Katherine Mansfield, "though never quite the prominence she deserved" (quoted in Lassner 1991, 139).[5] This verdict still holds true today, as Mayne is not mentioned in such recent literary histories as Foster's *Irish Novels. 1890–1940*, Ingman's *Irish Women's Fiction* and *A History of the Irish Short Story*, or Ingman and Ó Gallchoir's *A History of Modern Irish Women's Literature*. A possible reason for this consistent neglect may be the fact that Mayne excelled above all in the short story form, a genre often marginalised in literary histories. Similarly, her Irish credentials may have been judged not strong enough as she moved to London in 1905 and was therefore not a witness to Ireland's turbulent history in the early twentieth century. Mayne's modesty and "disdain for self-promotion" probably did not help either, as Susan Waterman (1999, 201) suggests on the basis of Norah Hoult's fictionalised portrait of Mayne in the novel *There Were No Windows*, which depicts Violet Hunt's final years. Mayne's alter ego, Edith Barlow, is described as "an English gentlewoman of the old school," whom men had hardly noticed, "and it had been her own instinct to shun their attention" (Hoult 2016, 92).

Whatever the reason for her neglect, Mayne certainly deserves renewed attention, both as an original and consummate writer in her own right and as a precursor to subsequent Anglo-Irish writers. Indeed, as I hope to show in this

---

4 Mayne wrote highly acclaimed biographies of Byron, the kings of Monaco, Lady Bessborough, and a series of "famous women"; she edited the letters of Lady Byron and wrote a critical study of Browning's heroines; and she made a name for herself as an excellent translator of French and German texts. For a full bibliography, see Waterman 1999.

5 Marcia Farrell (2007, 197) lists Mayne as one of Bowen's correspondents; Bowen also included a short story by Mayne in her 1937 anthology, *The Faber Book of Modern Short Stories*.

chapter, in portraying the fate of young women in her short fiction, Mayne dealt with themes that were later developed by writers like Elizabeth Bowen, Molly Keane, and Jennifer Johnston. Through a close reading of six stories, I will argue that Mayne's Irish stories are not just firmly embedded within a tradition of Big House writing, but also provide an original take on such themes as the gendered socialisation of young girls and strained mother-daughter relations.

Like many Anglo-Irish writers, Mayne carved out a literary career in London, but returned to Irish themes and settings in her writing. She made her debut as a novelist with *Jessie Vandeleur* (1902), a coming-of-age story of a girl in Ireland. Her subsequent novels too, explore the restrictions and challenges faced by clever young women as they negotiate gendered expectations and the marriage market. *The Fourth Ship* (1908) and *One of Our Grandmothers* (1916) feature Anglo-Irish protagonists, while *Gold Lace* (1913) has an English heroine who moves to an Irish garrison town. Although the novels were moderately successful, Mayne "was more widely regarded as a short-story writer" (Waterman 1999, 198). If her early collections—*The Clearer Vision* (1898) and *Things that No One Tells* (1910)—had earned her favourable comparisons with James (see Hueffer 1920, 11), her later work, published in *Come In* (1917), *Blindman* (1919), *Nine of Hearts* (1923), and *Inner Circle* (1925), was routinely hailed as on a par with Mansfield's modernist short stories.[6] Mayne's first collection, though written in Cork, features no clear reference to Ireland, but in all subsequent collections, there are several stories with Irish characters and/or an Irish setting. Amidst stories that display a great variety in terms of theme, genres and plot, these Irish stories stand out because of their poignant exploration of the lives of genteel daughters in Ireland—a life which Mayne had herself experienced in late nineteenth-century Cork.[7]

If *The Clearer Vision* seems to have purposefully excised any overt reference to Ireland, Mayne's second collection, *Things That No One Tells*, has Irish characters or scenes in almost all the stories. One of the most captivating stories is "Desertsurges," named after the "hideous, 'unkept-up,' Irish country-house" that dominates the story (Mayne 1910, 39).[8] It is the home of the Bolton girls: the pretty and passionate Emily and her plainer, elder sister, Elizabeth. The opening scene finds Major Heaton, a friend of their aunt and uncle, flirting shamelessly with Emily under the disapproving gaze of Elizabeth. The second

---

6   A reviewer for *The Spectator* noted in 1923 that it has become "the obvious thing for reviewers to talk of Miss Mayne in connexion with Katherine Mansfield" (1923, 22).

7   Mayne's father was a member of the Royal Irish Constabulary and the family moved from Johnstown to Kildare, where her brother and sister were born, and, finally, to Cork when her father was appointed as resident magistrate (Waterman 1999, 189). Little is known about her childhood and youth, beyond the fact that she "received her education at private schools in Ireland" (Waterman 1999, 189).

8   Desertserges is the name of a parish in West Cork, but the name also evokes both the barrenness of life in the country house and Emily's illicit desires.

scene, set on a rainy evening, shows Emily about to elope with Heaton, but they are intercepted by Elizabeth who tells her sister that Major Heaton is married. Instead of withdrawing in disgust, however, Emily throws herself at the middle-aged man in a "storm of reckless fury ... he had not dreamed of as possible from a woman of her upbringing" (59). Now it is Heaton who recoils in "horror" and makes his escape with "promises and caresses whose insincerity he marvelled that she did not feel" (60). The story closes with the evening's dinner in which Emily takes revenge on her sister by provoking her aunt's anger about Elizabeth's dishevelled appearance.

While "Desertsurges" evokes several characteristics of the Big House novel, it also displays Mayne's particular preoccupation with the nature of femininity and the plight of young girls. Desertsurges itself is, in all its gloom, isolation and decay, "the archetypal image of a declining social class" (Kreilkamp 1998, 21). The story also displays the typical figures of an ineffectual Ascendancy landlord and his domineering wife. For instance, when Elizabeth wants to inform them about Emily's elopement, her uncle interrupts her with "if it's anything unpleasant, can't it wait?", while her aunt scolds her for her lack of propriety (67). The house and the family structure in "Desertsurges" thus bear out Kreilkamp's characterisation of Ascendancy offspring as "trapped, festering within the walls of the Big House" (1998, 23). Indeed, the dreariness of Desertsurges mirrors the entrapment and desperation of the sisters who are likely to end up as "old maids," as one of the servants puts it, for "Divil a young gentleman comes next or nigh the place; 'tmight as well call itself a convent and be done with it" (62). Their plight recalls the fate of the Brennan sisters in Moore's *A Drama in Muslin*, about whom the narrator notes "what could they do if no one would marry them? A woman is nothing without a husband. There is a reason for the existence of a pack-horse but none for the unmarried woman" (1981, 58).

Yet, in Mayne's story the house is not just a symbol of a declining social order, it also represents the pervasive patriarchal structures that oppress late-Victorian girls. Like several of the stories in *The Clearer Vision*, "Desertsurges" also seeks to question and challenge the conventions of genteel femininity which impossibly require girls to be both demurely innocent and singularly focused on finding a husband. The first scene, told primarily from the perspective of Major Heaton, sets up Emily as a paragon of conventional upper-class femininity: she is "charming" and "pretty," "blush[es] helplessly" at Heaton's flirting and appears "helpless and adoring" under his dark gaze (45). In short, she has all the "signs of breeding," of "a long tradition of refinement" that Heaton expects of her (46). Even the elopement is in tune with these gendered norms, as Emily is ready to both follow her heart and submit to Heaton's demands. A severe breach of these codes occurs, however, when Emily appears unfazed by the announcement of his marriage. Heaton is shocked by "her callousness" as well as by the torrent of unladylike "invectives" and "epithets" that come from her "childish lips": "how had she learnt them? And then to utter them!" (59). Although he is dismayed that she is not the innocent "little girl" he thought her to be, he only "chuckle[s]" at his own corruption: "What a mystery it will grow to, amongst them all. The baffled villain that I am" (61). The end of the story, however, adds another twist and a further layer to the construction of femininity, as it shows Emily naïvely and, the narrator suggests, erroneously clinging to the belief that Heaton will come back for her: "She wondered, confidently, how soon he would write or come; and heard above her music the rustling drone of the rain, as in the long, mysterious avenue of Desertsurges and on the lurid road it stealthily obliterated foot-marks, wheel-marks" (67). In other words, Emily's conventional performance of girlish innocence hides not just a greater passion than Heaton had bargained for, but also a deeper and more tragic innocence about the callousness of men and the bleakness of her fate within the walls of Desertsurges.

The dismal fate of the daughters of the Big House is revisited in "The Turret-Room." Nellie Burke, the protagonist and focaliser of the first part of the story, is a serious and shy girl, with "a sharp long nose and insignificant pale head" (Mayne 1917, 195). Her two sisters are more like Emily from "Desertsurges": they are pretty and like to flirt with the officers that are stationed in their garrison and naval town of Inishlee. With its general shabbiness and squalor, Duneera Castle mirrors both the general decline of the Anglo-Irish Burkes and the indolence of Sir Bill, "the famous drunkard of the place" (197). In the absence of good looks, money and social status, Nellie realises that her prospects are bleak: "Geraldine and Kate would get away—would marry. Not any of these men: the gay, the transient soldiers, or the still more gay and transient sailors … there would *be* a man, some day, for Geraldine and Kate. For Nellie, no" (200).

Her sense of entrapment is symbolised by the turret-room, traditionally "the first-born daughter's appanage" (194). While she enjoys the room for the escape it offers her from the routine humiliations of her father's behaviour, the room's isolation also symbolises her loneliness and sense of stasis: "There was nothing, in short, that she could turn to; Nellie just existed, vaguely" (208). Her sense of entrapment is heightened by the remoteness of the room, "cut off from the house proper" and by the door which "stuck and had to be much pulled and shaken from her side, before she could get out" (208). Both symbol and clue, the closed door prefigures Nellie's death in a fire, caused by her father's drunken overturning of some candles. As Backus notes, in many Big House novels, the burning of the house is "depicted with an astonishing degree of complacency, if not enthusiasm" (1999, 215). Nellie too had called out for the destruction of Duneera earlier in the story: "I hate the sight of it, going to rack and ruin the way it is, and ourselves with it. I'd be thankful if it fell down and was buried in the ground, every stone of it, and then we might perhaps lead decent lives, out of this" (209). Yet Nellie herself is permitted no escape and is consumed by fire together with the house, becoming "like nothing that you could have known for her, nor for a woman's body, nor for anything at all" (213).

Although the story might conventionally have ended there, Mayne adds a long epilogue to describe Nellie's wake and burial. Interestingly, the narrative focus of these scenes shifts to the Irish servants, who debate at length about the horrible event and the necessity of burying the ashes of the turret-room together with the remains of Nellie's body: "would ye ever think to see such a thing as that, to be burying the whole place in the Protestant graveyard with Miss Nellie, for fear they wouldn't know which was her and which was the Castle?" (220). While the burial scene thus takes on the grotesque overtones of Big House Gothic, the keening of the Irish women gives the scene an unexpected emotional power as well. Giving in to the "old custom," Sir Bill "had sent the awaited summons to the famous keening-women" of the Clancy family (219). At the burial, "[t]he hooded women drew together, like a chorus" and "the blank sky might seem to curdle as the waves of human woe poured into it" (222).

The religious and emotional features of this long epilogue interestingly recall Nellie's own reflections on religion earlier in the story. Considering the outward show of the Protestant Sunday services, with the army band, the "scarlet coats and glittering helmets," she feels that "church is not *religion*" and wonders about the truer religious feeling of the Catholics she hardly knows (205–6). The powerful chant of the keening woman seems to bear out Nellie's intuition since they manage to express the grief that the family seeks to repress. Nellie's unease with the performance of religion she observes every Sunday also mirrors her reluctance to engage in the performance of femininity that is expected of the "muslin martyrs" as Moore (1981, 329) famously called them—a performance which her sisters, also in "their quite new muslin frocks," gaily partake of in the opening scenes (193).

In her critique of the sad plight of Anglo-Irish daughters, left to compete on the marriage market through the objectification of their bodies and the performance of a strictly coded femininity, Mayne echoes not just Moore's representation of "this awful mummery in muslin" (1981, 97), but also Hannah Lynch's indictment of the treatment of daughters in Ireland, "the very wretchedest land on earth for woman, the one spot of the globe where no provision is made for her, and where parents consider themselves as exempt of all duty, of tenderness, of justice in her regard, where her lot as daughter, wife, and old maid bears no resemblance to the ideal of civilisation" (1899, 196). In Lynch's 1891 novel *The Prince of the Glades* similarly, the protagonist laments that "to a girl, throbbing with the inconvenient consciousness of large capabilities and burning enthusiasms, the idiotic existence of the drawing room into which she is compelled at the most intolerant hour of waking youth

… is worse than a slow mental and moral death" (quoted in O'Toole 2013, 70). Although Nellie Burke is less self-confident than Lynch's heroine, she too recoils from both the artificial courtship rituals of the drawing room and the unremittent misery of a spinster life. The stasis that results from this can only end in death.

In other stories too, Mayne criticises the gendered norms of a marriage market, which require young girls to be both innocent and worldly, naïve and cunning. In "Photographs," two sisters, who have led a "nomadic" life, have returned to the small Irish town of Ballyvourney, Co. Cork, because of their father's job (Mayne 1910, 214). With great reluctance they engage in the social life that is expected of young ladies and visit the daughters of a neighbouring family, the Baileys: "It's death," mourned Sylvia. "At any rate, it's deadly," and her sister Via counters ironically, "Put on our pretty little masks—oh, it's all enchanting. It's all delightful. We haven't a wish in the world" (217). The four Bailey girls insist on showing them their extensive collection of eligible bachelors' photographs over which they speculate and swoon. Sylvia and Via are snobbishly dismissive: "Had ever a mere quartette of girls so glorious, so monstrous, a collection?" (223). Yet, at the end of the story, they are forced to recognise—"between merriment and misery"—that they are really no better, since Sylvia has to admit, "I've got 'his photo,' just like them" (224). A similar tragicomic representation of the confined upbringing of provincial Irish girls can be found in "The Boulevardiers," where Colonel Roche and his three pretty daughters are on a holiday in Paris. To his daughters' intense annoyance, their father insists on driving them everywhere: "the boulevards in a cab, the Bois in a cab, everything in a cab" (Mayne 1910, 101). On the last day of their visit, the girls finally manage to escape from this imprisonment: "They were out of the cab, it was the moment for masterpieces; and men were looking, looking again" (111). Yet, at the first display of male attention, the girls "scamper" back to their father and are "interred" in a cab once again (111).

In all four stories, Mayne depicts the circumscribed lives and limited prospects of Anglo-Irish daughters. Their literal imprisonment—in a big house, a turret-room, a drawing-room or a cab—reflects their confinement within strict gendered conventions that prime the girls for competition on a marriage market with male attention, and marriage, as the only goals a girl can aim for. Mayne's stories thus chime with Lynch's more explicit indictment of the harsh and unjust treatment of daughters in Ireland. In an essay for *Blackwood's Magazine*, moreover, Lynch explicitly blames Irish mothers for this situation, criticizing "the coldness, inhumanity, and selfishness of the Irish mother to her girls of every class" so that "nothing is left the unfortunate girls but penury and struggle and the dull old maidenhood of dull and narrow Irish towns and villages" (1898, 354).

In three further stories by Mayne, the confinement of the Irish daughters is also linked more explicitly to the figure of the omnipotent mother. In "The Letter on the Floor," the opening story of *Blindman*, Larminie Devine returns to her Irish home after her job—and relationship—in London has ended. In the "impoverished Devine establishment," Larminie has to be at the beck and call of her sickly but histrionic mother (Mayne 1919, 9). Although the latter appeared all kindness after Larminie's forced return, Larminie discovers a letter in her mother's purse in which she tells her husband about "the type of woman that your eldest daughter is" and castigates Larminie's "shameless" behaviour in London (26). The discovery of this letter has Larminie reflect on countless other scolding letters she and her sister used to receive from their mother who "slipped [them] under doors at night" (11). Encountering this latest missive, Larminie experiences again "the same imprisoned feeling, the same struggling up of something in one, like wings tied" (24). Pondering the contrast between these angry night-time letters and her mother's affectionate daytime behaviour, Larminie wonders about the reality of these two sides of her mother. Do they partake of "an endless part she had invented, and would play?" (25) Or are they the result of her mother's own unhappiness: "Life itself was as a cage to her" and her family are "the bars" (30). "One part of her cared for you—the stage-side. Mother, daughter; it was like a play," Larminie reflects, but "the cage-side ... had to hurt you, as the jackal had to hurt itself" (32). Linking her own sense of imprisonment to that of her mother, Larminie concludes bleakly, "Theatre and cage—perhaps life was the same for every one" (34). As "Desertsurges" and "The Turret-Room" have shown, theatre and cage are indeed the two defining poles of life for Anglo-Irish daughters: their only means of escape from the stifling enclosure of the parental home is through a studied enactment of genteel femininity that would procure them a marriage. In "The Letter on the Floor," however, the effectiveness of this escape is questioned; marriage seems to result only in another cage.

The plot of "The Letter on the Floor" is prefigured in the slightly earlier story, "The Separate Room." Although the story is set in London and the protagonists, save for the maid, are not explicitly marked as Irish, the impoverished but genteel mother and daughter Cameron bear a close resemblance to the Devines from "The Letter on the Floor." Like Larminie, Marion Cameron has been forced to return to her mother's dominion after being sacked from her job as a secretary and de facto ghost writer to a theatre critic.[9] Jealous of her daughter's bout of independence and professional success, the mother intensifies her close hold over her daughter. The claustrophobic closeness of their bond is symbolised by their sharing the same bed in the boarding house where they live. Recognising

---

9   The work experiences of both Larminie and Marion bear close resemblance to Mayne's own brief stint as an assistant editor to Henry Harland for *The Yellow Book*. Mayne's description of the chauvinistic and patriarchal attitudes of the male authors/ critics in these, and other, stories would make an interesting study in its own right.

Marion's depression, the doctor counsels "a separate room," but Mrs Cameron refuses: "I've never let you out of my sight for a single instant, and never intend to" (Mayne 1917, 41). Marion sees no other option but to kill herself. The next morning, "Mrs Cameron [finds] her daughter dead in bed … in the same room with herself" (46). As in "The Turret-Room," death turns out to be the desperate daughter's only way of escape from both the stranglehold of her mother and the vacuity of life as a spinster.

A final example of this destructive mother-daughter bond can be found in "The Peacocks," the only story with an Irish setting in Mayne's penultimate collection, *Nine of Hearts*. Living with her widower father in London, Alicia thinks back to her childhood and youth in Ireland. Though she had loved her childhood home with its view over the river, her life, and that of her sister, had been made miserable by their domineering mother: "So far as girls can be shut up, she shut them up" (Mayne 1923, 151). Like the girls in "Desertsurges," they seem doomed to become old maids or, as a local spinster warns them, to "turn into scarecrows like myself" (151). As in "The Letter on the Floor," Alicia struggles with her mother's duplicity: "like an evil-natured child that played malicious tricks behind one's back," she is amiable one moment; punitive the next (158). "Was it jealousy," she wonders, or her mother's own unhappiness that caused her to behave like that? Looking back, Alicia is glad her mother "had been dead for years and years" and that she at least had been able to "live her own life"; otherwise "there would have been no she herself by this time" (160–61). Although the sad fate of Marion Cameron in "The Separate Room" has thus been averted, the ending of "The Peacocks" suggests nevertheless that the mother's repressive hold has left its mark on Alicia, who has always had to stifle her feelings so that "the tears and the wild cry" can now no longer be expressed (161).

In all three stories, in short, the mother is represented as a cruel, selfish and omnipotent figure, whose dominion limits the daughter's growth and corrodes her sense of self. Moreover, with their constant admonitions of propriety and restraint, these maternal figures are also shown to be the guardians of genteel femininity. As Declan Kiberd has observed with regard to the children of the Big House, "in return for nothing, the young are compelled to adopt a time-honoured set of manners and attitudes, to be 'sealed' and 'finished' so that the social forms may survive the death of their contents. Living in a period house, they are effectively told to embalm themselves alive, perform approved routines, and deny all feeling" (1996, 370). Although less explicitly about the Big House, Mayne's mother–daughter stories also depict the impoverished Anglo-Irish class as "a self-devouring family" (Backus 1999, 176), a class that "turn[s] the habits of a moribund political system inward and savagely attack[s] [its] young" (Kreilkamp 1998, 23). In this way, Mayne's mothers prefigure characters such as Bowen's Lady Naylor in *The Last September* (1929) or Keane's Mrs St Charles in *Good Behaviour* (1981): women who take out their own frustrations on the next generation.

At the same time, Mayne's repressive mothers also participate in a wider trend of strained mother–daughter relations throughout twentieth-century Irish fiction. They are early instantiations of the familiar stereotype of the devouring mother, which can also be found in the work of Edna O'Brien, Julia O'Faolain, and Jennifer Johnston (Fogarty 2002; Ingman 2007, 67–95). As Mayne's daughters in "The Peacocks" and "The Letter on the Floor" come to understand, however, the devouring mother is herself but a victim of the same patriarchal structures she seeks to enforce on her daughter. Indeed, as Ingman has noted of the mother figure in Lynch's *Autobiography*, she is "one in a line of cruel mother figures in Irish women's fiction whose abusive behaviour towards their children stems from the limiting social context in which they live" (2013, 51). More than Lynch's rebellious heroines (Binckes and Laing 2012), Mayne's daughters perceive in their mothers the same feelings of entrapment and unhappiness they experience themselves. Moreover, in all three stories, the mothers' stage-like enactment of maternal feelings that they do not really—or no longer—experience is implied to be the result of the life-long practice of performing femininity that they now expect of their daughters. With marriage not offering the freedom still dreamed of by the daughters in "Desertsurges" and "The Turret-Room," the only escape from this spiral of oppression in Mayne's stories seems to be through the daughter's death or through a—resigned or defiant—life as a spinster. It is indeed a remarkable fact throughout Mayne's short fiction that very few of her daughters marry and that not one of them becomes a mother herself.

In short, Mayne's Irish stories paint a desolate picture of the life of Anglo-Irish daughters. The rooms and houses that confine the protagonists of these stories are but ciphers of their larger entrapment within narrowly prescribed class and gender roles. While a successful enactment of these roles may procure an escape from the stifling childhood home into marriage, the negative maternal examples in these stories suggest that escape into marriage will only procure another form of imprisonment. Moreover, the artificial performance of the expected feminine behaviour, which Mayne highlights throughout her short fiction, is shown to result in a corrosion of all true feeling and a betrayal of the self. Escape from this oppressive patriarchal system is only possible in Mayne's stories through death: whether an actual death through fire and suicide as in "The Turret-Room" and "The Separate Room," or the social death of the spinster's life. This is the life of "the scarecrow" or "old maid" as predicted in "The Peacocks" and "Desertsurges," which at least has the advantage of being "one's own life." Achieving a successful career is clearly not a fate that Mayne felt she could realistically grant her characters. The job experiences of the protagonists in "The Separate Room" and "The Letter on the Floor" are brief and suitably doomed and the patriarchal work environment embodies but another form of oppression. That Mayne herself did manage to avoid the sad plight of her heroines is testimony, then, to her own tenacity, hard work and quiet genius. As Mayne achieved fame as a short-story writer and biographer in the early twentieth-century, she successfully escaped the gendered restrictions of her Anglo-Irish upbringing in which her protagonists remained so tragically imprisoned. It is high time, therefore, that we honour that achievement and come to recognise Mayne as an important Irish writer whose short fiction successfully straddles the traditions of both late-Victorian New Woman writing and early twentieth-century modernist writing, while her poignant depictions of the Anglo-Irish world of her youth also earn her a place in the long tradition of Big House writing in Ireland.

References

Adams, Jad. 2006. "Mayne, Ethelind Frances Colburn." *Oxford Dictionary of National Biography*. https://www.oxforddnb.com/

Backus, Margot. 1999. *The Gothic Family Romance: Heterosexuality, Child Sacrifice, and the Anglo-Irish Colonial Order*. Durham: Duke University Press.

Binckes, Faith and Kathryn Laing. 2012. "Irish Autobiographical Fiction and Hannah Lynch's *Autobiography of a Child*." *ELT* 55, no. 2: 195–218.

Bowen, Elizabeth. 1945. "The Short Story in England." *Britain Today* 109. 11–16. Reprinted in Phyllis Lassner. 1991. *Elizabeth Bowen: A Study of the Short Fiction*. New York: Twayne, 138–43.

Chan, Winnie. 2007. *The Economy of the Short Story in British Periodicals of the 1890s*. New York: Routledge.

Farrell, Marcia. 2007. "Elizabeth Bowen: A Selected Bibliography." *Modern Fiction Studies* 53 no. 2: 370–400.

Fogarty, Anne. 2002. "Mother–Daughter Relationships in Contemporary Irish Women's Fiction." In *Writing Mothers and Daughters. Renegotiating the Mother in Western European Narratives by Women*, edited by Adalgisa Giorgio. 85–118. Oxford: Berghahn.

Foster, John Wilson. 2008. *Irish Novels. 1890–1940*. Oxford: Oxford University Press.

Hanson, Clare. 1989. *Short Stories and Short Fictions, 1880–1980*. London: Macmillan.

Hoult, Norah. (1944) 2016. *There Were No Windows*. London: Persephone Books.

Hueffer [Ford], Ford Madox. 1920. "Thus to Revisit..." *The English Review* July: 5–13.

Ingman, Heather. 2007. *Twentieth-Century Fiction by Irish Women.* Aldershot: Ashgate.

——. 2013. *Irish Women's Fiction.* Dublin: Irish Academic Press.

——, and Cliona Ó Gallchoir, eds. 2018. *A History of Modern Irish Women's Literature.* Cambridge University Press.

Kiberd, Declan. 1996. *Inventing Ireland.* London: Vintage.

Kreilkamp, Vera. 1998. *The Anglo-Irish Novel and the Big House.* New York: Syracuse.

Lasner, Mark Samuels. 2006. "Ethel Colburn Mayne's 'Reminiscences of Henry Harland'." In *Bound for the 1890s*, edited by Jonathan Allison, 16–26. High Wycombe, Bucks.: Rivendale.

Lassner, Phyllis. 1991. *Elizabeth Bowen: A Study of the Short Fiction.* New York: Twayne.

Lynch, Hannah. 1899. *Autobiography of a Child.* New York: Dodd, Mead.

——. 1898. "The Spaniard at Home." *Blackwood's Edinburgh Magazine* September: 349–63.

Mayne, Ethel Colburn. 1910. *Things That No One Tells.* London: Chapman & Hall.

——. 1917. *Come In.* London: Chapman & Hall.

——. 1918. "Henry James (As seen from the 'Yellow Book')." *The Little Review* 5 no. 4: 1–4.

——. 1919. *Blindman.* London: Chapman & Hall.

——. 1923. *Nine of Hearts.* London: Constable.

Moore, George. (1886) 1981. *A Drama in Muslin.* Gerrards Cross: Smythe.

"*Nine of Hearts*, by Ethel Colburn Mayne." 1923. *The Spectator* April 7. http://archive.spectator.co.uk/

O'Toole, Tina. 2013. *The Irish New Woman.* London: Palgrave.

Waterman, Susan Winslow. 1999. "Ethel Colburn Mayne." In *Late-Victorian and Edwardian British Novelists: Second Series*, edited by George M. Johnson. 187–201. Detroit: Gale.

12

Rediscovering Elizabeth Priestley: Spirited Writer, Feminist, and Suffragist

Mary S. Pierse

Uncertainty concerning the birth date of Elizabeth Priestley (various dates between 1865 and 1877 are provided in different sources) is underpinned by conflicting official records, and that problematic situation may be interpreted as symptomatic of prejudice, wilful neglect and disdain, in varying degrees. Such imprecision, for whatever reasons, has facilitated the almost complete disappearance of the Co. Down author— together with her books and articles—from public view over the past century, a period in which she has been carelessly confused and conflated with others of similar name. This feminist and progressive woman was the author of remarkable books, including *The Love Stories of Some Eminent Women* (1906), *First Causes* (1914a), and *The Feminine in Fiction* (1918a). Her articles appeared in outlets as diverse as the *Irish Citizen* and *Irish Presbyterian*, and in *The Herald of the Star,* a Theosophist publication connected to Annie Besant, and to which Bertrand Russell, James Cousins, George Bernard Shaw, Charlotte Despard, and Eva Gore-Booth also contributed material. While her views on suffrage, her challenges to Edward Carson, and her forceful denunciation of violence against women could seem light years from the idea of retelling love stories, a closer examination of her wide-ranging output reveals a connecting thread and an underlying determination to advance the status of women. This chapter seeks to shine a light on yet another forgotten woman writer, to note the difficulties of discovering details of her life and work, to unravel a web of entangled misconceptions concerning Elizabeth Priestley's identity, and to examine key aspects of her literary output.

Finding Elizabeth

Despite her profile in the early years of the twentieth century, it is sadly necessary to pose the question: who was she? Remarkably, Naomi Doak does not include the name of Elizabeth Priestley amongst Ulster Protestant women authors between 1900 and 1960, stating that the list only has names "readily identifiable through biographical research" (Doak 2008, 128). As author and journalist, Elizabeth Priestley, was better known as L. A. M. Priestley (L standing for Lisbeth), and although she signed articles accordingly, publishers frequently added the title of Mrs George McCracken, whereas she did not. Somewhat ironically, it is the surname of McCracken which has aided confusion with three, or even four, other authors who share the name of Elizabeth McCracken but not the name of Priestley. Whether on Amazon, in WorldCat, on the catalogue of the National Library of Ireland, or on any other site such as Project Gutenberg, a search for Elizabeth Priestley McCracken is likely to present her as author of a number of books, amongst them *Women of America* (1904), and *The American Child* (1913), books that were actually written by an American Elizabeth McCracken. In turn, that American Elizabeth McCracken is sometimes wrongly credited with authorship of *The Feminine in Fiction* and *The Love Stories of Some Eminent Women*. It can be definitively stated that Elizabeth Priestley McCracken from County Down is neither American or Scottish, nor does she fit into any of the putative identities that have surfaced in bibliographies, catalogues and online listings. She is not Elizabeth McCracken (born 1966), a living and successful academic and fiction writer; neither should Irish Elizabeth Priestley be mistaken for Elizabeth C. McCracken, a Scot who published *My Memoirs* in 1920, or for yet another writer Elizabeth A. McCracken (1899–1968) from North Carolina. On the grounds that titles and apparent subject matter of some books could, initially, seem to be closely related, excuses might conceivably be found for erroneously mixing the bibliographies, names and birth dates of the author of *Women of America*, and of Elizabeth Priestley McCracken. However, even prior to proving the distinct identity of Elizabeth Priestley in Ireland, the publishing locations provide a strong hint that two authors rather than one might be involved: some books listing Elizabeth McCracken as author were published solely in America and primarily in New York and Boston, and are to be found in libraries right through the USA but rarely in Europe; *The Feminine in Fiction* and *Love Stories of Some Eminent Women* were published in London, some short pamphlet titles were published in Dublin, and all are much more widely available in Irish, UK and European locations. Since the birthdates of 1865, 1876, or 1877 are often indiscriminately and widely assigned to all bearing the name—the *Dictionary of Women Worldwide* claims that Elizabeth Priestley was born in 1865 while archive.org, authorandbook.com, and the VIAF (Virtual International Authority File) mention 1876 and the *Dictionary of Ulster Biography* opts for 1865—could documentary evidence be found to confirm details for Elizabeth Priestley McCracken?

It is at this point that official state records combine to fail and to further complicate the picture. The births of five female children called Elizabeth (or

Eliza) Priestley (or Priestly) are registered in Ireland between 1867 and 1877 in Belfast, Newry, Downpatrick and Mallow but that of the author/journalist is not amongst them. The actual birth entry that belongs to Elizabeth Priestley has a blank where the first name would usually be: she is merely entered as a female child, born in Saintfield, Co. Down on 15 January 1868. A search of Priestley families in that area discloses a number of possibilities and by following the many trails of their family members, their occupations, subsequent histories and achievements, and counterchecking with church records in different parishes, a strong likelihood emerges that the female, nameless child was the fifth-born of James and Mary Priestley. Her identity could be definitely confirmed through a trawl of the meticulous records of the Presbyterian church which give dates of birth and baptism, names of parents, address and the full name of Elizabeth Anne McKee Priestley (although at a later time, her name was frequently rendered as "Elizabeth Anne Maud"). Rather unexpectedly, her birth date could be called into question by the census returns of 1901 and 1911. In 1901, Elizabeth's age is entered as 31 rather than as 33, and in 1911 as 37 rather than 43, or even as 41 in line with the previous census entry.[1] The census of 1911 records that she and solicitor George McCracken had been married for eleven years—but searches for a marriage certificate have not yet been fruitful and marriage certificates frequently attest merely to "Full Age" rather than actual age. Despite these irregularities, her father's will serves to confirm the birth date and her place in the family; moreover, her subsequent profile in newspaper reports and notices validates her origins and connections, and underpins disambiguation between Elizabeth Priestley and the American Elizabeth McCracken (1876–1964) who lived and wrote around the same period and who also published on women, family and suffrage, albeit with polar opposite views on some subjects.[2] It could well be construed as the ultimate insult and irony that from at least 1909, that American Elizabeth, based in Cambridge, Massachusetts, was a proud member of the Massachusetts Association Opposed to the Further Extension of Suffrage to Women, that she was on its executive committee in 1910–11, and was an Honorary member of the executive from 1913 to 1916 and possibly for longer. In the light of such misunderstandings, it would appear that in the late-nineteenth and early-twentieth centuries, whether in the USA or in Europe,

---

1   Staying with her sister's family at that point, the age might have been wrongly assumed. However, in 1901, the age of that sister Mary Jane (Marie) was entered as 28 rather than 30. The sisters may have conspired in this rejuvenation. For the 1911 census, the final column on the form allowed infirmities to be listed and Elizabeth is the only one who filled that section, describing her infirmity as "Unenfranchised." It is conceivable that other "errors" on the form were wilful.

2   The entry in Thomas William Herringshaw, *National Library of American Biography* (American Publishers' Association, Chicago: 1909–14, 99), says Elizabeth McCracken (born 29 February 1876 in New Orleans) was a journalist and author who began literary work in 1896 and was a contributor to numerous magazines.

and even when women moved in privileged circles, there was scant regard for accurate documentation of their lives and deeds. Rapid relegation to obscurity was not a fate peculiar to Northern Irish (or Southern Irish) women writers.

Elizabeth Priestley's Family

The Priestleys of Saintfield, Co. Down were prosperous. James Priestley, described as a Woollen Draper, married Mary Jane Graham in 1858. Their first two children—James, born in 1859, and William Stavely, born in 1862—did not survive. The third child, John Graham, was born in 1862 and a younger brother James was born in 1864. Both would study at Queen's University, Belfast and James, a prize-winning student, became a doctor. The subsequent births in the family were of Elizabeth Anne McKee in 1868, Mary Jane Stavely in 1870 and Helena Stavely in 1880. The brothers John and James died in 1903 and a bequest in Elizabeth's will went to establishing the Priestley Bursary in Greek at Queen's in their honour (yet another substantiation of her family origins). Their father died in 1884 and his will confirmed not just the structure of his family and the order of their births, but the extent of his wealth and property, and his firm religious allegiance. He left money to several Presbyterian missions and charities. Each of his daughters received £1100 and money was left for their education. Although none of the daughters is listed as having matriculated or graduated from Queen's, it is obvious from her thoughtful and forceful prose that Elizabeth received a very good education, possibly at the important Ladies' Collegiate School (later named Victoria College) founded by Presbyterian Margaret Byers but records have been destroyed. The Priestley family was staunchly Presbyterian and remained so: Elizabeth's husband, solicitor George McCracken, was Presbyterian, as was doctor Robert Alexander, husband of her sister Mary Jane (later known as Marie). George McCracken was secretary of the Presbyterian Unionist Voters Association in 1900. That shared creed might be seen as one element shaping some stances by both Elizabeth and George: Presbyterians in the northern counties still bore the label of dissenters in the minds and attitudes of many in the predominantly-Anglican political élite.[3] In the manner in which Elizabeth Priestley and George McCracken would battle

---

3   *The Irish News & Belfast Morning News* (5 February 1902) carried a letter from George McCracken complaining that the *Belfast News-Letter* had suppressed a letter in favour of two Presbyterian candidates in the upcoming Co. Down elections, purely on the grounds that they were Presbyterians. This rubbed salt into Presbyterian wounds as the founder of the *Belfast News-Letter* in 1737 was Presbyterian Francis Joy, father-in-law of Henry Joy McCracken. Isabella Tod, distinguished Presbyterian campaigner for unionism and for women's rights, noted similar discriminatory attitudes in the 1890s (Armour 2004, 72–87). For details concerning the complex situation regarding Presbyterians in Ulster from the mid-nineteeth century, see Peatling (2006, 156–65); Walker (1996, 30); and Brooke (1987, passim).

for equity and freedom and against discrimination, whether on grounds of religion, gender or class, one can detect some affinity with 1798's revolutionary United Irishman, the Presbyterian Henry Joy McCracken of Belfast.[4]

A Feminist Writer

Although references to L. A. M. Priestley mention that she wrote for several papers and journals, a search of newspaper archives produces relatively few articles by her, especially in the period prior to 1912. It is possible that she used a pen name in some publications but where her name is appended, it is her birth surname rather than that of McCracken. One early magazine piece was about cycling and while the tone might wax over-lyrical, it is suited to the medium and there is no doubt about its author's interest in women's independence:

> To glide along at one's sweet will; to feel the delight in rapid motion that is the result of our consciously exerted strength; to skim like a low-flying bird through the panorama of an ever-varying landscape; to know a new-born spirit of independence ... to return from a country spin with a healthy appetite, a clearer brain, and an altogether happier sense of life—an altogether unaccountable freshness of spirit; this is to experience something of the joys of cycling, and in so doing to rejoice that such a good gift has fallen to modern woman as the safety bicycle. (Priestley 1895, np)[5]

If Priestley is truly a feminist, and a suffragist, *The Love Stories of Some Eminent Women* (1906) is a title that would seem to herald a retreat from those beliefs. However, in her introduction, she clearly anticipated that reaction and tackles the misapprehension head on: "There is no occasion, we believe, to put forth any apology for the subject matter of these sketches" (vii). Her intention is "to brush away some of the misconceptions," to get near to the inner personal life, and to show dignity in the subjects (vii–x). Displaying courage, integrity and talent in diverse ways, the eight women featured are: Madame Roland of French Revolution fame; poets Elizabeth Barrett Browning and Christina Rossetti; writers Charlotte Brontë and George Eliot; Lady Henry Lawrence (wife of a British official in India); writer and humanitarian Isabel Arundell (Lady Burton); and actress Mrs Siddons. L. A. M. Priestley provides a brief account of their lives, and the qualities that might be deemed important in each woman are extolled in a manner redolent of a Victorian pulpit, even as those same women's lives are obviously remote from Victorian prescription.

In describing these women's lives, Priestley employs a somewhat pious,

---

4   While Henry Joy was a United Irishman, George was, for at least some of his life, a committed Unionist.

5   I am indebted to Dr Brian Griffin, Bath Spa University, who identified the source of this reference for me.

reverential tone that is simultaneously and effectively subverted by her examples: Madame Roland's political skill is admired, while her dalliances with other men are presented in a seductively acceptable way for the readers; against the backdrop of social exigencies, several are portrayed as sharing the ability to disregard family and public disapproval, daring to embark on travel and adventures that were far from usual in the first half of the nineteenth century. Mrs Siddons (Sarah Kemble) is acclaimed for her talent and achievements, and the difficulties of her working-woman's life are noted most sympathetically:

> a hard working woman, toiling steadily and persistently to provide for her home and children, studying, rehearsing, travelling, acting, and bearing in the midst of all this strenuous toil, the cares and anxieties inevitably associated with motherhood. (Priestley 1906, 286–87)

The focus on George Eliot allows acknowledgement of her unmarried relationship with George Henry Lewes while the way in which difficulties in Lewes' own marriage are mentioned, strongly suggests sympathy with both George Eliot and George Henry. Their partnership is silently acknowledged as a marriage when the text refers to Eliot's later union with Mr Cross as "her second marriage." Priestley goes further in her verdict on the Eliot/Lewes household: "the union of George Eliot and George Henry Lewes possessed every essential of a true and profoundly happy marriage" (Priestley 1906, 151). In the period 1906–7, renewed contemporary interest in George Eliot meant that Priestley's book received widespread comment in Ireland, Britain and further afield. Priestley's own attraction to the figure of Eliot was reflected in the name of her town house, "Middlemarch," on the Lisburn Road, Belfast, where she lived part of the time between 1913 and 1915. Readers are not instructed to follow any particular example, but they are assisted to recognise the flaws of convention and are imperceptibly drawn nearer to the side of licence to be different. As Priestley muses a little on the nature of any marital relationship, she sees the need for fine balance, and she matter-of-factly says, "The wife who discovers her husband a noodle has made an awful mistake" (Priestley 1906, 294). That directness would be increasingly visible in her subsequent journalism. For the eminent women in her study, Priestley has managed to show their power, their determination, and their considerable achievements. Strikingly, she has succeeded in doing so while maintaining a register that has a strong Victorian and biblical aura, even as she discreetly paints the possibility of flouting strict laws and makes it seem feasible, attractive, justifiable, and even necessary to do so.

Suffrage Days

During the twelve years between those love stories and *The Feminine in Fiction* (1918a), Elizabeth Priestley's articles frequently focused on the issue of votes for women and on the related concerns of justice and education for women at all levels in society. Her prose was commanding on the topic of women and on their position and opportunities, and several examples of it read well and powerfully today. She published important articles in the *Irish Citizen* and the *Vote*. Remarkably, her output also appeared in places that would seem unlikely to be sympathetic to her concerns about the status of women—notably in *The Irish Presbyterian* and in the theosophist journal, *The Herald of the Star*. But, as a working journalist, unattached to any paper, ambition ensured that her name is also to be found under articles in such publications as *St Andrew's Citizen* (Fife, Scotland), *Kilburn Times* (London), *Lake's Falmouth & Cornwall Advertiser, Rugby Advertiser, Exeter and Plymouth Gazette,* and *Cornishman*. On closer examination, what she wrote in *The Irish Presbyterian*, while not overtly related to suffrage or to the so-called "woman issue," was certainly calculated to draw attention to matters that were her ongoing, woman-related interests. In the *Irish Citizen* and in her correspondence with Hanna Sheehy Skeffington, she is much more outspoken on suffrage and similar concerns. Writing to Sheehy Skeffington in 1915, she mentions publication of her article "Mothers: How Society Treats Them" in *The Irish Presbyterian*, explains the nature of the publication and how she "got in":

> It is *par excellence* a denominational journal with the biased and rather prejudiced views of the exclusively church and religious paper. It has however a wide circulation being our one magazine of a literary sort, and is read among the typical old-fashioned country 'true blue' Presbyterians to which the very name 'suffrage' is suspicious and alarming. It argues for the broad-mindedness of the Editor Rev D.V Knox that when he wrote asking me to contribute an article and I suggested this one, he expressed his pleasure, and his approval of the subject. Both he and his wife I understand are sympathetic to the movement. But I can imagine the surprise with which Presbyterian Elders etc will read it! I hope it will be a salutary reminder to them that the present position of women is a disgrace to the principles they profess! (Unpublished letter to Hanna Sheehy Skeffington, 9 November 1915b)

This extract indicates how Priestley thought, wrote, and operated—reminiscent of the Shakespearean "cite Scripture for his purpose" and moreover pronounced "with a smiling cheek" (*The Merchant of Venice*, I. iii. 93–95, 27).

Lively contributions to *The Vote, Irish Citizen* and *Votes for Women*, between 1911 and 1919, ranged through the topics of the vote, care for children, the status of mothers and wife-beating (Priestley 1919a, 387–90; 1919b, 52; 1920, 26). Priestley's analyses are sharp and often caustic. She was presciently distrustful of Carson's promise of votes for women,[6] searing and scathing of

6   It was clear by late 1914 that the 1913 understanding or commitment by the Unionist party to implement votes for women (in the provisional government for

women who advocated supporting their men instead of looking for votes for themselves, cool and detached when assessing progress or the lack of it. In "Unionist Women," she labels the women "voteless drudges," deploring those party women who eschew the vital suffrage cause but would work gratuitously for a powerful political party, "for a seat on platform or committee with some titled or distinguished person" (Priestley 1913d, 113). Her article entitled "In Ulster Today" captures much of the prevailing political and social debate.[7] Maintaining that in fighting grimly to maintain the rights of British citizenship, Ulster was playing the role of the suffragette, Priestley claims all the arguments were identical with those of the Suffragettes:

> 'We shall fight against an intolerable tyranny,' says Ulster. So say the Suffragettes. 'We shall not be governed without our consent,' says Ulster. So say the Suffragettes. 'The blame of our rebellion lies with the government that refuses to redress our grievances,' says Ulster. So say the Suffragettes. (Priestley 1913b, 28)

However, Priestley notes the absence of logical equivalence: when Ulster is commended for her spirit and patriotism, militant women are condemned for their action.

During recent commemorations of the suffrage movement, Elizabeth Priestley has been referred to as a militant suffragist.[8] This is not unexpected for one who was a self-declared "Unenfranchised" journalist, but her militancy for suffrage undoubtedly increased—as her allegiance and that of George McCracken to Unionism was withheld—when Edward Carson reneged on the promised votes for women.[9] There was no mistaking the militancy in Elizabeth Priestley's "In Memoriam" tribute following Emily Davison's death in her suffrage protest at the Derby in 1913: "let it be well understood that she died for the sake of others" (Priestley 1913a, 42). It was a brave and controversial statement at that turbulent time.

Ulster) was not to be honoured. See Urquhart (2000, 7–35).

7   The divisions between Ulster suffrage enthusiasts mirrored the dissonances further south in Ireland between those who prioritised suffrage and those who placed it behind other political considerations. See Urquhart (2002, 273–92).

8   In twenty-first century publications, rather unexpectedly for writings concerned with women's battles for suffrage, her surname is frequently given as McCracken rather than Priestley. This is despite the name Priestley appearing in *Irish Citizen*, *The Vote*, and *The Herald of the Star*, even if sometimes followed by the 'explanatory' (Mrs Geo McCracken). In *Women in Ulster Politics* 1890–1940, Diane Urquhart refers to her as "Mrs L.A.M.P. McCracken" and as "McCracken" but not as Priestley (2000: 26). Margaret Ward has "Elizabeth Priestly (sic) McCracken" (Ward 2015, 35) but the index entry is correct in form and spelling as Priestley McCracken, rather than McCracken. Louise Ryan has "McCracken, Elizabeth Priestley" in her index (Ryan 2018).

9   As Urquhart claims, "Carson's betrayal of suffragists tarnished all unionists" (2000, 35).

Priestley collected several of her *Irish Citizen* articles in pamphlet form with the hope of reaching a wider readership than those who bought the paper. Modestly priced at only one penny, it probably sold well to a broad suffrage community, being advertised in their journals in Britain and Ireland. However, on publication, the pamphlet *First Causes* received a chilly reception in some quarters, for example: "the author sees her own side of the case clearly enough" ("First Causes" 1914, 5). Her lucidity made challenging reading for some. Noting changes that moved remunerative work from the fields and from the home, Priestley outlined some conditions and laws adversely affecting any woman who is then "handicapped by her sex, by man-made legislation, by masculine jealousy" (*First Causes* 1914a, 5). She deplored their economic dependence that made men "put a premium upon woman's sex value, in contradistinction to her value as a human being" (6). She railed against refusal of the vote to highly-qualified and educated women, thereby ranking them below "the meanest male degenerate" (9); she fumed over their exclusion from equal pay, lucrative and influential positions, and careers. The "galling ingratitude with which mankind in general requites womankind in general for services rendered" meant that "Woman is the house-servant of the world" (9). If asserting woman's place is the home means that "she is a necessary concomitant to the home as a perpetual unpaid drudge, why not state so?" (9). Priestley tackled domestic drudgery in "Co-operative Housekeeping," suggesting that housekeeping was wasteful, unsatisfactory and "inimical to the health and temper of the housekeeper" (Priestley 1915a, 130). Whether with tongue in cheek, or with serious ambition for revolutionary change, she advocated a co-operative approach to bulk purchasing by householders in a typical street of about twenty houses.

The Priestley/McCracken partnership in pursuit of women's rights was dynamic, unified and multi-faceted. Both were involved in charities to aid children,[10] and in campaigns to improve the legal position of women and children, topics pursued in Priestley's writings over many years. In a comprehensive article in 1917, she listed glaring deficiencies: the married mother not being the legal guardian of her child, with all the power and choice of home, religion, education etc being vested in the father; the inability of a mother in Ireland to sue for maintenance; absence of inheritance or family rights of illegitimate children who would be subject to a higher inheritance tax if favoured in a will; the law of seduction which only permitted an action by parent or employer of a seduced girl for "loss of service," but no action by her for damages on account of physical, mental or social injury (Priestley 1917, 376–78). In 1919, she again highlighted a lamentable lack of legal protection:

---

10   Both were involved in setting up the Ulster Children's Aid Society in Bangor ("Saving the Young" 1911, 6). They also worked for the rescue centre in Belfast (*Herald of the Star* 1919a, 387–90).

"Until some adequate protective laws are made and stringently enforced for little girl-children, our social system is appallingly pagan and wrong" (Priestley 1919a, 387–90). At a public meeting of the Irish Women's Suffrage Society in December 1913, George McCracken gave a lecture on "The Legal Aspects of Women's Suffrage" (*Northern Whig* 1913, 9). When Emmeline Pankhurst spoke at the Ulster Hall on 12 March 1914, George McCracken chaired the meeting (*The Suffragette* 1914, 477). He was the solicitor, or maintained a watching brief, for women hauled before the courts on charges relating to suffrage protests in 1914, notably for Lilian Metge (1871–1954), Dorothy Evans (1888–1944) and Madge Muir, the alias of Florence McFarlane (dates not known). In court for the Dorothy Evans case in July 1914, he protested against the exclusion of women from the court and he gained admission for two women journalists—one of whom was most probably his own wife (*Weekly Telegraph/Larne Times*, 1914, 9). In 1915, at the Bangor home of Priestley and McCracken, a presentation was made to Dorothy Evans by "her Belfast suffrage friends" ("Presentation to Miss D. Evans" 1915, 99) in tribute to how she had fought and suffered, and in thanks for what she had achieved, notably the appointment of a matron to the Police courts. Both George McCracken and John McCoubrey (the trade unionist husband of activist Margaret McCoubrey) were members of the Men's Political Union, the only all-male suffrage society in Ireland.[11] On occasion, the men provided physical protection for women suffragists, and Dorothy Evans acknowledged how they had encouraged women in their struggle ("Presentation" 1915, 99).

The Vote and the Future

In 1918, Priestley exulted: "The weapon of the Vote is now ours" but she warned against dangers, demanding that the new power should be directed towards "rebalancing in the scales of Justice the inequalities of life and liberties" (Priestley 1918b, 630–31). Much legislative change would be required. Priestley continued in her articles to foreground women's achievements, whether as solicitors, as ground-breaking novelists, or as sheriffs (*The Vote* 1923, 1–2; *The Vote* 1914c, 120–21 and 1933, 265–6; *The Vote* 1928, 1–2, 97–98). In *The Feminine in Fiction* (1918a), she documented the positive development of the woman character in novels, surveying depiction of female characters by, amongst others, Charlotte Brontë, George Gissing, Sarah Grand, Hall Caine, George Moore, Olive Schreiner, George Eliot, and George Meredith. Charlotte Despard's "Foreword" judges that Priestley demonstrated how the modern heroine and those of the mid-Victorian age are "altogether different persons" who might "belong to different races":

---

11   Although a militant socialist, and militant regarding suffrage, Margaret McCoubrey was a peace partisan when war broke out.

The vapours; the abundant tears; the sweet submission; the tacit acceptance of a subordinate role which marked the belauded woman of a past generation have gone. If these are allowed to fill any space in the modern canvas, it is that their futility may be seen. ... In such a woman as Evadne in Sarah Grand's daring novel *The Heavenly Twins* and as Lyndall in Olive Schreiner's haunting record *The Story of an African Farm* we see woman in revolt, one against the lies and conventions and deep-seated corruptions of Modern Society; the other against the moral and intellectual restrictions which surround the mind and soul of woman. (Despard 1918, 6)

Viewing fiction as the mirror of prevailing reality, Priestley is cheered by the stances of recent fictional heroines and lauds authors (including George Moore, Gertrude Atherton and Hall Caine) who allowed characters like Esther Waters (*Esther Waters*, 1894), the eponymous heroine of *Julia France and Her Times* (1912) and Gloria Quayle (*The Christian*, 1897) to stand and deliver in their battles for illegitimate children, suffrage, unmarried mothers, and equity at work.

L. A. M. Priestley Rediscovered

A self-identified Unionist and Presbyterian, one who viewed facets of Presbyterianism with a cool detachment and aspects of Unionism with disgust, L. A. M. Priestley defies facile or superficial stereotyping. As working journalist, as wife and as parent, she was always a proud County Down woman with a world view (Priestley 1929, 6).[12] However, it would have dismayed her that "The Story of Co. Down," a little booklet she wrote as a souvenir of the first road race in Ulster in 1928, was the literary production by which the *Belfast News-Letter* remembered her when she died ("Literary Circles" 1944, 3). For that paper, or any other, to describe her solely as Mrs George McCracken, who was popular in Bangor social circles, and was daughter of James Priestley, surely constituted an abhorrent and grossly reductionist insult to her memory. She had shown, in her considerable literary output, in her correspondence with Hanna Sheehy Skeffington, in her association and involvement with Ulster suffragists, and her contact with important novelists, that she was not to be imprisoned in archaic, conservative categorisations. Importantly, her writings map out many vital ingredients of an egalitarian future for humanity. With an abiding and strong concern for the status of women, both in the home and in the public sphere, she was undoubtedly the embodiment of an alternative history whose layers and components are multiple and interlaced, a story that must be retold.

---

12   Priestley's 1929 tribute to Dr Alexander Irvine reads as identification with their shared Co. Down heritage, and appreciation of his egalitarianism, non-sectarianism, courageous Christianity and resilience.

References

Primary Sources

Priestley, L. A. M. 1828. *The Story of County Down*. Belfast: Ulster Race Stands Syndicate. np.

——. 1895. "As Happy as Seven Kings." *To-Day's Woman*, 1 June 1895.

——. 1902. "Ruth." *The Irish Presbyterian*, December 1902: 735–36.

——. 1906. *The Love Stories of Some Eminent Women*. London: Henry J. Drane.

——. 1913a. "In Memoriam: Emily Wilding Davison B.A., Died 8th June 1913." *Irish Citizen*, 28 June 1913: 42 (from *Northern Whig*, 11 June).

——. 1913b. "In Ulster Today." *The Vote*, 14 November 1913: 28.

——. 1913c. "Presbyterians and Woman Suffrage." *Irish Citizen*, 28 June 1913: 47.

——. 1913d. "The Unionist Women." *Irish Citizen*, 3 August 1913: 113.

——. 1914a. *First Causes*. s.n.

——. 1914b. "Shall Suffrage Cease?" *Irish Citizen*, 29 August 1914: 117.

——. 1914c. "Women's Freedom: Foreshadowings in Fiction." *The Vote*, 12 June 1914: 120–21.

——. 1915a. "Co-operative Housekeeping." *Irish Citizen*, 16 October 1915: 130.

——. 1915b. Unpublished letter to Hanna Sheehy Skeffington, 9 November. Sheehy Skeffington Papers. National Library of Ireland, Ms 33,604SS.

——. 1917. "Motherhood Under the Law." *Herald of the Star*, July 1917: 376–78.

——. 1918a. *The Feminine in Fiction*. London: George Allen & Unwin.

——. 1918b. "Our New Power." *Irish Citizen*, November 1918: 630–31.

——. 1919a. "Rescue work in Belfast." *Herald of the Star*, 1 August 1919: 387–90.

——. 1919b. "Wife Beating." *Irish Citizen*, September 1919: 52.

——. 1920. "The Ill-treatment of Wives." *Herald of the Star*, January 1920: 26.

——. 1922. "A Distinguished Frenchwoman." *The Vote*, 29 September 1922: 305–6.

——. 1923. "The First Woman Solicitor in Ireland." *The Vote*, 15 June 1923: 185–86.

——. 1928. "Ireland's First Woman High Sheriff." *The Vote*, 30 March 1928: 97–8.

——. 1929. "Dr Irvine." *Cornishman*, 31 October 1929: 6.

——. 1933. "Madame Sarah Grand and Women's Emancipation." *The Vote*, 25 August 1933: 265–66.

Other Sources

Armour, Noel. 2004. "Isabella Tod and Liberal Unionism in Ulster, 1886–96." In *Irish Women's History,* edited by Alan Hayes and Diane Urquhart, 72–87. Dublin: Irish Academic Press.

Brooke, Peter. 1987. *Ulster Presbyterianism: the Historical Perspective.* Dublin; New York: Gill & Macmillan; St Martin's Press.

Despard, C. 1918. "Foreword" to *The Feminine in Fiction* by L. A. M. Priestley. 5–7. London: George Allen & Unwin.

Doak, Naomi. 2008. "Assessing an Absence: Ulster Protestant Women Authors, 1900–60." In *Irish Protestant Identities,* edited by Mervyn Busteed, Frank Neal and Jonathan Tonge, 126–37. Manchester: Manchester University Press.

"Dorothy Evans Case." 1914. *Weekly Telegraph/Larne Times*, 25 July 1914.

"First Causes." 1914. *Belfast News-Letter*, 9 July 1914.

"Irish Women's Suffrage Society." 1913. *Northern Whig*, 3 December 1913.

"Literary Circles."1944. *Belfast News-Letter*, 12 January 1944.

Peatling, Gary. 2006. "Whatever happened to Presbyterian radicalism? The Ulster Presbyterian Liberal Press in the Late Nineteenth Century." In *Politics and Power in Victorian Ireland*, edited by Roger Swift and Christine Kinealy, 155–65. Dublin: Four Courts.

"Presentation to Miss D. Evans." 1915. *Irish Citizen*, 18 September 1915.

"Programme of the Week." 1914. *The Suffragette*, 12 March 1914.

"Revolting Woman in the Novel." 1920. *Workers' Dreadnought*, October 1920.

Ryan, Louise. 2018. *Winning the Vote for Women: The Irish Citizen Newspaper and the Suffrage Movement in Ireland.* Dublin: Four Courts Press.

"Saving the Young." 1911. *Irish News and Belfast Morning News*, 17 June 1911.

Shakespeare, William. 1984. *The Merchant of Venice*. London: Methuen.

"The Love Stories of Some Eminent Women." 1906. *Belfast News*, Letter, 8 November 1906.

"The Policy of Suppression." 1902. *Irish News & Belfast Morning News*, 5 February 1902.

Urquhart, Diane. 2000. *Women in Ulster Politics 1890–1940: A History Not Yet Told.* Dublin: Irish Academic Press.

——. 2002. "'An Articulate and Definite Cry for Political Freedom': The Ulster Suffrage Movement." *Women's History Review* 11, no. 2: 273–92. https://doi.org/10.1080/09612020200200321

Walker, Graham. 1996. "Thomas Sinclair: Presbyterian Liberal Unionist." In *Unionism in Modern Ireland,* edited by Richard English and Graham Walker, 19–40. Dublin: Gill & Macmillan.

Ward, Margaret. 2015. "'A Voice in the Affairs of the Nation?' Debates and Dilemmas within First Wave Feminism in Ireland." In *Irish Feminisms: Past, Present and Future,* edited by Clara Fischer and Mary McAuliffe, 23–46. Dublin, Arlen House.

13

Education, Love, Loneliness, Philanthropy: Erminda Rentoul Esler

Patrick Maume

This essay outlines the little-known life and career of the Donegal novelist and short story writer Erminda Rentoul Esler (?1860–1924), hoping to increase understanding of the religious and social contexts with which she engaged, and to illuminate some of her characteristic preoccupations.[1] These include the contrast between face-to-face small-town commerce and society and a more impersonal, less trustworthy, urban world containing the dubious blessings of limited liability, stockbroking, and investment trusts; the isolation of the educated and socially elevated, for instance, tradesmen's daughters sent to genteel schools, or clergymen in remote parishes, and a suspicion that the God envisioned by orthodox Christian theology (especially Calvinism) is incompatible with the Gospels. It goes on to suggest that Esler's work shows dissatisfaction with the expectations of the magazine story, that this discontent is visible in asides and veiled references in the stories, and culminates in a rejection of romance for social reform.

Erminda Rentoul Esler has attracted limited critical attention but no definitive assessment. She has entries in several reference works (e.g. Blain, Clements, and Grundy 1990, 346: Loeber and Loeber 2006, 441–2), but these often replicate errors, describing her three-volume novel *The Way of Transgressors* (1890) as a short story collection or calling her short story collection *Youth at the Prow* (1898) a novel. Recent analyses (Kickham 2004; Foster 2008; Vance 2009; Walker 2009) focus on a few works, such as *The Maid of the Manse* (1895) with its depiction of Presbyterian life in mid-Victorian small-town Donegal; *The Wardlaws* (1896), about a Big House family in the aftermath of its financial downfall, and *The Trackless Way* (1903), a novel of religious doubt unusual in

---

1   This essay draws on research for the Royal Irish Academy's *Dictionary of Irish Biography* where a biographical entry on Erminda Rentoul Esler was published in 2019. I thank Derval Fitzgerald, Breandán Mac Suibhne and Gordon Lucy.

the context of Irish Presbyterianism (Foster 2008, 86–9).

Esler is routinely called a "kailyard" writer—a member of an Ulster offshoot of the Scottish literary school which depicted rural and small-town life, with nostalgic emphasis on small-town communitarianism and the displacement of Calvinism by a nebulous liberal Christianity emphasising empathy and social betterment (Vance 2009; Maume 2016). J. M. Barrie (1860–1937), "Ian McLaren" (Rev. John Watson, 1850–1907) and S. R. Crockett (1859–1914) were the principal Scottish kailyard writers, with the Scottish-born cleric, critic and editor William Robertson Nicoll as chief promoter through his *British Weekly* and ancillary publications (Darlow 1925). While some of Esler's themes, such as doctrinal conflict within Presbyterianism and the contrast between provincial society and a commercialised, financialised and untrustworthy urban modernity, are shared with kailyard writers, Esler in fact makes very little use of Ulster/Scottish dialect. Much of her writing has English provincial settings, and she was compared to English writers such as Mary Russell Mitford (*Our Village*, 1824–32) and Elizabeth Gaskell (*Cranford*, 1853). The English village of Grimpat recurs in her short stories, but is nowhere near as detailed as Hardy's Wessex or Shan Bullock's contemporary tales of rural Fermanagh (Maume 2004); there are no recurring characters, no "map" of Grimpat's layout and geographical location. While Esler's short stories often have rural or plebeian protagonists, her novels centre on individuals set apart from the community by education or ambiguous social status and hence are not communitarian in the kailyard style. Esler did contribute to nonconformist magazines, such as *Sunday at Home* (founded in 1854 by the Religious Tract Society) and *The Quiver* (founded in 1861) (Darlow 1925, 111n), though she came to detest the *British Weekly's* editor William Robertson Nicoll, as indicated by her savage caricature of him in her final novel, *The Trackless Way* (1903).

Erminda Rentoul was born in Newtowncunningham, between Letterkenny and Derry, in eastern Donegal, eldest daughter of the eight children of the Reverend Alexander Rentoul and Erminda Chittick. Her date of birth is uncertain; 1860 is usually given but she may have been born as early as 1852. Her father was minister of the Seceder congregation of Ray, Co. Donegal and served as Secession Moderator in 1840, just before the union of Seceders with the mainstream Presbyterian Synod of Ulster, when his congregation became Second Ray (with the former Synod of Ulster congregation as First Ray). His wife, Erminda Chittick, descended through her mother from an old gentry family called Squire, whose holdings were sold up by the Encumbered Estates Court on 31 May, 1854. Pedigrees of her parents' families, *Lineage of Gervaise Chittick* and *Lineage of James Alexander Rentoul*, were printed for private publication in 1890.[2] These emphasise her mother's claim to various aristocratic

---

2   These are written as by Erminda Rentoul and usually ascribed to Esler, but she usually published under her married name; they are dated "Cliftonville, Belfast, 1890"

lineages, while the treatment of her father focuses on his extensive work in famine relief and tenant right campaigning alongside his position as Orange County Grand Master of Donegal. According to the Rentoul pedigree, this did not affect his friendship with Catholic neighbours, who annually lent him a white horse for the Twelfth of July parade (see Lockington 2016, 10–14). Those familiar with Esler's novels may see echoes of these pedigrees in the sardonic account of the aristocratic Norman descent of the Wardlaws (who have reduced themselves to genteel poverty through generations of fecklessness, generosity and extravagance resembling that of Maria Edgeworth's Rackrents) and in the portrayal in *The Maid of the Manse* of a Presbyterian minister who has married a wife from an old and impoverished Church of Ireland family; despite nominal conversion to Presbyterianism the wife privately feels the local Catholic priest is superior to her husband because he was ordained by a bishop. Both novels present an undue concern with pedigree as a dangerous distraction from present-day work and relationships.

Esler's writing would frequently draw on aspects of her family's lives. Her eldest brother James Alexander Rentoul (1845–1919) was in his first year of university study when his father died suddenly in 1864, and his father's congregation loyally refused to select a permanent replacement until the younger Rentoul could be ordained in 1871. In Esler's *The Maid of the Manse* a student son, returning from college, reads of his minister father's death in a hotel newspaper and is met by a delegation offering to hold the ministerial position open for him, replicating J. A. Rentoul's experience (Rentoul 1921, 14, 46–7, 90; Lockington 2016, 16–17), except for the fact that the son in the novel refuses because of religious doubts.

After giving his younger siblings the best education possible, James Alexander moved to London in 1881, ministering in Greenwich before becoming a barrister, Unionist MP for East Down (1890–1902) and finally a London judge. His *Stray Thoughts and Memories* (1921) does not mention his sister but illuminates many plot details in her work. For example, he recalls a newly ordained Rome-educated priest, Fr. Sweeny, who was assigned to Manorcunningham and had to adjust to these remote surroundings (J. A. Rentoul 1921, 99). Such a priest features in *The Wardlaws*, and, without the memoir, might be seen as an unlikely invention.

Erminda Esler's education included periods in Berlin and Nîmes.[3] She graduated from Queen's College Belfast in 1879, and may have taught in the suburban school run by two of her unmarried sisters until, in 1883, she married the prominent Belfast doctor and advocate of women in the professions,

---

though Esler moved to London in 1889. They may be the work of her mother, also Erminda.

3   A character in *The Trackless Way* is suspected of crypto-Catholicism after attending a French convent school, which may reflect Esler's own experience.

Robert Esler (1836–1919), a widower. Aspects of the self-made Robert Esler's life would also feed aspects of his second wife's fiction: having worked as a draper's assistant before emigrating to the Australian goldfields, he subsequently became successful in business and financed his own medical education. Robert Esler was a leading member of the Ulster Medical Society, writing its history and serving as its president in 1888. In 1889 the Eslers moved to London, where Robert became a police surgeon (Clarke 2014, 40). His son by his first marriage was also a doctor in Australia; he and Erminda produced another two doctor sons. Erminda Esler's novels feature hardworking drapers' assistants who recover from disappointed love, immigrants who make money shopkeeping in goldfields (both in *The Way of Transgressors*) and older professional men who remarry despite appearing faintly ridiculous (*Helena Thorpe* and *The Trackless Way*).

Although none of Erminda Esler's novels are set in Belfast, a sub-plot in *The Way of Transgressors* suggests a hostile view of the city. The heroine's father is a grocer in the provincial village of Highfields, near "Fordmouth" (Belfast's Irish name *Béal Feirste* reflects its location on a ford near the mouth of the River Farset):

> Fordmouth was a manufacturing town; it fabricated cloth of a kind that was in request over half the world; it also built ships for trade purposes sound enough to be utilised as men-of-war, and it had a variety of other very successful industries … What it did not possess was a picture-gallery, a public library, or any institution whatever devoted to art or literature. … Fordmouth … liked big houses, big ware-rooms, big banks, big factories, and big churches; it fostered a school of scientific drawing, and gave prizes for the best designs for business premises, because all this served either for the acquisition or display of wealth. To be the richest man in Fordmouth was to be the greatest man …
>
> To say that the greatest scoundrels were the most successful is but to imply that merit met with deserved reward at Fordmouth as elsewhere. No doubt a fairly honest man now and then did fairly well … the type did not commonise itself by abundance. (Esler 1890, vol. 2, 43–5)

A wealthy grocer from Fordmouth ruins the heroine's family by selling her father shares in a building society for an apparently nominal sum, thereby exposing him to unlimited liability for about-to-be-revealed defalcations. Esler was clearly drawing on accounts of high-profile building society frauds in late-Victorian England, which provoked comment on declining business ethics. The swindler in turn confirms his immunity by transforming his own business into a limited liability company owned by his children. Esler suggests that blatantly successful dishonesty is admired in Fordmouth and, by implication, in Belfast: "To get rid of his liabilities just six weeks before the company collapsed, after having drawn his dividends therefrom for half-a-score of years—why, it was perfectly splendid, and gave Mr Dosset a place in public esteem he had never held before" (Esler 1890, vol. 2, 61).

Esler began her literary career in 1888 with a tale published by the Society for the Propagation of Christian Knowledge, *Almost a Pauper*. During the 1890s she broke into the magazine market, publishing not only in nonconformist magazines and the *Women's Signal* but in mainstream outlets such as *Chambers' Journal* and the *Cornhill Magazine*. She was correspondence editor of the monthly *The Young Woman* (founded and edited by the clergyman Frederick Atkins) contributing a "Monthly Chat" from its foundation in November 1892 and by 1894 adding a regular column "Between Ourselves," which advocated intellectual and material self-sufficiency in women, and gave a qualified welcome to the New Woman while defending sexual purity (Moruzi 2012, 146–8; 158–9). She produced three story collections in the 1890s: *The Way They Loved at Grimpat* (1894), *'Mid Green Pastures* (1895), and *Youth at the Prow* (1898). These combine an idyllic-pastoral sense of the land as generous provider of life with a sense of virtue recompensed only late and painfully.

In 1890 Esler had also published a three-volume novel, *The Way of Transgressors*, already serialised in an unidentified magazine. Comparison of this novel with its four successors suggests how Esler adapted to changing literary markets. *Way* is clearly a full-length novel plotted in three movements (closely but not entirely coinciding with the three volumes). In the first "movement," Malvina ("Viney") Grace, eldest daughter of a provincial grocer, returns from a high-class boarding school to find herself out of touch with her family and surroundings, while the local upper classes see her as beneath them. When a schoolfriend, Nellie Hayes, visits with her prospective fiancé Bertie Lyall (encouraged to marry Nellie by his wealthy aunt Lady Mildred Hayes), Bertie and Viney fall in love, but after pledging himself to Viney Bertie subsequently discards her.

In the second "movement," Viney's family are ruined and go to London, where Viney works in a shop, while Bertie pursues fame and wealth by deserting his ancestral Conservatism to become a Radical MP, leaving the Bar to become a solicitor. Reluctance to defer gratification leads him to embezzlement and bigamous marriage with Estelle, a naïve young French girl physically resembling Viney; they have a son. In the third "movement," Mr Grace's Cousin Sam returns from America with a small fortune, part of which he invests with Bertie for Viney. Bertie forges a mortgage, intending to abscond with Estelle; Cousin Sam discovers the fraud and forces Bertie to repay him, after which Bertie dies in an accident. Lady Mildred repays his thefts through the only honest solicitor in Fordmouth, adopts his child after Estelle dies, and recruits Viney as her companion, while the Graces are restored to prosperity. The initial magazine version of *The Way of Transgressors* suggested that Viney might marry a saintly clergyman, but a postscript in the book states that she never married, suggesting a view held by some other Victorian writers, notably Anthony Trollope, that a woman having once committed herself to a man is precluded from committing herself again, even if jilted. However, Esler's later novel *The Awakening of Helena Thorpe* (1901) rejects this view.

Futhermore, the complex structure of a three-volume novel allows subversive subtexts which are not always so obvious in the main thrust of the plotting. Nellie and Estelle are conventionally feminine *Döppelgangers* of Viney, and their fates (Nellie, kept ignorant of Bertie's betrayal, blames herself for his death) suggest that a hard-working, self-supporting woman is better both for herself and for her spouse than the conventional behaviour expected of the Victorian Angel in the House. Viney tells Bertie that though they would have faced reduced circumstances, she believes her strength and hard work would have helped him to success; Bertie later believes she was correct. This view is reinforced by Viney's younger sister, whose reflections on her family's ruin contrast the praise for the victim with the profits of the swindler, and who frankly hates Bertie while Viney remains ambivalent. She translates her educated eye and strong will into employment with a fashionable firm of household decorators, becoming the proprietor's wife and working partner. Viney's sister has little effect on the main plot; her function is to reinforce Esler's emphasis on clear thinking and self-reliance.

Esler's next two novels combine an overarching plot with chapters which could be stand-alone sketches, suggesting deliberate imitation of kailyard works such as Barrie's *A Window in Thrums* (1889) and *Auld Licht Idylls* (1888). Both her novels explore the isolation of the rural clergyman. In *The Maid of the Manse*, subplots involving successful and unsuccessful courtships of Presbyterian ministers overlap with the plight of Reverend Walter Hamilton, the older and more doctrinally conservative of two ministers with neighbouring congregations. His flock expect advice and sympathy while taking him for granted; his ex-Anglican wife does not fully respect him; he turns down a call to a prestigious Scottish pulpit because he does not want to desert his people, infuriating his wife while his congregants remain apathetic. In a crowning humiliation, his eldest son, studying for the ministry, rejects the Calvinism of the Westminster Confession of Faith (the 1646 doctrinal statement imposed as a condition for ministerial ordination by the Synod of Ulster in 1836). Although Esler attributes the father's orthodoxy to age and isolation, (she suggests younger ministers only subscribe to the Confession with mental reservations, and the most honest refuse), she does not portray the "old light" as moronic or dishonest, and invites the reader's personal sympathy for him.

In *The Wardlaws* (1896), this analysis of loneliness among the clergy extends to representatives of the two other principal denominations in Ireland. The first half of the novel concerns the efforts of Margery Wardlaw to support herself and her younger half-brother John after their father's death. By opening a shop she gains financial independence and self-respect, but loses her chance of marriage. The local Church of Ireland clergyman, William L'Estrange, loosely based on the Anglican theologian William Archer Butler (c.1814–1848) who served in the same area of Donegal (Lunney 2009, vol. 2, 190; Darlow 1925, 245), is a convert from Catholicism disowned by his family; his theological abilities only receive recognition after his death.

Margery is his only local friend, but he cannot bring himself to propose to a shopkeeper. Another potential friend—Fr. Fletcher, the lonely, educated Catholic priest—tells L'Estrange that the deepest spot in Hell is reserved for Judas and Luther, and that he cannot befriend Luther's imitator. This objection is to apostasy rather than Protestantism; Esler emphasises that Fletcher is haunted by fear that he sinned against Christian charity and tries unsuccessfully to visit the dying L'Estrange as he is nursed by Margery. Fletcher in turn befriends Padeen, the orphaned nephew of local small farmers, and offers to train him as an altar server and pay for his education in the hope he will become a priest, although it is not certain Padeen was born in wedlock; illegitimacy precluded ordination. The local chapel is built over a running stream, since no landlord would give a site; it floods during Mass.[4] Fr. Fletcher and Padeen hold the chapel doors open against the rising current as long as possible to help the congregation escape; Padeen is drowned, and the priest mourns him as the son he will never have. Esler's originals cannot be equated unproblematically with the characters whom they inspired. William Archer Butler, the real-life counterpart of L'Estrange, in fact received wide recognition in his lifetime and when he died in 1848 of typhoid caught from famine victims, he was engaged to the hymn-writer Cecil Frances Humphreys (later Alexander), while the priest recalled in J. A. Rentoul's memoirs was not Butler's contemporary. What is impressive, however, is Esler's empathy for rival clerics of different religious sects, without denying their sincerity or their blindnesses.

The second half of *The Wardlaws* moves to England, where the adult John Wardlaw is a stockbroker. He is tormented by knowledge that his business rests on speculation rather than productive investment, while his wife and adolescent children spend more than the business can sustain. Even his most sensible child, Margaret, fails to grasp his hints; he commits suicide while the business is solvent, shocking his family into self-reliance. Margaret, who alone realises the nature of her father's death, marries her father's partner who transfers his capital to productive use in a textile factory. Suicide, and the orthodox view that it entails eternal damnation, is one of Esler's preoccupations. The relatives of Bertie Lyell in *The Way of Transgressors* are tormented by belief that he committed suicide, and the most searing chapter in *A Maid of the Manse* describes the despair of a farmer whose brother is squandering the family's possessions on

---

4   This is based on a flood at Derrybeg Chapel, Gweedore, in 1880 (*Spectator*, 21 August 1880, 3).

drink and debauchery, while dependent siblings keep the industrious brother from starting afresh. He drowns himself in a flax-dam, leaving Rev. Hamilton tormented by his inability to console him.[5]

Esler's last two novels are compact single volumes centred on a single plot. *The Awakening of Helena Thorpe* (1901) critiques the Trollopean view that a woman's first deep attachment should be her last, as expressed in Trollope's (posthumous) 1884 novel, *An Old Man's Love*, which assumes that a first love returning after years of absence to find his former inamorata engaged to an older man has an unquestionable claim to marry her. Tom Seymour has formed an attachment to Helena Thorpe, eldest daughter of a provincial doctor, which Seymour considers an engagement; both are in their late teens. Richard Dean, a 49-year-old self-made Liverpool merchant, sells his business to an investment trust and builds a mansion in the village where he lived as a poor boy. He falls in love with Helena; she accepts him, though unsure whether she loves him. Seymour confronts Dean; Dean acquiesces and leaves without seeing Helena. Dean travels in Europe, and in a moment of intertextuality, Esler depicts him critiquing the treatment of a theme resembling his own predicament in two well-known Victorian novels, George Eliot's *Middlemarch* (1871–2) and Rhoda Broughton's *Belinda* (1882):

> The heroine was intended to be a real, genuine heroine, yet … all his pity was for Professor Forth. Twice wooed by girls of the same family, twice won by them, twice despised … And Mr Casaubon, the creation of a stronger hand, what had he done but follow the will-o'-the-wisp of a promised affection? … pilloried in a book for all time, his physical defects indicated with cruel glee, his mental limitations depicted as intentional fraud! … Ladislaw did not strike him as much worthier of Dorothea, except for that accident of youth. (Esler 1901, 240–1)

Helena and Seymour realise they do not love each other; she trains as a nurse. Dean uses his capital and managerial skills to create a large philanthropic organisation. Finally, Helena and Dean reunite and marry.

The turning from the romantic-aesthetic to the ethical is confirmed in Esler's last novel, *The Trackless Way: the Story of a Man's Quest of God*. Gideon Horville, a middle-aged Presbyterian minister in rural Ulster, has remained unmarried after being jilted for a rich rival. In ruined Tomintoul Castle, symbolising the moral failure of the aristocracy, he prays over a child's dead bird, arousing suspicions of heterodoxy. Horville befriends an elderly stonebreaker, Black, who has written a manuscript arguing the Gospel has become overlaid with

---

5   On 1 July 1892 Esler's mother drowned after falling into a reservoir at the Belfast waterworks at Cliftonville. (*Evening Herald* 2 July 1892, *Cork Examiner* 4 July 1892, *Irish Times* 9 July 1892.) Her death was ruled accidental; might Esler have suspected it was suicide?

ecclesiastical crotchets and a new Reformation is needed. On a seaside holiday Gideon meets Lilias Venner, daughter of a Dublin KC, an interlude into which Esler inserts her opinion of a thinly disguised Emily Lawless:

> Lilias had come to Knockboy because she had read of it. It was at Knockboy that Miss Eleanor Lanton, who might have been a supreme literary artist had not the soft touch of easy things relaxed those muscles of steel that are needed for the ascent of the remote, cold, solitary peak where genius sits, had cut one of her literary cameos, and Lilias wanted to see where Lanty and Hamish had lived their brief tragedy.[6] (Esler 1903, 82)

Lilias and Horville marry, initially bonding over shared dissatisfaction with religious orthodoxy. When she is deterred from communion by a hellfire sermon, they agree that communion is a simple expression of fellowship and he communicates her at the breakfast table using bread and water. Lilias grows ill at ease in provincial Ulster and after Gideon's widowed former fiancée builds him a congregational hall, leaves to seek artistic training, while Gideon is accused of heresy for opening the hall on Sundays and questioning the value of foreign missions. At his trial, Horville denounces substitutionary atonement—the belief that Jesus died to expiate the punishment required by God for human sin—by claiming that the death of Jesus was not God's plan and utters other heterodoxies. Amid hysterical accusations reminiscent of the trial of Jesus before the Sanhedrin, Horville is defrocked. Heresy trials were a Presbyterian preoccupation after the 1878 condemnation of the Biblical scholar William Robertson Smith by the Free Church of Scotland; Esler sides with those who argued such trials violated the principle of private religious judgment.

After communing with God, Horville seeks employment in London, encountering Reverend Wendover Wright, editor of the *Christian Chronicle*. The satanic Wright's name suggests the fraudster Whitaker Wright (1846–1904), whose business empire collapsed in 1900; however, he is also a savage caricature of William Robertson Nicoll, the Church of Scotland cleric, critic and editor who promoted the kailyard authors. Esler accuses Wright/Nicoll of encouraging heterodox writers to provoke controversies to sell his papers while carefully staying within the boundaries of orthodoxy himself, then dropping them when they no longer sell (Darlow 1925, 333). Wright offers to make Horville as successful as his protégé "Mountford," whose rise from obscurity to fame and fortune under Wright's tutelage recalls Nicoll's patronage of J.

---

6   Eleanor Lanton (note the initials) is based on the poet and novelist Emily Lawless (1845–1913) whose best-known novels are set in wild, remote seacoast areas mirroring a central character's alienation (e.g. *Grania: The Story of an Island*, 1892). The character name "Hamish" suggests *Hurrish*, her 1886 novel whose central character is a peace-loving tenant farmer destroyed by communal violence during the Land War. Lawless, like Lanton, was financially independent, allowing her to publish at her own pace.

M. Barrie. Using high-minded rhetoric, Wright covertly appeals to Horville's resentment and ambition, echoing Satan's temptation of Jesus in the wilderness. Wright wants Horville to write a book to be excerpted in the *Chronicle*: "The book will probably sell seven or eight thousand copies, owing to the controversy. He will be dead before that is over, and then we shan't have to pay for the book" (Esler 1903, 401):

> God saw [in Wright's office]—that the dirty floor was strewn thick with broken hearts and hopes, that each corner was piled with dead men's bones … Oh, Horville, Horville … a man who has gained a little bit of the world, and has lost his own soul, is speaking to you … cry to your God that He will deliver you! (Esler 1903, 399)

Horville is saved when Lilias, who has taken Horville's manuscript copy of Black's book, publishes it under Horville's name; Wright believes Horville has cheated him. Black reveals to Horville that he is the Earl of Tomintoul and employs him as land agent, and under his regime the tenants' insanitary cottages are replaced by a block of flats with shared kitchens and a communal dining area. The satisfied tenants offer to rebuild the castle, but Tomintoul refuses: "a chieftain should live among his people" (Esler 1903, 465).

The emphasis on personal aristocratic leadership and shared dining would suggest Esler was influenced by Standish James O'Grady, even in the absence of other evidence.[7] *The Trackless Way* was favourably reviewed in O'Grady's *All Ireland Review*, which later published a letter from Esler praising the *Review*, declaring:

> the Celtic mind accepts readily the mental and spiritual partnership of women. That race is best fitted to endure, and to revive, when defeated or cast down, which recognises how all existence, physical and spiritual, has a dual origin, and that the two sources are equal.

and advocating a guild society where each trade would have its own picturesque dress (Esler 1906, 546–7).

The Trackless Way resembles *The Way of Transgressors* in presenting different models of womanhood, but ultimately finds them wanting beside its male Messiah. Horville's maiden aunt and housekeeper is commonsensical but limited, while Lilias' former governess-companion, a French Catholic, who marries Lilias's widowed father and produces a son, receives some sympathy, but her absorption in her child indicates for Esler a lower nature content with animal satisfaction. Horville's ex-fiancée is a repentant Judas, and Lilias is a (chaste) Magdalen whose well-meaning interventions bring only trouble. Ultimately,

---

7   For these features of O'Grady's thought, compare Standish James O'Grady *Toryism and the Tory Democracy* (Dublin, 1886).

her artistic ambitions are futile; Black/Tomintoul, a childless widower, tells her celibacy is spiritually superior to marriage and she can only return to a *mariage blanc* of philanthropic labour.

In later life, Esler remained active in the Irish Circle of the Lyceum Club and the London-based Irish Literary Society, whom she lectured on literary topics. A lecture on Somerville and Ross, summarised in the *Irish Book Lover* in 1913, shrewdly identifies *The Real Charlotte* and *Naboth's Vineyard* as their masterpieces (Esler, 1913, 83–4). An *Irish Book Lover* obituary indicates that Esler died at her home in the South London suburb of Hither Green on 1 March 1924 (1924, 112).

In conclusion, this essay argues that Esler should not be seen as a purveyer of uncomplicated nostalgia (as stereotypically associated with the "kailyard" label), but as an acute social commentator pushing against the limitations of the magazine story format to include subversive expressions of her concerns about the development of commercial society, tensions within religious orthodoxies, the need for women's economic and intellectual self-reliance, and sharp comments on the shortcomings of some contemporary writers. Her career, particularly her participation in the London magazine world, merits further research.

References

Primary Texts

Esler, Erminda Rentoul. 1890. *The Way of Transgressors*. 3 vols. London: Sampson, Low & Co.

———. 1894. *The Way they Loved at Grimpat: Village Idylls*. London: Sampson, Low & Co.

———. 1895. *A Maid of the Manse*. London: Sampson, Low & Co.

———. 1896. *The Wardlaws*. London: Smith & Elder.

———. 1898. *Youth at the Prow*. London: J. Long.

———. 1901. *The Awakening of Helena Thorpe*. London: S.W. Partridge & Co.

———. 1903. *The Trackless Way: The Story of a Man's Quest of God*. London: R. Brimley Johnson.

———. 1906. Letter, *All Ireland Review* 17 March 1906, 546–47.

Other Sources

Blain, Virginia, Patricia Clements, and Isobel Grundy. 1990. *The Feminist Companion to Literature in English*. Yale: Yale University Press.

Clarke, Richard. 2014. "A Sextet of Contrasting Styles." *Ulster Medical Journal* 83, no. 1: 37–43.

Darlow, T. H. 1925. *William Robertson Nicoll: Life and Letters*. London: Hodder & Stoughton.

"Erminda Rentoul Esler." 1924. *Irish Book Lover* XIV, 7 & 8 (July–August):

112.

Foster, John Wilson. 2008. *Irish Novels 1890–1940: New Bearings in Culture and Fiction*. Oxford: Oxford University Press.

"Irish Literary Society." 1913. *Irish Book Lover* V, 5 (December 1913): 83–4.

Kickham, Lisbet. 2004. *Protestant Women Novelists and Irish Society 1879–1922*. Lund: Lund University Press.

Lockington, John W. 2016. *The Rentouls: A Presbyterian Ministerial Dynasty*. Belfast: Presbyterian Historical Society.

Loeber, Rolf and Magda Loeber. 2006. *A Guide to Irish Fiction, 1650–1900*. Dublin: Four Courts Press.

Lunney, Linde. 2009. "William Archer Butler." In *Dictionary of Irish Biography*, edited by James McGuire & James Quinn, vol. 2, 190. Cambridge: Cambridge University Press.

Maume, Patrick. 2004. "Shan Bullock's Perspectives on Nineteenth-Century Fermanagh." In *Fermanagh, History and Society: Interdisciplinary Essays on the History of an Irish County*, edited by Eileen M. Murphy and William Roulston, 459–77. Dublin: Irish Geography Publications.

——. 2012. "Lady Microbe and the Kailyard Viceroy: The Aberdeen Viceroyalty, Welfare Monarchy, and the Politics of Philanthropy." In *The Irish Lord Lieutenancy, c.1541–1922*, edited by Peter Gray and Olwen Purdue, 199–214. Dublin: Four Courts Press.

——. 2016. "Hubert Quinn, Liberal Protestantism, and Late Kailyard Culture in Mid-Twentieth Century Ulster." *Studia Hibernica* 42: 121–40.

Moruzi, Kristine. 2012. *Constructing Girlhood through the Periodical Press, 1850–1915*. Farnham, Surrey: Ashgate.

Rentoul, Erminda. 1890a. *A Record of the Family and Lineage of Gervaise Chittick*. Belfast: privately published.

——. 1890b. *A Record of the Family and Lineage of James Alexander Rentoul, LL.D, MP*. Belfast: privately published.

Rentoul, John Alexander, 1921. *Stray Thoughts and Memories*. London: Leonard Parsons.

Rentoul, Gervaise, 1940. *Sometimes I Think*. London: Hodder & Stoughton.

Vance, Norman. 2009. "'Kailyard' Stories in Ulster: Northern Fiction after Carleton." In *Revising Robert Burns and Ulster: Literature, Religion and Politics, c.1770–1920*, edited by Frank Ferguson and Andrew R Holmes, 148–64. Dublin: Four Courts Press.

Walker, Colin. 2009. "A Bibliography of Presbyterianism in Irish Fiction, 1780–1920." In *Revising Robert Burns and Ulster: Literature, Religion and Politics, c.1770–1920*, edited by Frank Ferguson and Andrew R. Holmes, 165–90. Dublin: Four Courts Press.

14

From Special Correspondence to Fiction: Veracity and Verisimilitude in Margaret Dixon McDougall's Writings on Ireland

Lindsay Janssen

If the agitation in Ireland were not a living issue, there would be little excuse for weaving these facts together by a slight web of fiction. I have taken imaginary characters to narrate real occurrences, and I have laid the scene in Donegal, because of my love for it. The incidents are taken from Ireland at large. (McDougall 1883, n. p.)

These lines open Margaret Dixon McDougall's Land War novel *The Days of a Life* (1883). In 1881, McDougall (1828–1899) was commissioned by the *Montreal Daily Witness* to travel to Ireland as a special correspondent and report on the famine and Land War of 1879–82.[1] Describing the Irish land question as a "burning question" which "[i]t behoves every man and every woman, having Irish blood in their veins, to look into," she used her writing to plead for the betterment of the lot of the poor tenants and labourers of Ireland (Preface). Her letters were published as "A Tour Through Ireland" and received positive acclaim, as evidenced by the letters' republication in other newspapers and by the fact that the collection *The Letters of "Norah" on her Tour Through Ireland* (1882), published through the offices of the *Witness*, was paid for by public subscription. As the epigraph indicates, McDougall also subsequently recast her letters into fiction.

The political developments in Ireland between the mid-nineteenth and early-twentieth centuries prompted extensive international newspaper coverage and many journalists were contracted by newspapers to travel to Ireland (Hooper 2001, 115). The period also witnessed a change in the public perception of

---

1   All issues of the *Witness* used in this essay were consulted through the website of the Bibliothèque et Archives Nationales du Québec (<http://numerique.banq.qc.ca/>) where they are freely accessible.

the journalist, as journalism became a newly respectable form of employment. Within this development the special correspondent, a journalist who travels to cover events firsthand, became a figure of high status (Griffiths 2015, 16, 21–22). Several special correspondents travelled through Ireland: examples include future Irish nationalist M.P. William O'Brien, Scottish-American journalist James Redpath, and Irish playwright J. M. Synge. Catherine Waters states that "special correspondents until late in the [nineteenth] century were mostly men" (2018, 102). This essay will use a rare case of female special correspondence as its departure point. McDougall's letters are fascinating as early works of literary journalism, but despite their merit, her work has only received limited attention.[2]

This essay has a dual focus. It discusses how McDougall, as an Irish-born special correspondent for a Canadian newspaper and a literary author, engaged with the hardships experienced by the Irish during the Land War. It also focuses on the effects of format and genre changes on the author's intention, starting from the original *Witness* letters and tracing their subsequent publication journey, following how the author moved from a relatively diverse style of journalism towards more conventional romantic fiction. While the original letters were dated and located, the collected letters were not, and, moreover, were reordered and altered. What do such changes do to McDougall's call for understanding and legislative change to better the lot of the Irish poor? And what happens to the historicity of the events described in the letters? This essay further investigates the tensions between non-fiction and fiction and demonstrates how McDougall's writing navigates the "reality boundary" (Sims 2009), which John Hartsock describes as the "space of complex and dynamic relationships," between narrative literary journalism and conventional fiction (2014, 2).

The *Montreal Witness* and McDougall's Take on the Irish Land Question

The Protestant *Montreal Witness* newspaper was published between 1845 and 1938 and its initial editor and proprietor was Scottish-born fervently Protestant evangelist and journalist John Dougall (1808–1886) (Snell 2003). By 1876, the *Witness* had "attained a high place among our Dominion newspapers" (Wood 1876, 14); according to J. G. Snell, the paper had a "sufficiently large circulation in the English-speaking areas around Montreal."[3] The *Witness* was

2   In my dissertation (Janssen 2016), I discuss McDougall's novel, *The Days of a Life*. In *A Happy Holiday* (2008), Cecilia Morgan devotes a chapter section to the collected letters.

3   The *Witness* provided circulation numbers: on 14 April, 1881 it stated that the daily circulation for 4–9 April had been between 12,520 and 13,100; the weekly number was 28,635 ("Circulation of THE WITNESS…"). In 1886, these numbers had

also read outside of the region, as indicated by the newspaper's inclusion of the U.S. and Britain in its subscription rates. Additionally, the list of public subscribers included in McDougall's collected *Letters* suggests a wider audience, as subscribers were also situated in St. Paul (present-day Alberta), Manitoba (Winnipeg), elsewhere in Ontario, in Paris (France) and Nebraska (U.S.) (McDougall 1882).

Although the newspaper's prospectus suggests that John Dougall aimed to make the *Witness* a pan-religious publication (15 December, 1845, 1), it was considered "aggressive and ... intolerant of Catholics, Irish and French Canadians" (Snell 2003), though this intolerance seems to have been based on religious rather than ethnic differences. The newspaper was perceived as so vehemently anti-Catholic that in 1850 it led to the publication of a Catholic counterpart, *The True Witness and Catholic Chronicle* (Snell 2003). Further, in 1875, when the paper was edited by Dougall's son John Redpath Dougall, the Bishop of Montreal, Ignace Bourget, placed an ecclesiastical ban on the paper ("The Montreal Witness"). The paper showed great interest in the condition of Ireland in the late 1870s and early 1880s, as articles concerning the Land War, the Land Law (Ireland) Act (1881) and famine featured on an almost daily basis. Moreover, the fact that McDougall's collected *Letters* were published "as a token of respect by the Irishmen of Canada" suggests that the *Witness* was read by Irish Canadians (McDougall 1882).

Margaret Dixon McDougall was born into a prosperous family in Belfast in 1828 and came to Canada with her family in her twenties. She was a schoolteacher, an author of fiction and non-fiction and wrote for various Canadian newspapers (Loeber, Loeber and Mullin Burnham 2004; "MacDougall [or McDougall], Margaret Dixon"). She left Canada on 27 January 1881 and spent most of the year in Ireland, travelling all around the island by train, boat, horse and car, and foot. Her letters were included in both the daily and weekly editions of the *Witness* and received a prominent place in the newspaper (typically the second page) throughout the year, suggesting that there was prolonged positive interest in her writings. Moreover, the newspaper included readers' correspondence which commended McDougall's writing. From these letters we also learn that although McDougall was not indicated by name in her byline, the audience did in fact know the identity of the author.[4]

McDougall's letters were written from a first-person perspective and were diverse in format and style, combining factual journalism, travel narrative, personal observations, socio-political commentary, and literary references.

---

risen to 14,265 and 39,134, respectively (Butcher 1886, 25). In that year, newspapers in Quebec had circulations varying from 400 at the lowest to 24,959 and 120,000, the latter numbers belonging to the daily and weekly *Montreal Family Herald and Star* (Butcher 1886, 24). There were but few other newspapers in the province that equalled or surpassed the *Witness,* suggesting that it had a sizeable circulation.

4   For example, "J. P. G." identifies McDougall in his letter (4 August, 1881).

While McDougall serves as our eyes and ears for most of the letters, she also, as is typical of literary journalism, uses "more than the journalist's single point of view" (Tulloch 2014, 630) by including many witnesses and informants. McDougall was affected by the scenes and accounts of suffering she encountered in Ireland and in her *Witness* letter of 12 April, 1881 she stated: "I am afraid from what I see and hear that the famine was more dreadful here in Donegal than we in Canada imagined."

In retrospect, McDougall acknowledged the "change which travelling through my native country has produced in my sentiments and the convictions forced upon me." She continues:

> Brought up in the North of Ireland in a purely Hiberno-Scotch neighbourhood, I drank in with my native air all the ideas which reign in that part of Ireland. The people with whom I came in contact were Conservatives of the strongest type; from my youth up, therefore, I had the cause of Ireland's poverty and misery as an article of belief. I never dreamed that the tenure of land had anything to do with it. Landlords were lords and leaders, benefactors and protectors to their tenants in my imagination.
>
> I changed my opinion while in Ireland, and now I believe that the land tenure is the main cause of Ireland's miseries. (1882, 297)

In her letters, McDougall showed herself favourable towards the Land League's goals and wrote that the Land League agitators only "gave voice to what is in the universal heart of the tenantry" (1882, 91). She spoke favourably of the intentions of future Irish Parliamentary Party leader Charles Stewart Parnell to improve the legislative and property rights of the tenantry, but did question the feasibility of his aim "at the entire abolition of landlordism"; she "could not help wondering how it could be done" (19 October, 1881).

Although her sympathies lay with the poor tenantry, McDougall strove to present a nuanced picture of the ruling classes, and took pity on men of the law who had to evict the poor as they were "under orders" to do "their odious duty" (1882, 67–68). She alternated between the outsider observations of a Canadian correspondent and identification with the Irish and wrote that she "felt quite at home with" the "Catholic people of the hills" of Donegal. She repeatedly referred to the Irish as "my people," which for her included all Irish, regardless of class and creed (12 April and 14 May, 1881). Through her experiences as a special correspondent, she came to affiliate herself with the Irish more broadly rather than just the Ulster Scots.

Disapproving of violent means but understanding of the underlying reasons, McDougall infrequently represented violent outbreaks in her journalistic and literary writing, and if she did do so, wrote of such instances concisely and in hindsight. For example, of boycotting she gave a few examples, stated that it had become "the order of the day" (1882, 284), but refrained from giving her opinion. She saw "the monopoly of all the land of a country in the hands of a few" as the most evil form of monopoly, and blamed "the system, not the men" for the current state of Ireland. She did not consider "the landlords of Ireland" as "naturally worse than other men," but felt that they had been given "too much power." Specifically, then, it was for her a rotten system which allowed a specific type of corruptible landlord to abuse his power. McDougall also opined that the law "was only for the rich," and functioned as an "engine of oppression" for the poor (1882, 297–98). Finally, McDougall appealed to the authorities in Ireland, "to try a little conciliation instead of such strong doses of coercion" (1882, 303).

McDougall's views align with those of influential figures such as the journalist James Godkin, who had stated earlier that the malevolent practices of greedy landlords were products of the long-existing "rottenness at the foundation of the social fabric" of the country (1870, 289). Moreover, her support of peasant proprietorship and her rejection of land monopoly connects McDougall to the convictions of men such as John Stuart Mill, James Fintan Lalor, Michael Davitt and Charles Stewart Parnell, who advocated the basic right that "the land should belong to those who inhabit it" (quoted in Lalor 1848, 9; Bull 2010, 137; Curtis 2011, 88–89).

From the "Tour" to the Collected *Letters*

In a letter to the editor, a reader suggested that McDougall's works should be combined into a single volume ("Justitia," 26 October, 1881); a year later, the collection was published. For the *Letters of "Norah,"* McDougall frequently adjusted formulations, made substantial changes in the chronology of events, and elided or added information. The letter included in the *Montreal Daily Witness* on 14 April, 1881 serves as an apt example of these changes and of the concomitant generalisation of information characteristic to McDougall's revision of the letters. Originally, it was titled:

> MORE ABOUT THE LATE LORD LEITRIM'S RULE—WHERE THE MONEY WENT TO—HOUSES OF THE POOR—THE GOOD RECTOR—THE LANDLORD'S PRIVILEGES AND DUTIES—THE "RINT"—SQUARING THE FARMS.

When it appeared as Chapter VIII in the *Letters of "Norah,"* it was called:

> THE HILL COUNTRY OF DONEGAL—ON THE SQUARE—OFFICE RULES. (1882, 36)

The contents of the letter were reordered. While Lord Leitrim's "unreasonable tyranny" (14 April, 1881) is discussed at length in both versions, McDougall chose to remove his name from the revised title. William Sydney Clements, the third Earl of Leitrim, was notorious for his ill-treatment of tenants and was murdered in 1878. After calling the murder a "dreadful" and "appalling crime," the Dublin *Freeman's Journal* included that "[i]t was not that [Lord Leitrim] was a bad man" but that he had become bent on destroying tenant right on his properties to secure his own "rights of property" (3 April, 1878). One example recounted by McDougall to demonstrate Lord Leitrim's crimes concerns a paralytic schoolmaster, a choice of subject suggestive of McDougall's tendency to focus on helpless victims to stimulate empathy for the Irish in both her journalistic and literary writings. In the past, the schoolmaster had built a room adjacent to his schoolhouse. As soon as Lord Leitrim found out, he had the man carried out into the road and the room demolished. When McDougall speaks with the schoolmaster, he is again "under notice of eviction" (14 April, 1881).

In the *Witness* letter, McDougall describes the schoolmaster:

> He must have been something of a character in his day, for in spite of poverty, dirt and disease, he looked like a reduced gentleman, and spoke with an educated voice quite different from the people around him. He wore some kind of an old wrap as if it were a military cloak, and was silent about his affairs, with a certain dignity that was impressive. The master, as they call him, was stricken with a partial paralysis of the lower limbs. He could teach, but he could not walk without the assistance of two persons.

In Chapter VIII, McDougall only mentions that the schoolmaster "had lost the use of his limbs" and "was quite an educated man, to judge from his speech" (39). McDougall also changes several speech instances. In the original letter, the schoolmaster displays a sense of gallows humour: "'If I am ejected,' said the schoolmaster with a smile, 'I will see the sky which I have not seen since 1870'" (14 April, 1881). In Chapter VIII, McDougall simplifies this statement to "[t]he father has not seen the sky since he was evicted in 1870," thereby also shifting from direct speech by the victim to her own indirect speech (39). Although seemingly minor modifications, they establish an important alteration. They strip the statement of its wittiness and the schoolmaster of his idiosyncratic dignity and depth of character. They also make this victim of landlord abuse seem even more passive, further emphasising his helplessness.

The original letter closes with "[p]eople who have been proved by their evil deeds unfit for absolute power, who have grossly abused that power, should be abolished as landlords, is the thought that floats on the breath of the mountain" (14 April, 1881). McDougall adds a concluding section to Chapter VIII in the *Letters of "Norah,"* thereby moving from specific examples to a general critical note: "What kind of system is it that produces such scenes …? It is a noticeable fact how many there are in the asylum in Letterkenny whose madness they blame on the horrors of these evictions. Wise legislation may find a remedy for these evils, but the memory will never die out. It is graven on the mountains, it is stamped on the valleys, it is recorded on the rocks forever" (42). This additional information serves to drive home McDougall's explication of the ills caused by the practice of eviction. In the *Letters of "Norah,"* McDougall emphasises the need for legislative action and concretises the effects of systematic landlord abuses by changing their description from being elusive (on "the breath of the mountain") to being everlasting tangible scars in the landscape.

McDougall continued this transition into a more generalised register in other ways. In the *Witness* letters she often provides details: the letters are dated and located and when discussing raised rents and other expenditures, McDougall provides exact numbers. Prices are included in the *Letters of "Norah"* as well, but much less frequently, and, as mentioned, headers with locations and dates are missing. Thus, between the *Witness* letters of 1881 and the collection of 1882, the letters lose much of their specificity and McDougall comes to rely less upon such factual evidence. This and McDougall's free handling of chronology can be seen to lessen the sense of historicity of the events reported. However, this does not diminish the power of the collected letters in relation to their originals, for McDougall enhances their force in other ways. She increases the explicitness of her general message between the first and second versions by adding overall concluding statements, the strongest example of which can be found in the addition of a final chapter (LVII) to the *Letters of "Norah,"* which concisely reiterates her overall argument. In revising the letters, McDougall seems to have had an eye to posterity, making her correspondence of a more general nature and thus more accessible for those without detailed knowledge of Ireland's condition in 1881.

From Letters to Novel

In 1883, *The Days of a Life* was published by William Templeman, who had also reprinted some of McDougall's letters in his *Almonte Gazette* in 1881. The novel's protagonist is Canadian-Ulster-Scots Ida Livingstone. Fourteen-year-old Ida travels to Ireland and stays with her family in Ramelton (Donegal), a town which had impressed McDougall, and she called it "an exceptionally pretty, clean little place" (4 April, 1881). Ida observes various injustices and evictions, and even sees one of her friends sent to jail for joining the Land League. The central tenet of the book accords with McDougall's call to change the lot of the Irish labourer through legislation, otherwise history will repeat itself and famines and landlord abuses will continue (1883, 418, 419).

Templeman made claims for the originality of the novel in his *Almonte Gazette*. Countering what he perceived to be "a misapprehension," he explained that while "[m]any are under the impression that the book is a reprint of the letters written from Ireland by the same talented lady," *The Days of a Life* was "an entirely new work." Although admitting that the novel was "one of fiction founded on fact," the publisher stated that it had "no connection whatever" with the *Witness* letters (*Almonte Gazette*, 13 July, 1883). Templeman's paradoxical convictions bear the imprint of a publisher seeking to defend the specific qualities and marketability of his own product. They also emphasise the strenuous nature of the dividing lines between fact and fiction, author biography and authorial invention, journalistic work and fiction writing.

In the *Witness* letters, McDougall describes the suffering poor in relatively muted tones: while often mentioning evictions and the hardships of the Irish poor, she generally does not resort to sensationalist terms. One of the few instances she does adopt a grimmer vocabulary is when drawing a comparison between the recent famine and the mid-century Great Famine. She points out a spot near the river Moy (in the northwest of Ireland)

> where a man had carried his father on his back to his burial ... When he got him to the place his strength was gone; he could not dig the grave deep enough, or cover it in sufficiently, so some people, a day or two afterward, found that parts of the body had been disinterred by the dogs and devoured, for there were no coffins for the poor then. This was an incident of the great famine. Such scenes did not take place in the last scarcity. (9 July, 1881)

In the collected letters McDougall removed the reference to dogs devouring the dead, and provides a more sanitised image of suffering, a process which also seems to underlie the novel, for it is largely devoid of stark representations. This change was not necessarily informed by the genre conventions of rural fiction: while narratives such as Annie Keary's *Castle Daly; The Story of an Irish Home Thirty Years Ago* (1875) are similarly sparing with the use of gruesome imagery, others, for example Margaret Brew's *The Chronicles of Castle Cloyne; or, Pictures of the Munster People* (1885) and Rosa Mulholland's "The Hungry Death" (1891) do depict ghastly "walking skeletons" (Mulholland 1891, 388) and victims with "wasted limbs, ... sunken features, [and] yellow parchment-like skin drawn tightly over the protruding bones of the face" (Brew 1885, 258–59).

The main characters of the novel are middle and upper-middle class, and their problems are caused less by the immediate threat of starvation, but by economics and the dictatorial behaviour of their landlords, making it less vital to the plot to provide grim descriptions of victimhood. In her novel, McDougall relies on other methods of emphasising the dramatic nature of Ireland's condition. *The Days of a Life* is peopled by good characters who fall prey to the whims of uncaring and evil antagonists. One of the novel's plotlines focuses on John and Bessie Coldingham. Virtuous John works for the benevolent Earl of Dane Clermont with whom he is on excellent terms. John does well for himself and is able to lease several adjoining buildings, converting and improving these to sublet to others, in effect functioning as a middleman (Donnelly 2010, 132). However, when their landlord dies, his son—the second Earl —becomes their landlord, and the Coldinghams' fortunes are reversed. The new landlord treats his tenants with disdain and overworks John, which leads to his premature death. After this, in an act of "wholesale robbery," the Earl takes possession of the family's holdings (357–58). Shocked, Bessie collapses and dies; her children are evicted afterwards. McDougall emphasises the corrupt nature of the system again: "[the Earl] evicted them because ... he had the power, and he brutally used it. But they who gave him this power are responsible before Almighty God for his iniquities!" (425). Later, the second Earl is found murdered.

This plotline was based on a case which McDougall had reported earlier: the dealings of a Scottish-Presbyterian strong farmer John Buchanan with his landlord, the infamous Lord Leitrim (4 April, 1881; 1882, 27–29). McDougall made changes to dramatise the Buchanans' lot into the Coldinghams' narrative. The Buchanans had five children; the Coldinghams have seven. And while McDougall did not mention any sexually transgressive behaviour on the part of the real Lord Leitrim, she does add this dimension of character to the second Earl, who tries to force himself upon his servant Roseen (1883, Chapter 16). This provides a gendered dimension to rural power dynamics, which connects the novel to a trope more often found in rural fiction such as P. J. Coleman's "Outrooted" (1905) and Joseph Guinan's *The Moores of Glynn* (1907).[5] The Land War and romantic plotlines take an equal share in McDougall's novel. In contrast to many works of Big House fiction (Kreilkamp 1998, 5), in *The Days of a Life* romance between Irish and English characters unfortunately does not provide a solution for a deeply divided rural Ireland, and the narrative ends in an open-ended manner.

Scholars such as Christopher Morash have demonstrated that after the Great Famine, pre-existing images of suffering were shaped into a "particular vocabulary" of Famine victimhood (1995, 76). McDougall connects to this well-known imagery in her literary and journalistic writings, demonstrating its applicability for other periods of similar suffering. McDougall's examples include self-sacrificing clergymen, evictions, people dying alongside the road, famine as an anthropomorphised entity, public works, and an emphasis on the helpless: child, female, injured and elderly victims. In *The Days of a Life*, McDougall condenses this imagery, especially in Chapter 12, which details the evictions of many helpless tenants, and which serves as a strong example of the accumulation of such images. In her letters, she describes a starving family, and in so doing nods towards the iconic dimension of the image: "We passed a cabin of indescribable wretchedness; a woman who might have sat for a picture of famine stood at the door looking at us as we passed. She had

---

5   In his dissertation (2018), Christopher Cusack discusses both narratives.

a number of little children, of the raggedest they were, around her" (1882, 172). In the letters and novel, McDougall repeatedly draws parallels between the Great Famine and the famine of her own time; the use of familiar images of famine victimhood further underscores the link. This can be considered an example of what Jerome Bruner has called "narrative accrual"—the repeated use of imagery across texts—which, through combination, functions to enhance the truth effect of an image (2004, 228–9). Thus, by connecting to an existing storehouse of Irish famine imagery, the descriptive potential of these existing images lends associative force to McDougall's writings and provides them with a sense of truthfulness.

Verisimilitude and Moral Framework

Present in all three versions is McDougall's empathic reaction to the Irish tenantry. It should be noted that the term "empathy" was not used before the early twentieth century, and therefore was not employed by McDougall herself. She rather uses terms like "pity" and "compassion." However, these do not accord with McDougall's sentiments as we would understand them today. Aleida Assmann and Ines Detmers explain that empathy supposes a similarity in character or values, while pity and compassion are terms "based on difference," "troubled by aspects of hierarchy, condescension and superiority" (2016, 4). Through her strong identification with the Irish and her insistence on their human rights to ownership of their land, McDougall empathetically places herself in a relationship of equality rather than hierarchy with "her people." McDougall does not explicitly call her readers to action; her quest for change lies mostly in changing their views, giving them the possibility to emulate her transformation. Because the letters and the novel were not written for a specifically Irish (-diasporic) community, McDougall's writings also functioned as works of "ambassadorial strategic empathy," as "attempts to reach readers outside the boundaries of the depicted social world in an effort to change [their] attitude" (Keen 2011, 136).

As memory scholars demonstrate, what we take from the past are disparate traces which we combine into narratives which carry meaning for us in the present, underscoring Richard Terdiman's famous dictum that memory is the past made present (Frawley 2011; Terdiman 1993; Wertsch 2002). Through the processes of generalisation and imaginative reconstruction, the collected *Letters* and the novel become increasingly distanced from the original correspondence's historicity. However, a loss of historicity does not necessarily equate a loss of truthfulness. Paul Ricoeur famously argued that the modes of history and fiction writing are mutually indebted: while the former provides factual weight and "ethical neutralisation," for representations of (emotionally) laden events such neutrality is not "desirable." The individuating and subjective potential of the latter is needed to provide a satisfactory narrative (Ricoeur 1990, 187–88). A similar observation can be made regarding the tension between the modes of journalistic and literary writing. Moreover, whether events are described as they really occurred or not, events narrated in literary journalism were "actual phenomena in the world" that "exist outside the cover of books. The subjectivity involved in all acts of human perception does not deny the phenomenalistic status of the experiences transcribed" (Zavarzadeh, quoted in Sims 2009, 13). Regardless of the actual "truth" of events, their representations refer to a world known to us; all three of McDougall's accounts referred to her readership's known reality. Thus, her writings are located on a spectrum stretching between fiction and journalistic writing, straddling the two sides of a flexible reality boundary. Jeffrey Alexander points out that we "like to believe in the verisimilitude of our accounts, but it is the moral frameworks themselves that are real and constant, not the factual material that we employ to describe them" (2004, 262). Arguably, then, what matters is not the veracity but the verisimilitude of McDougall's accounts. Although her *Letters of "Norah," The Days of a Life*, and the original *Witness* letters as well, contain adapted versions of the "factual" materials, all three representations of Land War-era Ireland uphold an unchanging moral framework.

Acknowledgement

The research for and writing of this essay was made possible through an Irish Research Council Government of Ireland Postdoctoral Fellowship.

References

Primary Sources
McDougall, Margaret Dixon ("Norah"). 1881. "A Tour through Ireland." *Montreal Daily Witness*, 4 April 1881.
——. 1881. "A Tour through Ireland." *Montreal Daily Witness*, 12 April, 1881.
——. 1881. "A Tour through Ireland." *Montreal Daily Witness*, 14 April, 1881.
——. 1881. "A Tour through Ireland." *Montreal Daily Witness*, 14 May, 1881.
——. 1881. "A Tour through Ireland." *Montreal Daily Witness*, 9 July 1881.
——. 1881. "A Tour through Ireland." *Montreal Daily Witness*, 19 October, 1881.
——. 1882. *The Letters of "Norah," on her Tour through Ireland, being a Series of Letters to the Montreal "Witness" as a Special Correspondent to Ireland.* Montreal: *Montreal Witness* Offices.
——. 1883. *The Days of a Life.* Almonte: Templeman.

Other Sources

Alexander, Jeffrey C. 2004. "On the Social Construction of Moral Universals: The 'Holocaust' from War Crime to Trauma Drama." In Jeffrey C. Alexander, et al. *Cultural Trauma and Collective Identity*, 196–263. Berkeley, CA: University of California Press.

Assmann, Aleida and Ines Detmers. 2016. "Introduction." In *Empathy and its Limits,* edited by Aleida Assmann and Ines Detmers, 1–17. Basingstoke: Palgrave Macmillan.

Bull, Philip. 2010. "Irish Land and British Politics." In *The Land Question in Britain, 1750–1950*, edited by Matthew Cragoe and Paul Readman, 126–45. Basingstoke: Palgrave Macmillan.

Brew, Margaret. 1885. *The Chronicles of Castle Cloyne; Or, Pictures of the Munster People*. 3 vols. London: Chapman and Hall.

Bruner, Jerome. 2004. "The Narrative Construction of Reality." In *Narrative Theory. Critical Concepts in Literary and Cultural Studies. Volume IV: Interdisciplinarity*, edited by Mieke Bal, 213–32. London: Routledge.

Butcher, W. W. 1886. *W.W. Butcher's Canadian Newspaper Directory.* London: "Speaker" Printing.

"Circulation of THE WITNESS during the Week Ending April 9th, 1881, and Corresponding Week of Last Year." 1881. *Montreal Daily Witness*, 14 April, 1881.

Coleman, P.J. 1905. "Outrooted." *Rosary Magazine* XXVI, no. 6 (June): 559–74.

Curtis, Jr, L. Perry. 2011. *The Depiction of Eviction in Ireland 1845–1910*. Dublin: University College Dublin Press.

Cusack, Christopher. 2018. "Memory, History, and Identity in Irish and Irish-Diasporic Famine Fiction, 1892–1921." Ph.D. Diss., Nijmegen: Radboud University.

Donnelly, James. 2010. *The Great Irish Potato Famine*. Stroud: History Press.

Dougall, John. 15 December 1845. "Prospectus of the Montreal Witness, Weekly Review, and Family Newspaper." *Montreal Witness, Weekly Review and Family Newspaper.*

Frawley, Oona. 2011. "Toward a Theory of Cultural Memory in an Irish Postcolonial Context." In *Memory Ireland Volume I: History and Modernity*, edited by Oona Frawley, 18–34. Syracuse, NY: Syracuse University Press.

Godkin, James. 1870. *The Land-War in Ireland: A History of the Times*. London: Macmillan.

Griffiths, Andrew. 2015. *The New Journalism, the New Imperialism and the Fiction of Empire, 1870–1900*. Basingstoke: Palgrave Macmillan.

Guinan, Joseph. 1907. *The Moores of Glynn*. Dublin: Gill and Sons.

Hartsock, John C. 2014. *Literary Journalism and the Aesthetics of Experience.* Amherst, MA: University of Massachusetts Press.

Hooper, Glenn. 2001. *The Tourist's Gaze: Travellers to Ireland 1800–2000.* Cork: Cork University Press.

"In the midst of a long period..." 1878. *Freeman's Journal,* 3 April, 1878.

Janssen, Lindsay. 2016. "Famine Traces: Memory, Landscape, History and Identity in Irish and Irish-Diasporic Famine Fiction, 1871–91." Ph.D. Diss., Nijmegen: Radboud University.

"J. P. G." 1881. "Ireland and 'Tour in Ireland'." *Montreal Daily Witness,* 4 August, 1881.

"Justitia." 1881. "Ireland and the 'Witness' Correspondent." *Montreal Daily Witness,* 26 October, 1881.

Keen, Suzanne. 2011. "Fast Tracks to Narrative Empathy: Anthropomorphism and Dehumanization in Graphic Narratives." *Substance* 40, no. 1 (24): 135–55.

Kreilkamp, Vera. 1998. *The Anglo-Irish Novel and the Big House.* Syracuse, NY: Syracuse University Press.

Lalor, James Fintan. 1848. *The Rights of Ireland and the Faith of a Felon,* Reprinted from the "Irish Felon" Newspaper (suppressed July, 1848). Dublin: An Clo-Cúmann.

Loeber, Rolf, Magda Loeber, and Anne Mullin Burnham, eds. 2004. "McDougall, Margaret Dixon," author entry. In *A Guide to Irish Fiction 1650–1900.* Dublin: Four Courts Press. Electronic version created by An Foras Feasa, 2012. http://www.lgif.ie.

"MacDougall (or McDougall), Margaret Dixon." *Simon Fraser University Library.* http://digital.lib.sfu.ca/ceww-738/macdougall-or-mcdougall-margaret-dixon.

"A Misapprehension." 1883. *Almonte Gazette,* 13 July, 1883.

"The Montreal Witness." *BAnQ Numérique.* http://numerique. banq.qc.ca/patrimoine/details/52327/1833888?docref=-7L17HENWgPp2R8sL5lOBQ.

Morash, Christopher. 1995. "Spectres of the Famine." *Irish Review* 17, no. 18: 74–79.

Morgan, Cecilia. 2008. *A Happy Holiday: English-Canadians and Transatlantic Tourism, 1870–1930.* Toronto: University of Toronto Press.

Mulholland, Rosa. 1891. "The Hungry Death." In *Representative Irish Tales,* edited by W. B. Yeats, 369–95. London: Putnam.

Ricoeur, Paul. 1990. *Time and Narrative,* Vol. 3. Chicago: University of Chicago Press.

Sims, Norman. 2009. "The Problem and the Promise of Literary Journalism Studies." *Literary Journalism Studies* 1, no. 1: 7–17.

Snell, J. G. 2003. "John Dougall." In *Dictionary of Canadian Biography,* Vol.

11. University of Toronto/Université Laval. http://www.biographi.ca/en/bio/dougall_john_11E.html.

Terdiman, Richard. 1993. *Present Past: Modernity and the Memory Crisis*. Ithaca, NY: Cornell University Press.

Tulloch, John. 2014. "Ethics, Trust, and the First Person in the Narration of Long-Form Journalism." *Journalism* 15, no. 5: 629–38.

Waters, Catherine. 2018. "Researching Transnational/Transatlantic Connections: the 1865 Atlantic Cable Expedition." In *Researching the Nineteenth-Century Periodical Press: Case Studies*, edited by Alexis Easley, Andrew King, and John Morton, 102–14. London: Routledge.

Wertsch, James V. 2002. *Voices of Collective Remembering*. Cambridge: Cambridge University Press.

Wood, T. F. 1876. *T. F. Wood & Co's Canadian Newspaper Directory Containing Accurate Lists of all the Newspapers and Periodicals published in the Dominion of Canada and Province of Newfoundland*. Montreal: T. F. Wood.

15

Hannah Berman: Jewish Lithuania and the Irish Literary Revival

Barry Montgomery

Hannah Berman (1885–1955) immigrated to Ireland as a six-year-old child with her family from the Kovno region of Lithuania around 1892. She was one of the earliest Irish Jewish writers, and the only Irish Jewish woman known to have been actively and prolifically publishing both her own fiction in English and translations from the Yiddish in Ireland during the opening decades of the twentieth century. Berman also engaged with both Jewish and Irish literary and cultural groups in Dublin, through which she was representative of an active, albeit small, intellectual, literary, artistic and political network within Irish Jewry during the Irish Literary Revival period seeking to establish common ground, parallels, and dialogue between Ireland's indigenous and recently arrived migrant communities.

Berman began as a Dublin journalist, although examples of her work in this field have yet to be uncovered. She later gained a modest, but international reputation as a novelist with her first major work, *Melutovna* (1913a), and as a translator, with her English version of Sholom Aleichem's Yiddish novel, *Stempenyu* (1913). Little is as yet known about the specifics of Berman's career, but the favourable reception of *Melutovna* (1913a) possibly prompted her departure for London in 1914. There she continued to be active within English Jewish circles, and was appointed general secretary and placed in charge of the literary section of the Jewish Association of Arts and Sciences in 1916 ("Jewish Association of Arts and Sciences," 33). The aim of this essay is to establish at least the beginnings of Berman's recovery as a pioneer of Irish Jewish literature, and to contextualise her fiction against her background as an Irish Jewish woman and Lithuanian emigrant of the late nineteenth and early twentieth century.

Melutovna is a village in the Western Russian region of Mohilev, now Belarus. The novel spans several generations, covering a number of decades of the latter half of the nineteenth century, and, as with most of Berman's fiction, concerns the domestic and external political experiences of Jewish village life in Tsarist Russia. Its subject matter remained topical into the early twentieth century; all major Irish newspapers featured reports on anti-Semitic violence, massacres, atrocities, expulsions, and discriminatory anti-Jewish legislation within the Russian Pale from the 1881–1882 cycle of pogroms, through to the downfall of the Tsarist regime in 1917. The *Weekly Irish Times*, amongst other newspapers across Britain and further afield, lauded *Melutovna* as a corrective against traditional prejudicial injustices directed specifically against the Jews ("Melutovna" 1914, 20).

By Cormac Ó Gráda's estimate, immigration saw Irish Jewry increase from 285 at the beginning of the 1870s to 5,148 in 1911, 2,965 of whom had settled in Dublin (Ó Gráda 2006, 11). But, as Ó Gráda also notes, emphasis on persecution in Lithuania as the principal cause for Jewish emigration to Ireland tends to be misleading, as, contrary to the impressions given by contemporaneous newspaper reports and even anecdotal folk memory, evidence seems to suggest that Lithuania was "virtually pogrom-free" between 1881 and 1914. Yet, as he notes, crucially, "the May Laws and their aftermath undoubtedly affected the psyche of emigré Russian Jews and their descendants, most of whom remain convinced that those who left Lithuania were refugees or asylum seekers, rather than primarily economic migrants" (Ó Gráda 2006, 14–5). This provides a very interesting perspective on Berman's fiction, because although violence and persecution do occur, quite often on the margins of her stories, a great deal of emphasis also tends to be placed on the trauma caused by the threat of violence and persecution rather than the actuality.

In Ireland, tensions between the indigenous and immigrant communities were in evidence, contrary to the prominence typically given to Daniel O'Connell and Michael Davitt's political emphases on a shared history of suffering and oppression between Irish and Jewish people; these tended to overshadow and obscure the true level of anti-Jewish sentiment in Ireland of that era to the extent that Fr. John Creagh's infamous Limerick Boycott of 1904 is often dismissed as an unfortunate anomaly unrepresentative of a wider cultural history of tolerance. The press tells quite a different story, particularly in regional newspapers; a 1903 article in the *Dundalk Democrat*, for example, makes a blatantly xenophobic case against immigrants, claiming that Ireland has become "a dumping ground for the foreigner and Jewmen, who have the country overrun at the present time" ("Dundalk House League" 1903, 15). Such sentiments clash with a nationalist tradition in Ireland which dates back to the seventeenth-century bardic tradition built around Owen Roe O'Neill, and classified by Jerrold Casway as "Gaelic Maccabeanism" (Casway 2000), in which poets from Thomas Moore to the Young Irelanders and beyond identified with the rebellious Maccabees fighting for freedom against oppression by invoking parallels between Erin and Zion. However, as Abbey Bender succinctly puts it in her pioneering study, *Israelites in Erin: Exodus, Revolution, and the Irish Revival* (2015), "those who invoked 'that chosen tribe' as a model for liberation could not have anticipated that their metaphoric Israelites would soon be arriving, literally, on Irish shores" (51). The reality of Jewish life in Ireland was thus perhaps closer to the bigoted mistreatment suffered by Leopold Bloom at the hands of The Citizen in James Joyce's *Ulysses* (1922).

Integration and communication were natural problems. The Dublin Jewish journalist and writer, E. R. Lipsett, writing under the pseudonym "Halitvack," for example, argued somewhat bitterly that the compound "Irish Jew" is little more than a contradiction, given that "the Jews understand the Irish little; the Irish understand the Jews less" (Lipsett 1906, 21, 29). This was the environment within which Berman began her career. She was never a major literary figure; but she has since fallen into almost complete obscurity, her short stories remaining uncollected and presumably unread for the better part of a century. Her first novel-length work, "The History of Joseph Lackenovitz," was serialised in the Chicago periodical, *The Reform Advocate* (1911), but never republished. *Melutovna* (1913a) and her later novel *Ant Hills* (1926), which was published more than a decade after Berman left Ireland, have both remained out of print for decades.

In light of such circumstances, it is thus unsurprising that Berman's literary work has also suffered critical neglect. Catherine Hezser's seminal essay, "Are you Protestant Jews or Roman Catholic Jews? Literary Representations of Being Jewish in Ireland," for example, only offers a cursory identification of Berman's novels being descriptive of Jewish life in Lithuania, not expanding any further on the socio-political or cultural contexts of her writing in Ireland during the opening decades of the twentieth century (Hezser 2005, 160). Ó Gráda, in keeping with general historical approaches to Berman, likewise confines his discussion of *Ant Hills* to its "vivid accounts of the Lithuanian peddlers' lot" relevant to the experiences of Berman's father, Lieb, who plied that trade in Ireland shortly after his arrival from Kovno (Ó Gráda 2006, 237n).

Such readings, although valuable, do little to illuminate the plethora of narrative vignettes, and the wealth of character study, socio-political and historical commentary, humour and pathos of Berman's three novels and in excess of forty short stories so far identified. Her fiction needs to be read as entirety to appreciate Berman's panoramic impression of the Russian Jewish experience seen through a series of highly personalised character studies that more often than not laid bare the individualities, idiosyncrasies and frequently the traumas of her Jewish characters against often adverse or unjust social and political circumstances. Berman clearly regarded fiction as a bridge connecting the old world and the new. She even claimed in a 1914 interview, "Yiddish Fiction," for the *Jewish Chronicle* that she based many of her fictional characters on her Dublin Jewish contemporaries (18–20). The extent to which this is true is of course unknown, and given the passage of time may never be ascertained, especially while Berman's writings remain unread and unstudied.

Berman's fiction had another declared purpose. She writes in a note attached to the short story, "Nothing and Nothing" (1912a), published in the *Irish Review*, that "we Jews have never yet explained ourselves to our [Irish] hosts; and so many misapprehensions have arisen from time to time [that] if I can succeed in clearing away the least of them I shall feel more than satisfied" (Berman 1912a, 242). It can be safely presumed that Berman did not suppose her "explanation" would be conveyed by a single story read in isolation, but rather through a holistic reading of her work. Berman's novels of course have a greater degree of unity in terms of plot and characterisation; but her short stories stylistically reflect the more fragmentary existence of her characters, who typically occupy the liminal space of the perpetually marginalised.

A fellow Irish Jewish novelist, Joseph Edelstein (1886–1939), had in fact already attempted a similar "explanation" to the one Berman proposes in his controversial novel, *The Money-Lender* (1908), which confronted Jewish usury in Ireland and Ireland's own anti-Semitic hostilities as the principal causes of friction and tension between the indigenous and immigrant communities. He managed instead to offend both communities with his depiction of a ruthless Shylockian protagonist alongside brutal representations of the Dublin slums (Edelstein 1908). Berman avoids the Irish Jewish immigrant experience entirely, her exile or emigration stories tending to involve England or America. Such tales are nonetheless bleak, focused on cultural and linguistic alienation, often accompanied by states of poverty and destitution, as is the fate of the emigrant to London, Isaac Ostrofsky in Berman's first novel length work, "The History of Joseph Lackenovitz" (1911a):

> [Isaac] was not long in making the terrible discovery that there was no fortune to be made in England any more than in Russia. He was crushed by the discovery; but continued to drag himself here and there, hoping always that something would turn up. He slept in outhouses and in fields, hungry, cold, tired, and a stranger, knowing nothing of what was said to him and unable to speak a word. Failure dogged his footsteps wherever he went. He no longer thought of making fortunes. (Berman 1911a, 708)

Shloumalle in "The Tile Maker" is also left destitute with a dependent family back home, after discovering that his traditional roofing skills are redundant in London, forcing him to beg, and then ruminate on his condition: "In these critical moments of a man's life there is no room in his heart for philosophy. The man who gives a dry crust is a benefactor, even if he beats one over the hands with a stick as well" (Berman 1911b, 2). Berman would return again to this theme later in her career, publishing "The Beggar" (1924b) to some acclaim in Ford Madox Ford's *Transatlantic Review*.

Such destitution and despair would have resonated with many Irish emigrants who had suffered similar experiences. But for the most part Berman's fiction tends to be confined to Russian Jewish village life. Indeed, Berman's background in Yiddish, the everyday language of the "Shtetl," or Russian Jewish village, was key in forming the character, style, and indeed politics of her fiction in English. Yiddish is of course to be differentiated from Hebrew, an entirely different language and one traditionally reserved for religious ceremony and scholarship. Berman was a native Yiddish speaker, as were all first generation "Litvak" immigrants, and she presumably acquired English after her arrival in Ireland; "Litvak" denotes Jews originating from nineteenth-century Lithuania (which then encompassed parts of Belarus and Poland), and who shared a common religious culture and Yiddish as a common language (Ó Gráda 2006, 17).

It is remarked in an interview on "Yiddish Fiction" Berman gave for the *Jewish Chronicle* in 1914 that she was fluent in both languages and "changed English for Yiddish very frequently" speaking the latter with "a soft Irish brogue" (18–20). Yiddish, however, was in decline amongst Jewish emigrants (Ó Gráda 2006, 30); but there were cultural efforts and a movement in Ireland, as elsewhere, to revive it, in which Berman participated, and these efforts invited small but significant parallels with the impetus behind the Irish language and literary revivals of the same period. In 1908, the Dublin based Jewish Amateur Operatic Society staged a Yiddish production of Avrom Goldfaden's *Shulamith, or Daughter of Zion* (1880), in the Abbey Theatre. The *Irish Independent* correspondent, "Jacques," dubbed this "powerful" event (perhaps jokingly) the "Yiddish [Literary] Renaissance in Dublin" as taking place in "Lady Gregory's and Mr Yeats's National Abbey Theatre," declaring the play's dramatic offerings "of lavish slices out of Jerusalem life of 200 B. C." a tremendous success ("Jacques" 1908, 3). The following year in 1909 Padraic Colum delivered a lecture on the "Revival of Irish Literature" to the Dublin Jewish Literary Society, of which Berman was a member. The lecture was extremely well received, invoking a shared sense of heritage with regard to the cultural necessity of respective revivals and retentions of language and literature.

It is apparent that Berman was attempting to faithfully replicate the Russian-Jewish mode of Yiddish within the medium of English to convey experiences of Lithuanian Jewish village life, a subject on which she also took a scholarly interest, having delivered a lecture to the Manchester Daughters of Zion in November 1910 on "Life in a Russian Jewish Village" ("Zionism" 1910b, 14). She may have had no immediate hopes for "a school of English writers on Russian-Jewish themes"; but in her interview for the *Jewish Chronicle* she describes her own creative methodology as translating "palpitating Yiddish mentally into idiomatic English" in order to avoid a "fatal" rigidity of style

("Yiddish Fiction: Interview" 1914, 18–20).

Berman thereby invited suggestive, if not explicit, comparisons and parallels by bringing a literary culture that had its original expression in the Yiddish language into the domain of the Irish Literary Revival. She would later in an informal family memoir, "Zlotover Story," describe Ireland and Lithuania as being often "coupled for their extreme poverty, peasant economics, and the fact that they are both of great antiquity" (2). This document, alongside "Berman Story" and "Recollections," all of which were composed during the 1940s, recount the circumstances of Berman's family's emigration to Ireland, providing some insight into the author's origins and early life, both in Lithuania and in Ireland, some of which Berman brings into play in her fiction.[1] Relatives on her mother's side, the affluent Zlotovers, lost their Lithuanian lands and properties under the May Laws (1882) of Tsar Alexander III, but would go on to become a prominent family in the Dublin Jewish community ("Zlotover Story", 7). Berman infuses the fear and sense of insecurity that accompanied this familial experience into short stories such as "Day Dreams" (1914a).

Zeldalle, the pregnant wife of a well-to-do village mill owner, and a group of nearby children, are nearly trampled by the galloping horse of the local overlord. The incident and the overlord's indifference traumatises Zeldalle, who draws the conclusion that to be Jewish in Tsarist Lithuania amounts ultimately to nothing: "everything was a mockery—the durability of the mill, the gilded prophecy of the village women ... the eternal peace of nature herself ... everything. And Jonathan [her husband] was no more than a dreamer" (Berman 1914a). Another Berman character, Frooma, would echo this sentiment more than a decade later in *Ant Hills* (1926), ruminating that in a Russian Jewish village "we poor folks are like ants. We build our little hills grain by grain, with blood and tears. And in the end? Comes a tyrant with iron heels, and with one twist of his boot – no more hills and no more ants" (1926, 182). The threats of eviction, displacement, violence, tyranny, and persecution were as real and traumatic for Jews in Tsarist Lithuania as they were for the Irish under British imperialism.

Like her many translations—Berman was the authorised translator of the work Sholom Aleichem (Solomon Naumovich Rabinovich) from 1911 until the period of the well-known Yiddish author's death in 1916 (Berman, 1916, 7)—Berman's short stories, on diverse topics ranging from the domestic to the

---

1   I would like to thank Dr. Natalie Wynn (TCD) for the acquisition of these typescripts, and the Jacob Radar Marcus Center of American Jewish Archives, Cincinnati, Ohio, for supplying "Berman Story" (Robert and Jessie Bloom Collection, Ms-93, Box 13: folders 2–3 (Reminiscences [Jessie Bloom—Dublin, Ireland], undated). "Zlotover Story" was revised and updated for private publication by Dr. Melisande Zlotover in 1966 as *Zlotover Story: A Dublin Story with a Difference* (Dublin: Hely Thom Ltd), which pays homage to Hannah Berman in the preface but expunges much of her original text.

supernatural, were published globally. Composed chiefly between 1909 and 1914, they were often (but not exclusively) published in Jewish newspapers and periodicals as far afield as America, South Africa and Australia, and they were frequently signed off with "Dublin, Ireland."[2] She presented two stories, "Breinalle's Little Love Affairs" (Berman 1910a), about the dreams of a lowly village goose girl, and "My Guest" (Berman 1914b), a "Dybbuk" story derived from Jewish folklore, as part of an "original night" of "native talent" at a National Literary Society event on February 17, 1913, which also featured readings from Katherine Tynan Hinkson ("An Original Night" 1913, 10). Berman also composed at least two Irish-set stories, both of which appeared as prize-winning publications in the Irish *Weekly Freeman*. "His Own Household" (Berman 1912a), set in Ireland, is about the marriage of a young farmer to his beloved being cruelly deferred due to financial difficulties and a traditional obligation to provide dowries for his unmarried sisters. "When the Grave Gives Up its Dead!" (Berman 1913b) is set in Texas, and relates the surreal story of a young emigrant Irish doctor who murders a middle-aged Mexican man in order to marry his much younger wife, only to have his transgression exposed in a macabre twist and climatic ending. The latter tale is particularly curious insofar as it may have been inspired by the "Arise, you dead/From your watery graves" incantation in Avrom Goldfaden's famous Yiddish play, *The Two Kuni-Lemls* (Goldfaden 2006, 236).

For Berman, a key nexus for suggesting parallels between Jewish Lithuanian and Irish cultural experiences is gender, an issue inextricably linked to her Zionism. Certain Irish Jews, such as Joseph Edelstein, were Zionists and Irish Nationalists, clearly envisaging parallels that underlay their overall politics, also informing the principles of the Judaeo-Irish Home Rule Association, which Edelstein formed in 1908. Where Berman stood on such parallels is unknown, and whereas the majority of Irish Jewry were Zionists, Jewish Irish Nationalists were in much fewer numbers, most being Unionist and in allegiance to the British monarchy. Berman delivered a lecture on the father of modern Zionism, Theodor Herzl, as early as 1905 ("The Provinces: Dublin," 29). The *Jewish Chronicle* also records Berman's participation in two debates in January 1910 held at the Ladies' Zionist Association in England: "Is Zionism Practical?" and "Have Women Distinctive Work in the Zionist Movement?" ("Zionism" 1910a, 11). Later in life she travelled to Palestine, publishing a series of articles, "Impressions of Palestine," for the *Empire Review* in 1929,

---

2   Aleichem often drew comparisons with Mark Twain and Charles Dickens in life, later achieving lasting global fame when his "Tevye the Dairyman" tales, composed between 1894 and 1916 (Frieden 1995, 2), were adapted into the Broadway hit and film, *Fiddler on the Roof*. Alongside her English translation of *Stempenyu* (1913), Berman published a great many translations of Aleichem's short stories in Dublin, a collection of which were later published as *Jewish Children* (1920), and was regarded as instrumental in bringing his Yiddish fiction to an English-speaking readership.

which were collectively published the following year in book form (Berman 1929). Berman's prominence within the Dublin Daughters of Zion Association is suggested by her seconding a vote of thanks to Helena Weisberg, who spoke on "The Place of Women in the Zionist Movement" in Dublin on 1 January, 1911. A description of Weisberg's lecture, written by an anonymous "Jewish Correspondent," appeared in the *Evening Herald* in which the Zionist movement is lauded for raising "the status and personal dignity of Jewish woman" (2 January 1911, 5). Berman interrogates the injustices of patriarchy regularly within her fiction. This may happen externally, such as when Zeldalle is traumatised by the overlord in "Day Dreams" (1914a), or internally, in the domestic sphere, such as in the aforementioned short story, "Nothing and Nothing," in which the first person female narrator, Chanalle, has grown jaded by her inability to conceive children, thereby becoming excluded from her traditional societal role as a mother.

Chanalle's indifference to material wealth and emotional estrangement from her seemingly affectionate husband, an affluent Lithuanian Jewish farmer, are the product of an existential terror that her secret resentment of the other childbearing women in the village will be exposed. Chanalle is not oppressed in any overt or obvious sense; she is paradoxically sympathetic because she is a victim of and embittered by an internalised, though no less oppressive, patriarchy that equates female utility with childbearing. Her condition is not one of self-hatred or self-loathing, but rather of abject acceptance, expressed in the story's conclusion:

> As I sit in the silence of my room, I fancy that I can already say, without bitterness and without jealousy: that my childlessness and the loneliness of my old age are nothing to me—but, really, nothing—and nothing. (Berman 1912b, 242)

Outside her own domestic circumstances, this might also be read as an allusive, if extreme gendered response to colonialism and the marginalisation of women in Irish society, which would in itself be consistent with oppressive co-traditions of *othering* both the Irish and the Jews as feminine.

Alongside interrogating or satirising patriarchal misogyny within the confines of the village, Berman genders external anti-Jewish sentiments and oppressions on numerous occasions. A Catholic priest dismisses Zelda's appeal to quell approaching hostilities during the pogrom episode of *Melutovna* (1913a) with misogyny, conspiracy theories and a general sense of righteousness that the persecution of the Jews is divine justice. The local Jews have been falsely accused of well-poisoning and of being behind a recent cholera outbreak. The non-Jewish peasants riot and invoke the "blood libel"—the prejudicial and propagandist belief that Jews ritually murdered Christian children during Passover in a recreation of the crucifixion of Christ—by chanting "We will avenge the death of our little ones! We will cut down all the Jews! They killed our Lord!" (Berman 1913a, 339). The Jews respond in terror, "over and above all else the fear of a pogrom fill[ing] their panic-stricken hearts with agony and horror" (Berman 1913a, 335). Ultimately, the pogrom is averted after some property damage, Berman's principal focus instead being on the trauma incurred by living under the perpetual threat of extreme prejudice and violence. Responses to poverty and hunger are also gendered. "In the Shadow of the Famine" (Berman 1910b), concerns a farmer, Nahum, who, despite his current healthy crop, has known and is traumatised by the memory of famine to a degree that reduces him to a state of abject terror over the potential future in store for both himself and his children. Fear is unjustly presented as feminine weakness, which is also the central trope of one of Berman's later, and probably best-known tale, "The Charity Box" (1923), published almost a decade after Berman left Ireland in the first issue of Seumas O'Sullivan's *The Dublin Magazine*.

John Brannigan reads "The Charity Box" in terms of a shared history of trauma and suffering amongst the Irish and Jews (Brannigan 2009, 67). The story is set on a train moving displaced Jews through war-torn Lithuania, most likely during World War I. The unnamed narrator is a self-hating Jew and misogynist who describes the air being "thick with the stench of hundreds of people lying on top of one another—sighing, groaning, wailing, cursing, and praying," but that after a number of days, the passengers "were no longer horrified by the dead bodies which [they] had not the strength to throw out of the windows" (Berman 1923, 34). He listens to the tale of an elderly Jewish man, Reuben, who is consumed with shame and remorse for having stolen the titular charity box out of desperation and hunger. The narrator is unsympathetic, concluding the story with "I turned away in disgust from the strange Jew, who was, after all, a tearful old woman" (Berman 1923, 38). Rather as with "Nothing and Nothing," reading "The Charity Box" in isolation might give an inaccurate impression of Berman, especially if a reader mistakenly assumes that she is sympathetic to her own narrator. Berman's reappearance in *The Dublin Magazine* a decade following her departure for England has an additional significance in coinciding with a newly-revitalised Irish Jewish cultural movement: the Dublin Jewish Dramatic Society, which evolved out of the Jewish Amateur Operatic Society in the 1920s, continuing for some thirty years into the 1950s. Although not consistently so, efforts were made by these dramatic players to sustain links between the Yiddish and Irish literary revivals, for example, a performance in March 1922 at the Empire Theatre placing Aleichem's Yiddish play, *Der Doktor* (*The Doctor*) on the same bill as Monaghan playwright Bernard Duffy's *Special Pleading* (1921) and Lady Gregory's *Spreading the News* (1904) ("Dublin Jewish Dramatic Society," 4).

Berman was personally credited with familiarising Dublin audiences with the drama of Sholom Aleichem in an *Evening Herald* review of the Dublin

Jewish Dramatic Society's performance of Aleichem's *Der Geht* (*The Divorce*) produced by the legendary Frank Fay at the Olympia Theatre in 1924 (Shochar 1924, 2). She also set an example and paved the way for other Irish Jewish literary talents, such as Esther Mofsovitz (Morris), who composed three plays in the early 1920s in response to a need for "suitable plays of Jewish interest" in English for an Irish audience ("Note", Morris 1926), just as Berman had done just over a decade prior with her fiction. Mofsovitz had previously performed in a Yiddish production of Leon Kobrin's *Der Zeitgeist* at the Abbey in 1923 ("Esther and Zeitgeist" 1923, 4). She published her three plays as *Tears and Laughter* (1926), one of which, a comedy, *The Matchmakers*, was staged at the Abbey Theatre in December 1925, alongside David Pinsky's Yiddish drama, *Yeshurim*, again produced by Frank Fay ("Jewish Entertainment," 5).

Mofsovitz—or Morris, the name she adopted—is especially interesting in that she is the great-grandmother of the contemporary Irish poet, Simon Lewis, author of *Jewtown* (2016), who, alongside the novelist Ruth Gilligan, author of *Nine Folds Make a Paper Swan* (2016), have recently reimagined and reinvigorated interest in the Irish Jewish immigrant experience through their respective works.[3] Currently, Irish Jewish literature, within which Hannah Berman was a key, if largely forgotten player, is a developing field of scholarly interest, including an AHRC-funded, NUI Galway and Ulster University project, *Representations of Jews in Irish Literature*, which has produced a successful touring exhibition and has a forthcoming critical volume on the subject.[4] In this growing field, it is Berman's place at the very beginnings of Irish Jewish literature where she finds her greatest importance, and which in turn presents the strongest argument for her recovery as a significant contributor to early twentieth-century Irish literature and culture.

References

Primary Sources

Berman, Hannah. 1910a. "Breinalle's Little Love Affairs." *The Reform Advocate* (Chicago), 2 July 1910, 1018–1020; repub. 1924. *The Dublin Magazine* 1, no. 2; 272–79.

———. 1910b. "In the Shadow of the Famine." *The Jewish Exponent*

---

3   I would like to thank Simon Lewis, whom I met and had the honour of introducing at the Representations of Jews in Irish Literature exhibition launch in Waterford Institute of Technology in February 2017, for bringing my attention to his great grandmother, Esther (Mofsovitz) Morris. See: Marjorie Brennan, https://www.irishexaminer.com/lifestyle/artsfilmtv/history-of-jews-in-irish-literature-goes-beyond-leopold-bloom-442308.html

4   Other forthcoming studies with an Irish Jewish literary interest include the Trinity College Dublin volume, *Reimagining the Jews of Ireland: Historiography, Identity and Representation*, Zuleika Rodgers and Natalie Wynn, eds.

(Philadelphia), 16 December 1910, 1–2.

———. 1911a. "The History of Joseph Lackenovitz." *The Reform Advocate* (Chicago), 6 May–11 November 1911.

———. 1911b "The Tile Maker." *The Jewish Exponent* (Philadelphia), 31 March 1911, 1–2.

———. 1912a. "His Own Household." *Weekly Freeman*, 20 July 1912, 10–1.

———. 1912b . "Nothing and Nothing." *The Irish Review* 2, no.17: 235–42.

———. 1913a. *Melutovna: A Novel*. London: Chapman & Hall.

———. 1913b. "When the Grave Gives Up its Dead." *Weekly Freeman*, 19 July 1913, 10–11.

———. 1914a. "Day Dreams." *The Reform Advocate* (Chicago), 24 January 1914, 743–4, 775–76.

———. 1914b. "My Guest." *The Sentinel* (Chicago), 15 May 1914, 11, 18.

———. 1916. "Shalom Aleichem: a Tribute." *Sydney Hebrew Standard*, 21 July 1916, 7.

———. 1923. "The Charity Box." *The Dublin Magazine* 1, no. 1: 34–38.

———. 1924a. "Bread." *The Dublin Magazine* 1, no. 6: 948–52.

———. 1924b. "The Beggar." *The Transatlantic Review* 2, no. 3; 248–55; repub. (1926) in *Transatlantic Stories*. Ford Madox Ford, ed. London: Duckworth.

———. 1926. *Ant Hills*. Introduction by Paul Goodman. London: Faber and Gwyer.

———. 1929. *Impressions of Palestine*. London: Macmillan.

———. "Berman Story." Jacob Rader Marcus Center of the American Jewish Archives, Hebrew Union College, Jewish Institute of Religion. Robert and Jessie Bloom Collection, Ms-93, Box 13: folders 2–3.

———. "Zlotover Story." (Unpublished, undated manuscript, American Jewish Archives, Hebrew Union College, Jewish Institute of Religion.) Robert and Jessie Bloom Collection, Ms-93, Box 13: folders 2–3.

Other Sources

Aleichem, Sholom. 1913. *Stempenyu*. Translated by Hannah Berman. London: Methuen & Co.

———. 1920. *Jewish Children*. Translated by Hannah Berman. London: William Heinemann.

———. 1940. *Collected Stories of Sholom Aleichem: Tevye's Daughters*. Translated by Francis Butwin& Ben Shahn. New York: Crown Publishers.

"An Original Night: Native Talent at Literary Society." 1913. *Freeman's Journal*, 18 February 1913, 10.

Bender, Abby. 2015. *Israelites in Erin: Exodus, Revolution, & the Irish Revival*. New York: Syracuse University Press.

Berkowitz, Joel and Jeremy Dauber, eds and trans. 2006. *Landmark Yiddish*

Plays: a Critical Anthology. Albany: State University of New York Press.

Bock, Jerry; Joseph Stein. 1964. *Fiddler on the Roof*. London: Chappell.

Brannigan, John. 2009. *Race in Modern Irish Literature and Culture*. Edinburgh: Edinburgh University Press.

Casway, Jerrold. 2000. "Gaelic Maccabeanism: The Politics of Reconciliation." In *Political Thought in Seventeenth Century Ireland: Kingdom or Colony*, edited by Jane H. Ohlmeyer, 176–90. Cambridge: Cambridge University Press.

"Dublin Jewish Dramatic Society."1922. *Evening Herald*, 31 March 1922, 4.

"Dundalk House League." 1903. *Dundalk Democrat*, 29 August 1903, 15.

Edelstein, Joseph. 1908. *The Money-Lender: A Novel*. Dublin: Dollard.

"Esther and Zeitgeist: Racine's Play in Yiddish at the Abbey." 1923. *Freeman's Journal*, March 26 1923, 4.

Frieden, Ken. 1995. *Classic Yiddish Fiction: Abramovitsh, Sholem Aleichem, & Peretz*. Albany: State University of New York Press.

Gilligan, Ruth. 2016. *Nine Folds Make a Paper Swan*. London: Atlantic Books.

Goldfaden, Avrom. (1880) 2006. "The Two Kuni-Lemls," *Landmark Yiddish Plays: a Critical Anthology*, edited and translated by Joel Berkowitz and Jeremy Dauber, 201–46. Albany: State University of New York Press.

Hezser, Catherine. 2005. "'Are you Protestant Jews or Roman Catholic Jews?' Literary Representations of Being Jewish in Ireland."*Modern Judaism* 25, no. 2 : 159–188.

Hyman, Louis. 1972. *The Jews of Ireland: from Earliest Times to the Year 1910*. Shannon: Irish University Press.

"Jacques." 1908. Review of Jewish Amateur Operatic Society's production of Avrom Goldfaden's *Shulamith, or Daughter of Zion*. *Irish Independent*. 1 July 1908, 3.

"Jewish Association of Arts and Sciences." 1916. *Jewish Chronicle*, 24 March 1916, 33.

"Jewish Entertainment: Three Plays at Abbey Theatre." 1925. *Irish Times*, 21 December 1925, 5.

"Jewish Correspondent." 1911. *Evening Herald*, 2 January 1911, 5.

Jewison, Norman, dir. 1971. *Fiddler on the Roof*, United States of America: Mirisch. Film

Joyce, James. 1922. *Ulysses*. London: Egoist Press.

Lewis, Simon. 2016. *Jewtown*. Galway: Doire Press.

Lipsett, E. R. ('Halitvack'). 1906. "Jews in Ireland." *Jewish Chronicle*, 21 December 1906, 29.

"Melutovna." 1914. *Weekly Irish Times*, 14 March 1914, 20.

Morris, Esther. 1926. *Tears and Laughter*. London: Erskine McDonald.

Ó Gráda, Cormac 2006. *Jewish Ireland in the Age of Joyce: a Socioeconomic History*. Princeton: Princeton University Press.

Rodgers, Zuleika and Natalie Wynn, eds. 2021. *Reimagining the Jews of Ireland: Historiography, Identity and Representation*. Oxford: Peter Lang.

Shochar, Ben. 1924. "Jewish Dramatic Society," *Evening Herald*, 10 March 1924, 2.

"The Provinces: Dublin." 1905. *Jewish Chronicle*, 1 December 1905, 29.

"Yiddish Fiction: Interview for the Jewish Chronicle with Miss Hannah Berman." 1914. *Jewish Chronicle*, 29 May 1914, 18–20.

"Zionism." 1910a. (Report on "Is Zionism Practical?" and "Have Women Distinctive Work in the Zionist Movement?") *Jewish Chronicle*, 7 January 1910, 11.

"Zionism." 1910b. (Report on Berman's talk, "Life in a Russian Jewish Village", for Manchester Daughters of Zion.) *Jewish Chronicle*, 25 November 1910, 14.

16

Mothers of the Insurrection: Theodosia Hickey's *Easter Week*

Lisa Weihman

Irish women served as both combatants and support staff in every military conflict of the revolutionary decade, but their stories were largely forgotten for nearly a century. Tracing women's war work is not a simple task: women's narratives of historical events are less likely to survive the ravages of time and place; their private letters are rarely archived; their names often change in midlife due to marriage; and their stories are the most subject to censorship by culturally repressive conspiracies of church, state, and family. Challenging these impediments, recent feminist historiography offers a more comprehensive view of women's experiences, with a groundswell of scholarship since the Bureau of Military History's opening of its witness statement archive in 2003.[1] New biographies of the women associated with early twentieth-century Irish political life appear each year, proving that Irish women played an integral role in the revolutionary struggle.[2] Irish women of all political and religious affiliations "did their bit" for both Ireland and the Empire throughout the revolutionary decade, serving as munitions workers, secretaries, and medical staff in Ireland and at the Front (Madigan and Horne 2013, 7). During the 1916 Rising, the women of Cumann na mBan and the Irish Citizen Army served in both ancillary and combat roles, and their war work is now being recognised in both official histories and in public memory.

Literary portrayals of the Rising have also played a significant role in the

---

1   See Lucy McDiarmid's *At Home in the Revolution: What Women Said and Did in 1916* (2015), and *Women Writing War: Ireland 1880–1922* (2016), edited by Tina O'Toole, Gillian McIntosh, and Muireann O'Cinnéide.

2   There is new work on Hanna Sheehy Skeffington by Margaret Ward (1997; 2019); on Dorothy Macardle by Nadia Clare Smith (2007); on the Gifford sisters by Anne Clare (2011); on Constance Markievicz by Lauren Arrington (2016), to name but a few of the recent biographies.

evolution of public memory.[3] Yeats's "Easter 1916" has long been a gateway text for many readers, memorialisng the martyred male heroes by name while diminishing the sacrifice of the unnamed Constance Markievicz, whose voice has turned "shrill" through her activism. Unlike Yeats, AE [George Russell] speaks of Markievicz approvingly in his privately published poem honouring the insurgents of 1916 (quoted in Flanagan 2015, 127):

> Here's to the women of our blood
> Stood by them in the fiery hour,
> Rapt lest some weakness in their mood
> Rob manhood of a single power.
> You, brave on such a hope forlorn
> Who smiled through crack of shot and shell,
> Though the world cry on you with scorn,
> Here's to you, Constance, in your cell.

AE's depiction of the women of the Rising, while celebratory, places them in subordination to their male leaders, whose "manhood" they empower through their devotion; yet he hails Constance ("Here's to you") for her bravery and idealism, and gives her equal billing with the other leaders of the Rising. Tensions over literary representations intensified during the early years of the Free State, with women often serving as gatekeepers of nationalist cultural memory. Sean O'Casey's portrayal of the Rising in *The Plough and the Stars* (1926) so outraged Sighle Humphreys and other members of Cumann na mBan that they disrupted the Abbey Theatre's production of the play in 1926 (Morash 2002, 166). But by then, many of the women involved in diehard republican activism during the Irish Civil War were struggling to find a role in the emerging nation (McCoole 1997), and with a few notable exceptions, such as R. M. Fox's *Rebel Irishwomen* (1935), the legacy of women's participation in militant nationalism was repressed within the Irish Free State.[4] Writing about the Rising in the post-Treaty cultural landscape was a political and social landmine, and there are few works about the Rising written after the Civil War until the 1960s.[5]

---

3   Memoir and journalism were the most common modes of recording history for the women who were "out" during the Rising. For example, Margaret Skinnider published her memoir *Doing My Bit for Ireland* (1917) in the United States, and Nora O'Daly, who along with Skinnider spent the Rising at Stephen's Green with the ICA, published her essay "The Women of Easter Week" in *An tÓglach* magazine in 1926 (McAuliffe and Gillis 2016, 222).

4   Sinéad McCoole writes: "A large number of women imprisoned during the Civil War were never married. Their republicanism alienated them from men in the Free State, who did not wish to be associated with 'wild women' whom the Church had excommunicated and who had served a sentence in prison" (McCoole 1997, 60).

5   Dorothy Macardle's short story collection *Earth-Bound* was written during her imprisonment in Kilmainham and Mountjoy Prison (1924), but the stories focus on the

Because of this cultural conservatism, it is rare to find literature from the era that explores women's roles in revolutionary Ireland, but one nearly forgotten text that does this is *Easter Week* by Theodosia F. W. Hickey, published in 1933. Unknown today, Theodosia Hickey published a dozen books between 1930 and 1947, mostly stories for children. Hickey was the daughter of the novelist James Owen Hannay (1865–1950), who wrote under the pseudonym George Birmingham. According to Joan Fitzpatrick Dean, Hannay was "a strong advocate of Home Rule" and was friends with such luminaries as Horace Plunkett, Arthur Griffith, Standish O'Grady, and Douglas Hyde (2004, 10). Theodosia, born 1 April 1896, was a top student of History and Political Science at Trinity College, winning the Cluff Memorial Prize in History and Political Science and ranked a Senior Moderator in the Dublin University calendar for 1917 (*Dublin University Calendar* 1922, 400). Hickey's education and her family connections to Dublin's political and literary elite provided her first-hand insight into the lives of politically active women like Constance Markievicz and Hanna Sheehy Skeffington, both of whom were associates of her father. This essay aims to explore her 1933 novel *Easter Week* in terms of its investigation of women's specific experiences of the 1916 Rising and the liberatory potential from rigid gender roles glimpsed in revolutionary violence.

Published a decade after the founding of the Free State, Hickey's *Easter Week* is culturally nationalist in the broadest sense, sympathising with the rebels' cause while also reflecting the ambivalence of most Dubliners toward the Rising. The novel is both *roman* à *clef* and historical fiction, weaving facts and historical figures into the lives of four fictional families, each family representing a distinct political point of view. Lacking the modernist interiority and experimental form of generational peers such as Kate O'Brien and Elizabeth Bowen, Hickey's tone is often unexpectedly comedic given the seriousness of her subject, and she traffics in stock "types" or caricatures of Irish life. The novel owes a debt to both Somerville and Ross's *Irish R. M.* stories (1899; 1908) and to her father's *Irishmen All* (1914), a series of short vignettes describing stereotypical characters from Irish life.[6] But for all of its stylistic quirks, the novel succeeds in doing the remarkable work of centring on women's experiences of revolutionary violence. The novel also offers its primary heroine, Bella Lavelle, a queer counter-narrative to the conventional heterosexual romance plot. Keenly aware of the sacrifices women make to both the nationalist cause and the Great War, Hickey's novel acknowledges the shared pain of loss both conflicts brought to the lives of Irish women, and argues that violence arises from the rigid gender roles enforced within the patriarchal family home. In the chaos of the Rising, each character

---

War of Independence and Irish myth rather than the Rising; Rosamond Jacob's novel *The Troubled House* covers the years from 1916–21, but, while written during the early years of the Free State, was not published until 1938 (Lane 2010, 155).

6   *Irishmen All* featured illustrations by Jack B. Yeats.

is challenged to rethink not only their relationship to the nation, but also their inherited assumptions about class and gender.

The central narrative of *Easter Week* follows the Lavelle family, whose eldest daughter, Bella, is reading for an honours degree in history at Dublin University. Bella is described as "large and lazy," and like Theodosia Hickey at the time of the Rising, she is twenty years old. Bella uses the disruption of the Rising to try on a series of potentially liberating identities. She begins the novel a bored undergraduate who "greatly preferred reading poetry, and only took up her history books when examinations loomed near" (10), but spends the week of the Rising moving across the most dangerous parts of Dublin, ending the novel painfully uncertain about her future. Through Bella, Hickey acknowledges the challenges her generation of Irish women faced in finding both a political identity and personal autonomy, and the strongest moments in the novel involve Bella's determination to live a life very different from that of her mother. Mothers in the novel are weak, miserable creatures who obsess over their sons and resent their daughters, a situation the novel suggests is a root cause of social disorder. Mothers represent the status quo and failure to adapt to changing circumstances, while the revolutionary women of the Rising offer a break with tradition and a path into the future.

The Ranelagh Square home of the Lavelle family is late Victorian by way of the Celtic Twilight: prints of woodland faeries by AE and William Morris's *The Earthly Paradise* are in the background; there is something both nostalgic and mocking in this description of a middle-class Anglo-Irish family home in the middle of a revolution (10). *Easter Week*'s benign *paterfamilias* Mr. Lavelle is a lawyer, the father of three daughters and one son, Roderick, serving at the Front (11). Mrs. Lavelle is a cold, distant woman, more concerned with the fate of her son than with the welfare of her family in Dublin. Unnamed fifteen-year-old twin sisters spend the week of the Rising at home, eating increasingly scarce bread with jam, while Bella crosses Dublin at the height of the fighting in an attempt to find her way home from an Easter Monday outing in the mountains. The Lavelle household also features Maggie, the frightened maid who runs off midweek to peel potatoes for the rebels in Stephen's Green, and Aunt Theresa—Tiz—the maiden aunt of forty who "never realised that she was a superfluous woman" (7–8). Aunt Tiz shows great courage when she goes off in search of Constance Markievicz during the fighting, breaking in to the College of Surgeons through an unguarded door with the misguided hope that Markievicz can give her information about the missing Roderick. Roderick Lavelle, unexpectedly in Dublin on leave when the fighting breaks out, is a captive in the GPO, but his family believes him to be dead. Hickey's detailed knowledge of even small events associated with the Rising is extraordinary, suggesting insider knowledge of the events of that week. For example, once she is inside the College of Surgeons, Aunt Tiz pockets a fragment from the torn

Jubilee portrait of Queen Victoria by S. Catterson Smith, R. H. A.: "'That's probably the best work they've done yet,' said Tiz, who did not admire life-sized portraits of Queen Victoria … If I get out of here alive,' she thought, 'it'll not be without a souvenir'" (189). Right down to such fragments, Hickey captures the conflicted responses of those confronting the violence of the Rising.[7]

In what might be the first literary reference to the women of Cumann na mBan, Hickey introduces Mollie O'Connor, a young woman who moves in and out of the GPO with messages and food for the men. The narrator claims: "She was only a Sinn Féiner because Johnnie was. She wanted to appear gallant and brave in his eyes" (174), but her movements through the fighting and her horror at the devastation she encounters are strikingly similar to the narratives of the real women who fought in the Rising.[8] Mollie first volunteers as a Red Cross nurse, though she knew nothing about nursing, and she spends most of the week inside the GPO cooking and washing up. Cumann na mBan is not named in the novel, but they did wear the Red Cross during the Rising, and members were stationed at the GPO to serve in the same capacity as Mollie. Margaret Skinnider reports that wearing the Red Cross was no protection to the women from British bullets: "they made excellent targets in their white dresses, with large red crosses on them" (Skinnider 1917, 124). Mollie may have joined the cause because of love, but her war work is both dangerous and important:

> She had to get out at the back of the Post Office and pursue devious paths by backyards and alleys for some time before she could venture into the open street … Sometimes the shots sounded very close to her and she cowered for shelter; in the lulls she ran again. She could not distinguish between the sounds of rifle and machine-gun fire, distant shells or bomb. It was all 'the shooting' to her, and equally terrifying. (Hickey 1933, 176–77)

Mollie makes her way across the burning city to the back of Liberty Hall in search of a familiar house, and "ordinarily Mollie would have said she could walk there blindfolded. But two eighteen-pounders had been let loose on the district and the steamer Helga, anchored opposite in the Liffey, had attempted to drop shells on the rebel stronghold. Many of the houses Mollie knew were now unrecognizable ruins" (177). She encounters the mangled body of a black cat in the street and flees to Johnnie's nearby home, where "[e]very window had shattered at the report of the first shell" and thick dust lay on everything (178). Mollie O'Connor's romantic hopes for Johnnie die with him in the GPO.

Hickey's novel rejects conventional heterosexual romance plots at every turn. Pursued by an "earnest, undersized young professor at Trinity College,

---

7   Margaret Skinnider mentions the destruction of the painting in her memoir: "At the College of Surgeons we had destroyed nothing except a portrait of Queen Victoria. We took that down and made puttees out of it" (1917, 187).

8   See Lucy McDiarmid's *At Home in the Revolution* (2015).

Dublin" named Kent, Bella Lavelle unwillingly attends his lectures, where she "ostentatiously" ignores him (13). On Easter Monday morning, Bella organises a walking party to Little Sugar Loaf. Bella, indignant at Kent's invitation, is nonetheless required by custom to entertain him: "She tried to make the best of it. After all, she had plenty in common with Mr. Kent. They both read books, and liked approximately the same poetry. Mr. Kent was discovering modern Irish poetry, which Bella knew all about, and this gave her a pleasant sense of superiority" (49–50). After a picnic at the summit of Little Sugar Loaf the men of the party lapse into awkward conversation about Ireland. Bella's English-born cousin Cyril asks: "'What do Irishmen want?' ... I really want to know. Why is there always an Irish question and an Irish crisis? Though my father is an Irishman I've never heard anything about it. What's wrong with you— us?'" The cultural nationalist David Kaye responds: "We want self-government" (51). Arriving at the station to make their way home, the party discovers that the trains are not running because of the Rising. Bella and Cyril take refuge at a friend's home, and Tuesday morning, Cyril borrows a bike so that he can return to the city and report to military headquarters. Bella walks him to the gate and pulls a second bicycle out of a clump of laurels. "'I hid it there,' she panted. 'I knew Mrs. Coyle would never let me go with you, so I didn't say a word'" (61). Cyril tries to make her stay, but Bella protests: "Oh, Cyril, don't be an ass. You don't know the way, so it's me taking you, really" (60-61). Over the next three days, Cyril and Bella make their way home through the worst of the fighting.

There is no record of where Theodosia Hickey spent the week of the Rising. Her father was serving as a Church of Ireland chaplain to the troops in France during that time, and her family was living in Killiney (Birmingham 1934, 221). What little that can be gleaned about Hickey's life is primarily through biographical work on her father and through his memoir, *Pleasant Places* (1934). Published the year after *Easter Week*, Hannay mentions his eldest daughter Theodosia only a handful of times and often only as "my eldest daughter," while his two sons and his youngest daughter, Althea, are frequently referenced by name. Hannay writes: "Our eldest girl, Theo, left Alexandra College and we sent her for awhile to Paris, where she was supposed to learn French and did learn to dress herself, quite as useful a lesson" (Birmingham 1934, 207). Whether this reference is meant to be playful or mocking is hard to know. Theodosia's sister Althea never married and lived with her parents through Ada's death in 1933 and her father's in 1950. Theodosia's marriage in 1920 to William Hickey, a Catholic from England, may be one cause of family tension. By the time Hickey publishes *Easter Week* in 1933, she is thirty-seven years old and the mother of two children.

Hickey's depiction of Bella Lavelle's strained relationship with her mother suggests powerful generational tension. She writes: "Mrs. Lavelle would have given all three daughters' bodies and souls for her son Roderick's little finger.

She did not trouble to conceal that she resented the fact that while he was suffering in France the girls were safe at home" (1933, 14). Theodosia's older brother Robert was wounded at the battle of Passchendaele (Taylor 1995, 144), and in a 1909 letter congratulating Hanna Sheehy Skeffington on the birth of her son Owen, Theodosia's mother Ada writes: "I suppose you would have preferred a girl! But I think little boys are the nicest & perhaps you will agree with me now that you have one."[9] Late in the novel, Bella's mother expresses similar sentiments about her children: "Roddie was her life, and he was dead. The fate of her [then missing in action] husband, of Bella, the hunger of the twins left her unmoved" (1933, 183). Bella is unable to sympathise with her grieving mother. "Bella's eyes were dry and her lips numb. Tears would not come, nor words of consolation. She ought to kiss her mother, she knew, and cry, too. She could not. She always felt an extreme distaste for her mother when she lay in bed in the room sordid and untidy and dirty water in the basin. She ought not to be thinking of these things now, but she was" (228). These lines become even more ironic when one considers that Adelaide "Ada" Hannay, died in January 1933, the year *Easter Week* was published.

The stories Theodosia Hickey records of the Rising in *Easter Week* correlate strongly with both press reports and archived letters and diaries of the events of that week. During the reading of the Proclamation outside the GPO, women mock the rebels and spit on the flag: "this was no mob waiting passionately for freedom, ready, like the Parisian mobs in the French revolution, to wallow in blood for liberty" (Hickey 1933, 76). Hickey intersperses the words of the Proclamation with the laughter of a mob gathered near Nelson's Pillar. The looting of Noblett's sweet shop draws the crowd away from the momentous scene. The unnamed rebel reading the Proclamation finishes his task and "followed the flag for which he was soon to die back up the streets to the Post Office," his dignity a stark contrast to the frenzied mob of looters (77–79). The novel's sympathies lie with those who seek freedom, even if Bella Lavelle refuses to choose a side. Halfway through their journey back to Dublin, Cyril asks Bella if she's a nationalist. She replies: "Who? Me? I'm nothing. I hate politics. So would you, Cyril, if you lived in Ireland where they're talking about them night and day" (132). Cyril insists that she must be on one side or the other, but Bella asserts: "Well, I'm not. It's not so simple as you think either." English-born Cyril concedes: "I see that. In fact, I'm completely puzzled" (132). The novel captures the ambivalence and even outright hostility most Dubliners felt toward the rebels, portraying the republicans as a high-minded but misguided minority.

What is most unusual about the novel is Hickey's focus on women's roles in the Rising. The martyred male leaders of the Rising are largely absent from the

---

9   Correspondence from Ada Hannay to Hanna Sheehy Skeffington, National Library of Ireland, NLI MS 41, 178/12.

novel, and at the center of the conflict is Constance Markievicz:

> A slight figure in green uniform, wearing breeches and high boots and a cock's feather in her hat strode out. About a hundred men, women, boys and girls came crowding after her. She advanced to meet the soldiers, her face pale and drawn. She shook hands with the officer in charge, unstrapped a revolver in a leather case, kissed it passionately, and handed it over to him. The officer looked slightly bewildered and thanked her with some embarrassment. She did not answer, but bowed her head and stood quite still, the picture of a gallant, vanquished leader. Then, still silently, she suffered herself to be marched away. (258)[10]

Mr. Lavelle witnesses this scene and quips, "By Jove, she's a great little actress," a dismissive remark, but one that has a biographical connection to Hickey's family. Constance Markievicz had the starring role in James Owen Hannay's play *Eleanor's Enterprise* when it was performed at the Gaiety Theatre in December 1911. It is impossible to know if the young Theodosia Hickey met Markievicz, but her father knew her well, and Markievicz's arrest after the Rising triggered an investigation into letters between Markievicz and Hickey's father.[11]

Theodosia Hickey's family connections to major figures associated with the Rising, including both Frances and Hanna Sheehy Skeffington, are important background to the action of *Easter Week*. Through the execution of Montague Tibbetts, Hickey recreates one of the most tragic events of the Rising: the murder of Francis Sheehy Skeffington by Capt. John Bowen-Colthurst. Having given Bella and Cyril shelter in his home on Wednesday night, Tibbetts volunteers to guide a lost battalion of British soldiers through Dublin. Lawrence O'Brien is one of the soldiers, described as "very young. He had only come to the battalion from Sandhurst two days before they were ordered to Ireland" (114). In a crisis moment, Lawrence tells his commanding officer that he must quit. "I can't do it … Don't you understand? This is my country. These are my people. Irishmen. I can't shoot them. I won't" (114). Tibbetts rushes ahead of the battalion in an attempt to keep them from being ambushed. He stops to wipe his brow with a large white handkerchief, and Lawrence is convinced that Tibbetts has signaled to the rebels. Later that night, Lawrence executes the innocent man, before learning that the C. O. has been looking for Tibbetts because he was "the

---

10   During the Rising, Markievicz was second-in-command of the ICA forces at Stephen's Green under Michael Mallin.

11   Hannay was dismayed at Markievicz's insistence that she wear as little as possible on stage during her performance. When Markievicz was arrested in 1916, Hannay's correspondence with Markievicz was handed over to Dublin Castle, "and although no more was heard of the matter, there is a delicious sense of Birmingham comedy about a Chief Secretary in 1916 reading, with one presumes a sense of bafflement and wonder the letters between a Church of Ireland clergyman and a noted Irish revolutionary apparently all about her underclothes!" (Taylor 1995, 105).

hero of the battle", who did "marvels for the wounded" after the fight (149). Lawrence loses his mind with grief.

Tibbetts is described as a man of deep principles thwarted by the intensity of his social activism and his physical handicaps: "Though not actually a dwarf he was not quite normal … Mr. Tibbetts often felt that, had his legs not ceased to grow before the proper time, he might have done great things" (110). In the context of the novel, Tibbett's height makes him ridiculous in the eyes of nearly everyone he meets, and even his wife is grateful when he leaves the house early on the morning of his death because she can then give Cyril and Bella a proper breakfast of eggs and bacon, not the vegetarian fare that Tibbetts insists upon. Lawrence O'Brien is depicted as a boy who loses his grip on reality after witnessing death for the first time, while in reality Bowen-Colthurst was a thirty-six year old veteran of several wars, and unlike Mr. Tibbetts, Francis Sheehy Skeffington had a distinguished career as an author, journalist, and activist.[12]

Hickey's satirical portrait of Francis Sheehy Skeffington may have roots in her father's break from his former nationalist friends after the outbreak of war. As George Birmingham wrote:

> It was inevitable that there should be an unbridgeable gulf between the two sections of nationalist Ireland … Our recognition of the justice of the Allied cause meant for us the breaking of many old friendships. Here was no matter of a difference of opinion, where toleration and mutual respect might have saved the rupture of friendship. The thing went deeper. So strong were the feelings on both sides that even ordinary social intercourse became impossible. It was not a drifting apart. (Birmingham 1934, 221)

There is no evidence that Hanna Sheehy Skeffington maintained ties with Hannay or his family after the war. Theodosia Hickey's portrait of her father's former friend is a mixture of satire and respect. Montague Tibbetts is the object of ridicule, but he is also "the hero of the day," and a female Red Cross doctor—a fictionalised Dr. Kathleen Lynn—declares: "He's a pacifist and conscientious objector and professes every kind of fad known to man. I've laughed at him for years, but when I saw him work to-day I swore I'd never laugh at him again" (154). Bella Lavelle's support for Mr. Tibbetts results in her imprisonment: "I know Mr. Tibbetts was not, and never could be a spy. As to his being a Sinn Feiner [sic]—well, lots of people are, more or less" (150).

Bella Lavelle is thrown in among the captured and wounded, where "the

---

12   Barton and Foy describe Sheehy Skeffington as "[a] well-known, loved and somewhat eccentric Dublin character dressed in a knickerbocker suit who was actively involved in every worthy cause such as pacifism, socialism, vegetarianism, alcohol abstinence and votes for women. He had become an object of resentment in military circles because of his opposition to the war which the authorities believed hindered recruiting" (1999, 189).

reek of blood and filth was indescribable" (152), until "a very brisk middle-aged woman in tweeds carrying a leather bag" comes to her rescue (153). Dr. Kathleen Lynn was the Chief Medical Officer for the Irish Citizen Army, not the Red Cross, and she was imprisoned for her activities during the Rising (Taillon 1996, 12).[13] The fictionalised Lynn recruits Bella for nursing duty and convinces the sentry to release her. That night, she leads Bella home to her "small and immaculately neat flat where she fed her on cold beef and pickles and beer" (155). "I've no faith in tea and boiled eggs," she told Bella, "though that's what women are supposed to live on when they haven't got a man. And I don't like bits on trays. I sit down to my meals, and when I've finished I put my feet in the fire and light a pipe" (155).[14] Hickey notes that Bella

> conceived an enormous admiration for the doctor. She decided to live by herself in a flat at the first possible moment, and, secretly, to practice smoking a pipe. She must also seize every opportunity the future offered to drink beer, as then possibly she might get to like it. She wished she was dressed in a well cut tweed suit and silk shirt instead of a flimsy dress and a mackintosh, and wondered if her dress allowance would run to the immediate purchase of a pair of strong brogued shoes. Slightly grey hair, she decided, was very distinguished. (156)

Everything about the doctor is coded as queer, from her unconventional clothing to her declaration of how she lives independently without a man. Bella sleeps in "the doctor's exceedingly gentlemanly pyjamas. She decided she would always wear pyjamas" (157). Bella decides to follow the doctor to Mount Street the following day, to tend to the wounded. These details suggest that Theodosia Hickey not only knew Kathleen Lynn; she knew her well enough to know that she was a lesbian. Kathleen Lynn and her partner Madeleine ffrench-Mullen met during the 1913 Lockout and were together until ffrench-Mullen's death in 1944 (McDiarmid 2015, 250–51, 255). Even more unexpectedly, Hickey depicts Bella Lavelle's crush on the doctor, whose way of life becomes a standard she hopes to emulate as an adult. Bella's experiences during the Rising offer her a path away from the terrible heterosexual marriages of the novel and toward a future very different from her mother's.

Hickey's interest in women's experiences of the Rising stands in contrast to many later depictions of the fighting as a hypermasculine space devoid of women.[15] The novel depicts women jeering in the street when the Proclamation

---

13   Ruth Taillon explains that in 1914, efforts were made to have Cumann na mBan recognized as the Irish branch of the International Red Cross, but the Red Cross refused, saying it could not admit a group from a country without a standing army (1996, 10).
14   Kathleen Lynn's diary from the week of the Rising describes the rations at City Hall, where she was stationed as part of the Irish Citizen Army: "Firing on & off all day—siege fare, bully beef & biscuits, tea without milk" (Lynn 1916).
15   Neil Jordan's hypermasculine vision of the Rising in his film *Michael Collins* (1996)

is read, providing sustenance to the men in the GPO, serving as nurses, cooks and dispatch runners for the Volunteers, and VAD nurses for the troops stationed in Dublin. Gender roles are renegotiated in the revolutionary moment, and the novel offers a female perspective on a cataclysmic event in Irish history without any nostalgia for a lost past. For nationalist women like Mollie O'Connor and Constance Markievicz the Rising ends in grief, but the novel also gives their stories to a new generation of readers who may never have known that women fought in the Rising. For a middle class, Anglo-Irish woman like Bella Lavelle, the Rising is a test of her ingenuity and a chance to experience new identities. While the men of Theodosia Hickey's *Easter Week* argue over "what Irishmen want," the novel proposes that what Irish women most wanted in 1916 was also "self-government," in the shape of freedom from the stifling conventions of the patriarchal home.

References

Arrington, Lauren. 2015. *Revolutionary Lives: Constance and Casimir Markievicz.* Princeton: Princeton University Press.

Barton, Brian and Michael Foy. 1999. *The Easter Rising.* Stroud, England: Stutton Publishing.

Birmingham, George. 1919. *Up the Rebels!* New York: George H. Doran.

——. 1934. *Pleasant Places.* London: William Heinemann.

Clare, Anne. 2011. *Unlikely Rebels: The Gifford Girls and the Fight for Irish Freedom.* Dublin: Mercier Press.

Dean, Joan Fitzpatrick. 2004. *Riot and Great Anger: Stage Censorship in Twentieth-Century Ireland.* Madison: University of Wisconsin Press.

Flanagan, Francis. 2015. *Remembering the Revolution: Dissent, Culture, and Nationalism in the Irish Free State.* Oxford: Oxford University Press.

Fox, R. M. 1935. *Rebel Irishwomen.* Dublin and Cork: Talbot Press.

Hickey, T.F.W. 1933. *Easter Week.* London: Hurst & Blackett.

Lane, Leeann. 2010. *Rosamond Jacob: Third Person Singular.* Dublin: University College Dublin Press.

Lynn, Kathleen. 1916. "The Revolutionary Diary of Dr. Kathleen Lynn," *The Royal College of Physicians of Ireland.* https://www.rcpi.ie/heritage-centre/1916-2/revolutionary-diary-kathleen-lynn/

Madigan, Edward, and John Horne. 2013. *Towards Commemoration: Ireland in War and Revolution, 1912–1923.* Dublin: Royal Irish Academy.

McAuliffe, Mary, and Liz Gillis. 2016. *Richmond Barracks 1916: We Were There: 77 Women of the Easter Rising.* Dublin: Dublin City Council.

McDiarmid, Lucy. 2015. *At Home in the Revolution: What Women Said and Did*

is an example of the cultural amnesia regarding women's war work during the conflict.

in 1916. Dublin: Royal Irish Academy.

McCoole, Sinéad. 1997. *Guns and Chiffon*. Dublin: Stationery Office Books.

Morash, Chris. 2002. *A History of Irish Theatre, 1601–2000*. Cambridge: Cambridge University Press.

O'Toole, Tina, Gillian McIntosh, and Muireann O'Cinnéide. 2016. *Women Writing War: Ireland 1880–1922*. Dublin: University College Dublin Press.

Skinnider, Margaret. 1917. *Doing My Bit for Ireland*. New York: The Century Company.

Smith, Nadia Clare. 2007. *Dorothy Macardle: A Life*. Dublin: Woodfield Press.

Taillon, Ruth. 1996. *When History Was Made: The Women of 1916*. Dublin: Beyond the Pale Publications.

Taylor, Brian. 1995. *The Life and Writings of James Owen Hannay*. Lewiston: Edwin Mellon Press.

Ward, Margaret. 1997. *Hanna Sheehy Skeffington: A Life*. Dublin: Attic Press.

———. 2019. *Fearless Woman: Hanna Sheehy Skeffington, Feminism, and the Irish Revolution*. Dublin: University College Dublin Press.

Contributors

Christopher Cusack was awarded his Ph.D. with distinction in February 2018. His thesis focused on Famine fiction published between 1892 and 1921. He is a postdoctoral researcher at Radboud University in Nijmegen, the Netherlands. Among his publications are the co-edited volumes *Recollecting Hunger* (Irish Academic Press, 2012), *Global Legacies of the Great Irish Famine* (Peter Lang, 2014), and *Irish Studies and the Dynamics of Memory* (Peter Lang, 2017).

Elke D'hoker is professor of English literature at the University of Leuven, and co-director of the Leuven Centre for Irish Studies and of the modern literature research group, MDRN. She has published widely in the field of modern and contemporary British and Irish fiction, with special emphasis on the short story, women's writing and narrative theory. She is the author of a critical study on John Banville (Rodopi, 2004) and has edited or co-edited several essay collections: *Unreliable Narration* (De Gruyter, 2008*), Irish Women Writers* (Lang, 2011), *Mary Lavin* (Irish Academic Press, 2013) and *The Irish Short Story* (Lang, 2015). Her most recent monograph, *Irish Women Writers and the Modern Short Story* was published by Palgrave in 2016. Her volume *Ethel Colburn Mayne: Selected Stories* will be published by EER in the series "Irish Women Writers: Texts and Contexts" in 2020.

Heidi Hansson is Professor of English Literature at Umeå University, Sweden. Her main research interest is women's literature, and she has previously published in the fields of postmodern romance, Irish women's literature, nineteenth-century travel writing and northern studies. Among her works on Irish topics are a full-length examination of the nineteenth-century writer Emily Lawless, *Emily Lawless 1845–1913: Writing the Interspace* (Cork University Press, 2007), the edited collection *New Contexts: Re-Framing Nineteenth-Century Irish Women's Prose* (Cork University Press, 2008) and *Fictions of the Irish Land War* (Peter Lang, 2014), edited together with James H. Murphy. She has also written about contemporary Irish writers such as Anne Enright and William Trevor. Together with Fionna Barber and Sara Dybris McQuaid she edited the interdisciplinary collection *Ireland and the North* (Peter Lang, 2019).

Seán Hewitt is a Government of Ireland Fellow at University College Cork. His current project is titled "Acts of Enchantment: Natural History in British and Irish Writing, 1870–1930." His monograph, on the works of J.M. Synge, is forthcoming from Oxford University Press. His debut collection of poetry, *Tongues of Fire*, will be published by Jonathan Cape in 2020.

Anne Jamison is a Senior Lecturer in Literary Studies at Western Sydney University, and a member of the University's Writing and Society Research Centre. She is a feminist literary critic with a research focus on nineteenth-century Irish and Australian women's writing. She completed her Ph.D. at Queen's University Belfast and has since published broadly on Irish literature, including research on Edith Somerville and Martin Ross, Alicia Lefanu, Kate O'Brien, James Clarence Mangan and Anne Enright, as well as on the intersections between law, literature and authorship in the Victorian period. She is author of *E. Œ. Somerville and Martin Ross: Female Authorship and Literary Collaboration* (Cork University Press, 2016) and was awarded the State Library of New South Wales Nancy Keesing Research Fellowship in 2016/17 for her work on colonial Australian writer, Catherine Helen Spence.

Lindsay Janssen is a researcher and lecturer at Radboud University Nijmegen. She was an IRC Government of Ireland Postdoctoral Fellow affiliated to University College Dublin. Her research concerns cultural memory and identity formation and Irish and Irish-North American periodical cultures between the mid-nineteenth and early-twentieth centuries.

Kathryn Laing lectures in the Department of English Language and Literature, Mary Immaculate College, University of Limerick. She has published widely on Rebecca West, Virginia Woolf, George Moore, F. Mabel Robinson, and Irish writer Hannah Lynch. Publications include *Hannah Lynch: Irish Writer, Cosmopolitan, New Woman*, co-written with Faith Binckes (Cork University Press, 2019), "'Only Connect': Irish Women's Voices, Latin America and the Irish Women's Writing Network" in a special issue of *Irish Migration Studies in Latin America* 9, no. 1 (2018) and "Hannah Lynch and Narratives of the Irish Literary Revival," *New Hibernia Review* 20, no. 1 (Spring 2016). With Sinéad Mooney she is co-founder of the Irish Women's Writing Network and General Editor of two new series to be published by EER, "Key Irish Women Writers" and "Irish Women Writers: Texts and Contexts" (in which her work *Hannah Lynch's Irish Girl Rebels: "A Girl Revolutionary" and "Marjory Maurice"* will appear).

Patrick Maume is a researcher with the Royal Irish Academy's *Dictionary of Irish Biography*, to which he has contributed approximately 450 entries on nineteenth and twentieth-century figures. He is a graduate of University College Cork and Queen's University Belfast; he spent many years in Northern Ireland and now lives in Dublin, and has published biographies of Daniel Corkery and D. P. Moran and a survey of early twentieth-century nationalist politics. He has also produced some 70 articles, book chapters and edited texts, several of which deal with women writers, including Emily Lawless, Margaret Cusack, Charlotte Riddell, and Geraldine Penrose Fitzgerald.

Lia Mills writes novels, short stories, memoir, and essays. She is a Doctoral candidate at the University of Limerick (Creative Writing). In a previous existence she was Teaching and Research Fellow at the Women's Education Research and Resource Centre (WERRC) at UCD, where her research interest was in Irish women's writing, particularly at the turn of the last century. Her most recent novel, *Fallen*, is set during the period leading up to and including the Easter Rising in Dublin, 1916. *Fallen* was the Dublin: Belfast Two Cities One Book selection for 2016.

Barry Montgomery is a researcher on the AHRC-funded Ulster University and NUI Galway *Representations of Jews in Irish Literature* project, to which he has contributed seven chapters for the forthcoming critical volume on fiction, drama and poetry in English, ranging from the Early Modern Period to the present. He also forms part of the project team for the accompanying Irish-Jewish Literature Exhibition, which has successfully toured Ireland and America, and has given public lectures on Irish Jewish Literary Studies at the Royal Irish Academy, Dublin, the Linen Hall Library, Belfast (to mark Holocaust Memorial Day, 2017), and the Irish Literary Society, London. Barry has written on Ruth Gilligan's *Nine Folds Make a Paper Swan* (2016), Richard Head's *The English Rogue* (1665) for *Crime Fiction – A Critical Casebook* (Peter Lang, 2018), and has contributed several entries on late eighteenth and early nineteenth-century fiction to *The Cambridge Guide to the Eighteenth-Century Novel, 1660–1820*.

Aintzane Legarreta Mentxaka is a lecturer in literature, drama, and critical theory at the American College Dublin. Mentxaka has taught at University College Dublin and Dublin City University, and was a Government of Ireland postdoctoral fellow of the National University of Ireland. She is the author of *The Postcolonial Traveller* (Academia Press, 2016) and *Kate O'Brien and the Fiction of Identity* (MacFarland, 2011). Her book, *Kate O'Brien,* will be published by EER in their new series "Key Irish Women Writers."

Sinéad Mooney is a Senior Lecturer in English at De Montfort University, Leicester. She is the author of *A Tongue Not Mine: Beckett and Translation* (Oxford University Press, 2011), which was completed on an Irish Research Council fellowship and won the ACIS Robert Rhodes Prize; *Samuel Beckett* (Northcote House, 2006), with Kathryn Laing and Maureen O'Connor, editor of *Edna O'Brien: New Critical Perspectives* (Carysfort, 2006), and essays on Samuel Beckett, Elizabeth Bowen, Edna O'Brien, Mary Lavin, and Molly Keane. With Kathryn Laing, she is founder of the Irish Women's Writing Network and General Editor of two new EER series, "Key Irish Women Writers" and "Irish Women's Writing: Texts and Contexts."

Maureen O'Connor lectures in the School of English in University College Cork. She is the author of *The Female and the Species: The Animal in Irish Women's Writing* (Peter Lang, 2010), co-editor, with Derek Gladwin, of a special issue of the *Canadian Journal of Irish Studies*, 'Irish Studies and the Environmental Humanities', 40.1 (2018); with Kathryn Laing and Sinéad Mooney, of *Edna O'Brien: New Critical Perspectives* (Carysfort Press, 2006); with Lisa Colletta, of *Wild Colonial Girl: Essays on Edna O'Brien* (University of Wisconsin Press, 2006); and, with Tadhg Foley, of *Ireland and India: Colonies, Culture, and Empire* (Irish Academic Press, 2006). She has recently completed a book-length study of Edna O Brien's fiction and is working on a monograph on nature and nation in the writing of Irish first-wave feminists, including Eva Gore-Booth, Margaret Cousins, Charlotte Despard, and Alice Stopford Green.

Mary S. Pierse taught diverse literature courses at the School of English, and has given courses on Irish feminisms for the MA programme in Women's Studies at University College, Cork. Editor and compiler of the five-volume *Irish Feminisms 1810–1930* (Routledge, 2010), she instigated the George Moore international conference series and has edited and co-edited several volumes on Moore's works. She also published on the writings of Kate Chopin, Antonio Fogazzaro, Katherine Cecil Thurston, and contemporary Irish poets. Her ongoing research focuses on Moore's *oeuvre*, Franco-Irish artistic connections, and Irish women writers in the *fin-de-siècle* period. She is a board member of the National Centre for Franco-Irish Studies.

Matthew L. Reznicek is Assistant Professor of English at Creighton University, where he teaches nineteenth-century British and Irish Literature. He has published widely on Irish women writers, including Sydney Owenson, Maria Edgeworth, Katherine Cecil Thurston, Somerville and Ross, and Kate O'Brien. His first monograph, *The European Metropolis: Paris and Nineteenth-Century Irish Women Novelists*, was published by Clemson University Press/Liverpool University Press in 2017. He is working on a monograph exploring the relationship between Irish women writers and European opera.

Julie Anne Stevens lectures in the School of English, Dublin City University. From 2017–2019, she was visiting professor at John Paul Catholic University, San Diego, California. She publishes on literature and the visual arts, Irish and American women's writing, illustrated children's books, and short fiction. From 2009–2017 she served as the Director for the Centre for Children's Literature and Culture in St. Patrick's College, and in 2013 she acted as a judge for the Children's Books Ireland Awards. She is part of the team for the Irish Women's Writing Network. She published *The Irish Scene in Somerville and Ross* in 2007 (Irish Academic Press) and co-edited *The Ghost Story from the Middle Ages to the Twentieth Century* in 2010 (Four Courts Press). Somerville Press published her latest book, *Two Irish Girls in Bohemia: The Drawings and Writings of E. Œ. Somerville and Martin Ross*, in 2017.

Lisa Weihman is an Associate Professor of English and Irish Studies at West Virginia University, specialising in modern and contemporary British and Irish literature. She has published essays on Dorothy Macardle, Elizabeth Bowen, and Virginia Woolf, among others, and is working on two projects: a forthcoming critical edition of Somerville and Ross's novel *The Real Charlotte* and a book, *Anglo-Irish Women Writers after the Revolutionary Decade*.

Index